D1562791

U.S. Coal
and the Electric Power
Industry

Richard L. Gordon

U.S. COAL
AND THE
ELECTRIC POWER
INDUSTRY

PUBLISHED FOR
RESOURCES FOR THE FUTURE, INC.
BY THE JOHNS HOPKINS
UNIVERSITY PRESS

RESOURCES FOR THE FUTURE, INC.

1755 Massachusetts Avenue, N.W.
Washington, D.C. 20036

Resources for the Future is a nonprofit corporation for research and education in the development, conservation, and use of natural resources and the improvement of the quality of the environment. It was established in 1952 with the cooperation of the Ford Foundation. Part of the work of Resources for the Future is carried out by its resident staff; part is supported by grants to universities and other nonprofit organizations. Unless otherwise stated, interpretations and conclusions in RFF publications are those of the authors; the organization takes responsibility for the selection of significant subjects for study, the competence of the researchers, and their freedom of inquiry.

This book is one of RFF's energy and mineral studies, which are prepared under the direction of Hans H. Landsberg. Richard L. Gordon is a Professor of Mineral Economics at Pennsylvania State University. The manuscript was edited by Brigitte Weeks and Penelope S. Harpold.

RFF editors: Mark Reinsberg, Joan R. Tron, Ruth B. Haas, Jo Hinkel

Copyright © 1975 by The Johns Hopkins University Press
All rights reserved
Manufactured in the United States of America

Library of Congress Catalog Number: 74-24403

ISBN: 0-8018-1697-1

Library of Congress Cataloging in Publication Data will be found on the last printed page of this book.

Foreword

The present study represents a survey of a much neglected sector of the U.S. energy market. The results reflect several years' study of the subject that involved supplementing the literature review with extensive discussions with both coal consumers in the electric power industry and ultimately with the coal industry itself.

The neglect of coal economics is hardly a unique phenomenon. Mightier industries such as steel and automobiles are even more poorly analyzed than coal. What makes coal's treatment more surprising is that its rivals—oil, natural gas, and nuclear power—are the subject of an enormous literature. Even here, the disparity is easily explicable. Coal has never had the same appeal for researchers. Two forces influence the choice—the intrinsic interest of the subject and data availability. For various reasons, such data availability on the other sectors, while far from fully satisfactory, has been much better. That classic source of information—government investigations—has generated much material. Moreover, much to their credit, the other sectors have conducted active discussions of their economics. Similarly, coal, until the late 1960s, did not seem very interesting.

This study was conceived because it appeared that it was desirable to see what could be done to overcome these data problems and explain this neglected portion of energy supplies. The task seemed urgent given the controversies surrounding coal's economic role as a major fuel for the electric utility industry. This decision appears to have been confirmed by subsequent events. Coal issues have become much more prominent. The question of how to keep mining and using coal in a socially acceptable manner has created great concern. The problem extends both to coal in its conventional boiler-fuel applications—emphasized in this study—as well as to its conversion to synthetic oil and gas.

This study attempts to treat coal's role in the electric utility market. The importance of coal to this industry, and what proved to be a correct expectation—that coal's relationship to electric power would reward research efforts—governed this choice. The concentration of this study on the electric power industry should not conceal the fact that research was undertaken in

v

other areas. Efforts were made to survey other markets for coal, but the resulting information was such that its presentation here can be limited to a few summary judgments inserted in the final chapter. The author will be happy to arrange to provide interested readers with additional material.

It was not initially planned to contact the coal industry directly, but such contact was made as part of research supported by the National Science Foundation. This research proceeded while the first draft of this manuscript was under review and was used to improve the content of chapter 5 greatly. The willingness of Dr. James H. Blackman of the NSF to permit use of this material is most appreciated.

Enormous debts are accumulated in research efforts of this kind, and it is always a pleasure to acknowledge them, since they cannot be repaid. Primary appreciation must go the late Orris C. Herfindahl of Resources for the Future, Inc. He provided the initial encouragement for this project and valuable comments on the first draft. Such aid was but a small portion of his immense contribution to natural resource economics. Further assistance at RFF was provided by Sam Schurr, Joel Darmstadter, Milton Searl, and Harry Perry. Mr. Perry subjected the second draft to the most incisive review I have ever had the fortune to receive, and every page benefited from his insights. David Brooks of Canada's Mineral Resource Branch of the Department of Energy, Mines, and Resources, Rene Malès of Commonwealth Edison Company, and Abraham Gerber of National Economic Research Associates all also provided extensive comments on the manuscript. M. A. Adelman also provided useful suggestions. Alvin Kaufman and Thomas Browne of the New York State Public Services Commission willingly endured double jeopardy by commenting on two versions of the manuscript.

The electric power, coal, oil, and steel industries provided enormous amounts of assistance. All generously granted interviews to me or my graduate assistants. This included both the companies and the trade associations in the coal and electric power industries. Haskell P. Wald and his associates at the Federal Power Commission both devoted considerable time to discussion and willingly complied with frequent requests for material. Similar requests were also satisfied by numerous other U.S. government agencies. Among my colleagues at Penn State, William Moroz and Warren Witzig were particularly helpful.

The research here was greatly aided by Charles J. Johnson and Noel P. Gillatt who served as graduate assistants. Additional aid with computations was provided by Vincent J. Calarco, Ronald F. Ayers, and Donald Barnett. The best part of the typing was undertaken by Mrs. Janice Winklestin. Our former departmental secretaries Barbara Poorman and Barbara Younker also were most helpful. The library of the College of Earth and Mineral Sciences provided considerable aid. My family endured the usual burdens of such projects and the unusual one of keeping me company on some of the trips to interview companies.

References are provided here by listing the author, date, and relevant pages in the text. The full citation can be found in the bibliography. The text references to reports of government and some private organizations often use abbreviations of the names but all are explained when first used. Only the first author of multiauthor works is listed.

University Park, Pa.
December 1973

Postscript: Since the completion of the manuscript, many changes have occurred. Where they could be easily fitted into the text at later stages, note was taken of the more important changes, but since none fundamentally altered the long-run conclusions, massive revisions were eschewed. The one conclusion that requires more stress than the original manuscript provided is that a rigid insistence on rapid implementation of air pollution regulations may produce intolerable and possibly impossible demands on the energy system. So many problems are associated with moving to the alternatives of oil, western coal, or scrubbers, that severe strains are inevitable if we insist on rapid results.

March, 1975

Preface

When RFF decided in 1969 to support a study of the competitive position of U.S. coal, oil was selling at a price that augured poorly for the future of coal. Richard Gordon's eye was specifically on coal's use as a boiler fuel in power-generating facilities, the market to which coal in this country has increasingly been restricted, and it was here that he inclined to a rather pessimistic view.

For many research undertakings that were largely completed before October 1973, the events following those fateful months of embargo required a decision: should the work be modified in the light of new developments or should it be brought rapidly to completion for the intrinsic value of the research and the enduring usefulness of much of the material presented? In this instance, the latter decision prevailed. To fully reflect the post-October 1973 situation would have meant not just to modify or qualify a figure here or a judgment there but to start anew and write a different book.

Our decision to encourage the author to complete the project basically as planned with an occasional look at unfolding events was based on two criteria: the study contained a wealth of information on the coal industry that was untouched either by recent events or by other studies—such as the analysis of fuel procurement, transportation, and plant location—and the future of competitive energy sources has even today not been revealed. Thus, the book is valuable both as an historical survey and as a useful point of reference for considering emerging trends. If the reader keeps these cautions in mind he will be able to use it at its best, that is, as a vantage point from which to observe the unfolding and no doubt rapidly changing events to come.

Hans H. Landsberg
Director, Division of Energy
and Resource Commodities

April 1975

Table of Contents

List of Tables

List of Abbreviations

AEC   Atomic Energy Commission
AEP   American Electric Power
BLS   Bureau of Labor Statistics
Btu   British thermal unit
CEQ   Council on Environmental Quality
EEI   Edison Electric Institute
EHV   Extra High Voltage
EPA   Environmental Protection Agency
FPC   Federal Power Commission
GPU   General Public Utilities
LNG   Liquified Natural Gas
NAPCA   National Air Pollution Control Administration
NPC   National Petroleum Council
OMD   Output per man day
OPEC   Organization of Petroleum Exporting Countries
PAD   Petroleum Administration for Defense
SOCTAP   Sulfur Oxide Control Technology Assessment Panel
TVA   Tennessee Valley Authority
UMW   United Mine Workers
USBM   U.S. Bureau of Mines
USGS   U.S. Geological Survey

U.S. Coal
and the Electric Power
Industry

1

Introduction—
The Problems of Coal

During the early 1970s concern about securing adequate supplies of environmentally acceptable energy has produced a sudden increase in interest about coal. Paradoxically, two quite different elements are involved in viewing coal. Traditional methods of producing and consuming coal are under attack because of their undesirable environmental consequences, but arguments are widespread that new, more acceptable methods of coal use should be developed because it is the United States' most plentiful fuel.

This awakening interest in coal contrasts with the long period after the late 1940s when coal was a forgotten industry. Such attitudes were a natural, if somewhat exaggerated, response to the nearly catastrophic decline in coal use that began after World War II. The then largest consuming industry—railroads—converted to diesel locomotives; a wide variety of other consumers shifted to cleaner, more convenient fuels—notably the natural gas that a growing pipeline system made available.

As the industry's fortunes declined, it also disappeared from public view. The making of a reconstruction quietly emerged as the industry found itself in an excellent position to supply fuel to the rapidly growing electric utility market. By the late 1960s, coal output had recovered enough so that restoration of earlier levels of production seemed quite likely in the seventies.

Unfortunately, the developments in coal conflicted with the national desire for a better environment. Coal had the misfortune of creating a wide array of environmental damage in its production and particlarly in its principal market—electric utilities. Coal mining of any kind leads to water pollution. Waste piles are left behind. Surface mining scars the land; underground mining creates dangers of subsidence. The sulfur and particulate matter in coal are major air pollutants. In addition, underground coal mining is considered an extremely dangerous occupation. These impacts, in turn, led to a proliferation of public policies designed to correct the environmental damages and hazards to workers associated with coal. These policies may have damaged coal's competitive position so greatly that another major output decline will occur. However, many observers feel that this would be an undesirable development and that, in fact, coal output

1

should be greatly expanded to meet pressing national energy needs—particularly for synthetic oil and gas.

The present study is an effort to deal with some elements of this debate. However, for reasons discussed later in this chapter, the problems of continued coal use to supply electric power plants receives far more attention than the prospects for major new markets. This is primarily a study of coal use in the already existing market. The discussion begins with basic background material in this chapter about the position and prospects of coal in the U.S. energy markets. This discussion treats the definition used here of coal, principal markets for coal, the competition being faced from rival fuels, the impact of public policy, and the prospects for new technology. Then the implications of these points are noted.

To provide historical perspective, chapters 2 and 3 examine various critical aspects of electric utility fuel use from 1946 to 1972. Chapter 2 describes the prevailing patterns of fuel consumption by electric utilities in different parts of the country and the prices that these utilities paid for their fuel. In chapter 3, a special, well known but little analyzed aspect of electric utility fuel use—how the fuel is procured—is examined. In particular, the role of long-term fuel supply contracts and vertical integration is surveyed and analyzed in some detail. This involves presentation of the results of an extensive survey undertaken of the experience of individual companies. The chapter also briefly examines the question of the competitive structure of coal and electric power fuel markets. The review serves to justify the assumption in later chapters that the coal markets are competitive.

In the next four chapters, the stress is upon prospective developments. Chapter 4 reviews the historical experience with fuel transportation and the selection of power plant sites as a basis for providing projections of future locational patterns and transportation costs. Fuel price trends are examined and projected in chapter 5. Here an extensive effort to develop an independent assessment of coal price trends is combined with surveys of the literature on rival fuels. This permits derivation of estimates of possible future price patterns. The discussion includes appraisal of the economics of low British thermal unit (Btu) content gas from coal and oil as a power plant fuel.

In chapter 6, the environmental pressures affecting the use of coal in the electric utility industry are reviewed. Chapter 7 adds material on the capital costs of different types of electric power plants and uses these estimates and the data from the three prior chapters to develop scenarios of fuel choice. These scenarios indicate the preferred fuel implied by different assumptions about prevailing public policies and the costs of fuel, transportation, and power plants. This only permits appraisal of which fuel will be chosen in various situations, and no effort is made to measure precisely the quantities of different fuels that would be consumed in each case. Quite the contrary, the analysis suggests that it will be extremely difficult to estimate future patterns of fuel use because of the uncertainties prevailing about costs, technology, and public policy. In lieu of such original forecasts, chapter 8 reviews previous projections of electric utility fuel use and outlines the implications of the scenarios of chapter 7 for the standard forecast of future electric utility fuel use. Chapter 9 provides a summary and conclusions.

COAL AND ITS MARKETS

It should be recalled that in the United States, the vast majority of the coal consumed is bituminous. The historical portions of this study are primarily concerned with bituminous coal. The anthracite industry is small and continues shrinking. Modest amounts of lignite are in use, and developments in the electric power market may stimulate further growth since substantial amounts of low-sulfur lignite are available in the West.[1]

As table 1.1 shows, the comeback of coal by the 1960s was largely produced by developments in the electric utility fuel markets. Electric power use of coal has been the industry's only growing market since World War II. The average annual rate of increase, indicated by a semi-logarithmic trend, is 6.4 percent. The history of the coal industry since the war has been dominated by this growth on the one hand and market losses on the other. The biggest loss came from the dieselization of railroads; in addition, consumption in the catchall category of retail sales declined sharply. Use in other industries has varied considerably but by 1971 was still well below the levels of the late forties. During the fifties, the market losses more than offset the rises in electricity. By the sixties, the railroad market had vanished, and the losses elsewhere were considerably less than the gains in electric power generation. In addition to these markets, two have remained important without showing any marked trends—coking and exports.

As table 1.2 shows, indicators about uses of coal other than in electricity production can be obtained from the periodic *Census of Manufactures*. Its report covers about 69 out of the 99 million tons of coal that the Bureau of Mines indicates were consumed by manufacturing and mining industries in 1967. The largest users are in the chemical and paper industries. These are followed by stone, clay, and glass products, and primary metals. It should be recalled that the major coal users in these sectors—cement and steel—

---

[1] Lignite appears incidentally both in the process of examining the electric power market and in the overview of the market. In the latter case, this reflects the practice of the U.S. Bureau of Mines of aggregating lignite with bituminous in its data. Similarly, small amounts of anthracite are consumed in the markets studied in detail. The review of possible developments implicitly gives increased weight to lignite in the review of western coal.

TABLE 1.1
United States Consumption and Exports of Bituminous Coal, 1946–1971
(thousands of net tons)

	Electric power utilities	Railroads (Class I)	Coking coal	Steel & rolling mills	Cement mills	Other manufacturing & mining industries[a]	Retail deliveries to other consumers	Total U.S. consumption	Exports
1946	68,743	110,166	83,288	12,151	6,990	120,364	98,684	500,386	41,197
1947	86,009	109,296	104,800	14,195	7,919	127,015	96,657	545,891	68,667
1948	95,620	94,838	107,306	14,193	8,546	112,612	86,794	519,909	45,930
1949	80,610	68,123	91,236	10,529	7,966	98,685	88,389	445,538	27,842
1950	88,262	60,969	103,845	10,877	7,923	97,904	84,422	454,202	25,468
1951	101,898	54,005	113,448	11,260	8,507	105,408	74,378	468,904	56,722
1952	103,309	37,962	97,614	9,632	7,903	95,476	66,861	418,757	47,643
1953	112,283	27,735	112,874	8,764	8,167	96,999	59,976	426,798	33,760
1954	115,235	17,370	85,391	6,983	7,924	78,359	51,798	363,060	31,041
1955	140,550	15,473	107,377	7,353	8,529	91,110	53,020	423,412	51,277
1956	154,983	12,308	105,913	7,189	9,026	94,772	48,667	432,858	68,553
1957	157,398	8,401	108,020	6,938	8,633	88,566	35,712	413,668	76,446
1958	152,928	3,725	76,580	7,268	8,256	82,327	35,619	366,703	50,291
1959	165,788	2,600	79,181	6,674	8,510	74,365	29,138	366,256	37,253
1960	173,882	2,101	81,015	7,378	8,216	77,432	30,405	380,429	36,541
1961	179,629	b	73,881	7,495	7,615	78,050	27,735	374,405	34,970
1962	190,833	b	74,262	7,319	7,719	79,453	28,188	387,774	38,413
1963	209,038	b	77,633	7,401	8,138	83,467	23,548	409,225	47,078
1964	223,032	b	88,757	7,394	8,679	83,639	19,615	431,116	47,969
1965	242,729	b	94,779	7,466	8,873	86,269	19,048	459,164	50,181
1966	264,202	b	95,892	7,117	9,149	89,941	19,965	486,266	49,302
1967	271,784	b	92,272	6,330	8,922	84,009	17,099	480,416	49,528
1968	294,739	b	90,765	5,657	9,391	83,054	15,224	498,830	50,637
1969	308,462	b	92,901	5,560	9,131	78,557	14,666	507,275	56,234
1970	318,921	b	96,009	5,410		83,207c	12,072	515,619	70,944
1971	326,280	b	82,809	5,560		68,862c	11,351	494,862	56,633

Source: U.S. Bureau of Mines data.
a Includes bunker fuel.
b Data included in other manufacturing and mining industries.
c Beginning in 1970, the data listed in these two columns were combined.

4

have their consumption reported separately by the Bureau of Mines (USBM).

The data in table 1.2 suggest, moreover, that many industrial coal users employ it to generate electricity. This may be indirectly inferred from the association between high levels of coal use and substantial electric power output (although the data do not specify the fuel source for this electricity). This electricity is probably jointly produced with process steam. Where both process steam and electricity are needed, it is often most efficient to generate steam in modern boilers at higher temperatures and pressures than are desired in process use and to pass the steam through a turbine producing both electricity and steam of the necessary characteristics.

Presumably, these uses are subject to the same air pollution challenges as electric utilities. However, the solutions may be quite different because the nuclear alternative generally will be impractical for industrial users of coal. However, special cases may arise such as the arrangement made by Dow Chemical to use the waste heat from a nuclear plant to be built by Consumers Powers (see chapter 6).

TABLE 1.2

Reported Coal Consumption and Net Electric Power Production by Manufacturing Industries, 1967

Industry	Thousands of tons of coal[a]	Million kwh generated[b]
Food and kindred products	5,889.2	2,191.1
Tobacco	348.6	112.9
Textile mill products	1,810.7	498.8
Lumber and wood	253.8	621.7
Furniture and fixtures	198.1	46.4
Paper and allied products	12,839.7	22,987.1
Printing and publishing	32.6	6.9
Chemicals and allied products	19,652.8	21,372.7
Petroleum and coal products	865.6	4,088.7
Rubber and plastic products	1,882.6	582.3
Stone, clay, and glass	11,211.2	1,193.1
Primary metal industries	7,700.5	22,526.7
Fabricated metal products	1,036.4	43.5
Machinery, except electrical	1,323.0	495.4
Electrical equipment and supplies	806.8	187.6
Transportation equipment	3,194.5	2.0
Instruments and related products	—	576.0
Miscellaneous	—	1.5
Total	69,045.8	77,534.4

Source: U.S. Census.

[a] There is no category or combination of categories in table 1.1 comparable to the coverage of these data since table 1.1 includes and this table excludes mining. Moreover, the data here are compiled from surveys of users and are incomplete because the Census by law cannot release data that provides information about individual firms.

[b] From all sources.

It is these considerations that cause the present study to be devoted to electric power generation rather than to other uses of coal. Modification of arguments developed about the electric power sector to apply to manufacturing is fairly straightforward and is summarized in the conclusion. The prospects for developing new markets are discussed later in this chapter.

COMPETITIVE ALTERNATIVES TO COAL

Coal in its natural form is clearly the least flexible of the fossil fuels. Being solid and containing substantial amounts of waste, coal involves greater difficulty at every stage of the use process. It is more difficult to extract, transport, and handle in consumption than oil or gas. Moreover, after combustion an ash residue remains that creates a disposal problem. As a result, coal will be used directly only when it is cheaper than other fuels. Therefore, economies of scale in coal handling are such that larger users find that they can more cheaply overcome the disadvantages. This fact largely explains the concentration of coal use among large consumers of fuel. Other fossil fuels are more widely used, but nuclear power is primarily usable only in large facilities such as electric power plants.

It has long been a desire of the coal industry to overcome these drawbacks by developing economically viable techniques for manufacturing synthetic oil and gas from coal. It has been further argued that impending exhaustion of conventional oil and gas supplies would make the need for such synthesis inevitable. Such exhaustion presumably would also improve the position of coal in existing markets.

In chapter 5, a fuller discussion is provided on the limitations of this argument. However, the essence of the criticism raised in chapter 5 should be noted here. The basic point is that the available data on comparative endowments of different fuels are grossly inadequate to support the argument that coal synthesis will ever become viable. Total physical endowments of other fossil fuels may be far smaller than those of coal but probably are still sufficient to last many generations. In addition, other resources such as solar power and deuterium in water are available in much vaster amounts than coal. At least in principle, one can imagine a situation in which sufficient quantities of the other fossil fuels prove available at costs less than those of coal synthesis to last the world long past the time, say sometime in the twenty-first century, when the more plentiful resources such as solar energy also become cheaper than coal synthesis. To resolve this issue, it is necessary to go beyond simple physical endowment measures to consideration of comparative costs of production. Tentative efforts at such cost comparisons in chapter 5 tend to suggest that the prospects for coal improving its competitive position are far less bright than enthusiasts about coal use would argue.

CRITICAL POLICY ISSUES

The prospects for coal as a utility boiler fuel cannot be assessed without considering the outlook for competing fuels, essentially oil. This, in turn, confronts us immediately with a set of policy issues and imponderables. Perhaps the central issue for developments in the rest of the twentieth century is the probable evolution of the policies of the countries in the Middle East and elsewhere that possess vast amounts of low cost oil for export. These countries formed an Organization of Petroleum Exporting Countries (OPEC) that sought during the 1960s to force increases in world oil prices but found prices actually fell. Then in 1971, the countries found the techniques needed to institute momentum towards sharp, continuing price rises. It has been argued in countless statements by U.S. energy industry and government officials that this trend is irresistible. These observers see a rise in oil prices that at the very least will price oil out of the markets considered here. M. A. Adelman, however, has vigorously contended that if the consuming countries act together wisely, they can reverse the trend to rising oil prices. His basic argument is that cartels are inherently unstable because the interests of different members diverge, and no participant can be sure that his partner's interests will insure continued cooperation. Therefore, the temptation to undercut the cartel secretly before another member does is often considerable. Since 1971, the countries have found that private oil companies can be made to serve as a buffer. They are forced to pay a fixed and widely publicized tax. Therefore, the companies are unable to cut prices themselves and tax concessions by any country would be highly visible. Adelman suggests that various consuming countries put pressure on the private companies within their borders to cease selling oil and to begin to sell managerial services, and to restrain themselves from frantic bidding against each other for oil. This, he believes, could remove the oil producing nations' ability to maintain and raise prices (see Adelman, 1972a and b). Clearly, then, future oil price developments depend on whether or not Adelman is both correct and *believed*.

Further important influences on oil prices could be produced by U.S. oil policies—including both those affecting imports and domestic production. In 1973, the long-standing policy of controlling imports by a quota system was replaced by a system of import fees. These are tariffs by another name and have exactly the same protective effect of allowing domestic producers to compete at a price that exceeds import prices by the amount of the tax. A special feature of the system is that higher fees are charged on product imports than on crude oil imports. This approach is designed to encourage domestic refining of imported crude oil.

Many combinations of future world price and domestic policy evolution are conceivable. The most pessimistic appraisals of world prices suggest that even without protectionist policies, the United States would head to virtual self-sufficiency in energy because imported oil would be so expensive. Conversely, Adelman suggests that U.S. policies could lead to reduction in world oil prices and a climate in which large imports would not pose serious risks. 1973 oil market developments have increased the difficulty of attaining low oil prices, but have not rendered the basic argument obsolete.

However, the much used balance-of-payments argument against oil imports is neither truly independent nor necessarily valid. At most, the argument states that in addition to the existing pressures on prices, the increase of oil imports will produce a balance-of-payments outflow. Such an outflow will undoubtedly lead to devaluation of the dollar and further rise in the effective cost of oil. Thus, the argument restates the prior contention that imported oil will become so expensive that importing it will be undesirable.

Two basic further defects exist in the balance-of-payments argument. First, it is inconsistent to argue simultaneously that oil is a vital commodity and that its import should be reduced to prevent a balance-of-payments drain. If oil is so essential, society may prefer to import it and cut down on foreign purchases of something else. This is the classic argument for using devaluation rather than trade restrictions to control balance-of-payments deficits; after devaluation, the market determines which goods are still demanded and the choice may be quite different than that arbitrarily decreed when trade restrictions are imposed.

The second objection is that the proof that oil imports would indeed strain the balance of payments is quite unsatisfactory. The influences on trade balances are far more complex than can be expressed by the simple calculations provided on how much oil imports will increase money outflows. In the first place, it is necessary to analyze the impacts of these outflows on their recipients. They or those from whom they buy may, in fact, greatly increase their purchases from the United States. Secondly, the net increase in outflow must be related to the situation that would otherwise prevail. It is quite conceivable that developments in other parts of the U.S. balance of payments could make possible increasing oil imports without straining the total payments balance. The United States might be headed towards developing a substantial payments surplus if it does not increase oil imports.

For those who consider this all purely hypothetical, it would be instructive to examine the European energy literature of the 1950s (see Gordon, 1970). The American discussions of the seventies are practically identical to the earlier European debates. Subsequent experience has shown quite clearly that arguments such as were applied here to the United States were applicable to Europe. Something better than the standard statement of the balance-of-payments argument, therefore, is needed to prove that the European experience cannot be repeated.

In any case, the state of the U.S. energy market also will be heavily dependent on purely domestic energy policies. A particularly critical question is the future evolution of natural gas policy. A 1954 Supreme Court decision held that the Natural Gas Act required the Federal Power Commission (FPC) to regulate field prices of natural gas producers. It has long been argued that such regulation could produce severe gas shortages, and by the early 1970s such shortages were causing widespread concern. It is widely agreed, therefore, that some change in regulation is required to make more gas available.[2] The FPC has already changed its policies to allow higher gas prices, and the President's 1973 energy messages proposed deregulation of prices of new natural gas. The extent to which regulations change and the response of gas supply and demand to these higher prices will be a major influence on future energy market conditions.

However, the growing importance of environmental policies may prove an even more important influence. As of 1973, the extent to which such policies have affected energy supplies remains controversial. However, few deny that major impacts eventually could occur. Development of such promising oil provinces as Alaska's North Slope and the outer continental shelves on the east and west coasts depends upon resolution of disputes over their environmental impacts. As chapter 6 shows, both fossil fuel and nuclear generation of electricity produce environmental impacts that have produced concerns that, in turn, have inspired stringent regulations.

By 1973, it was becoming increasingly clear that difficult choices were involved in designing a policy that provided a proper balance between environmental concerns and desires for material goods such as energy. Arguments have been raised for changing both the goals of environmental policies and the policies used to attain them. For example, chapter 6 discusses the debate over whether satisfactory technology to control sulfur oxide emissions from coal burning plants has been perfected. Such debate has led to policy discussions about imposing less ambitious control requirements, or at least delaying the implementation of existing policies. The President's April 18, 1973 energy message, for example, suggested a delay in attaining the secondary standards—those that eliminate effects other than to health—for sulfur oxides.

Similarly, some interest has arisen in implementing the principle of textbook economics that taxes are preferable to regulations as techniques of improving environmental quality. Not only have some of the major environmental groups supported this concept, but the Nixon Administration has proposed its concrete application to sulfur oxide emission control (see chapter 7).

The debate over the taxes versus regulation centers about which tool is most effective in the world of imperfect knowledge and institutions. An

---

[2] See Brown 1972 for a review of these issues.

optimal environmental policy is one that insures that all abatement expenditures be adopted if they are less costly than the degradation they eliminate. If we truly knew the actual costs of abatement and the value it produces through improving the environment, we could either impose the desirable measures by regulations, or set taxes to accomplish the same goal. If those who cause degradation faced a tax that could be reduced by refraining from continuing their actions, they would adopt all abatement measures that produced a tax saving greater than the abatement costs. Thus, if the tax saving equaled the value to society of abatement, all abatement measures costing less than the value of the environmental improvement would be adopted.

The best choice in practice will be determined by many forces. Given our imperfect and evolving knowledge, a flexible policy that adapts to better information is needed. Similarly, differences in the situation from region to region or industry to industry necessitate methods for tailoring policies to special needs. Moreover, expenses arise in administering different policies and, therefore, reductions in administrative costs may justify changes in policy design.

These points suggest that a complete theory of control policy indicates that the preferable choice depends upon circumstances. It becomes necessary to work out in great detail how taxes and regulations compare on balance as techniques to solve a particular problem. At any rate, the basic case for taxes is easier to state than that for regulation. The main justification for taxes is that it saves the government from attempting to measure the costs of abatement. Each firm makes this calculation for itself and presumably is better able to do so than the government. The counterargument is more complex, but one critical point is that it may be difficult to move a tax to its proper level as better information accumulates. Legislative bodies may be more willing to grant broad administrative powers than to engage in continued study of proper taxes or to delegate taxing authority.

A final policy issue is the extent to which governmental support should be provided to energy research and development. It is widely contended that certain promising research and development projects are so large and risky that they cannot proceed without government aid. However, large size and high risk are not the only reasons for lack of support; the project may be simply unattractive. Thus, research and development policy must somehow choose between those prospects that are truly deserving, and those that are not.

Clearly, the prospects for coal depend critically on these policies and their effect. The coal industry will thrive most when public policy aids it, when its rivals at home or abroad are subject to severe public policy constraints, when it benefits from extensive support for research and development work, and when its use is not limited by severe environmental regulations. In what follows, the impacts of various policy postures are considered so that some sense may be conveyed of exactly how sensitive the prospects of coal are to alternative policies.

NEW ENERGY TECHNOLOGIES

Technology occupies a somewhat ambiguous position in economic analysis. Economists simultaneously stress the role of new technology in promoting economic progress and warn that major new technologies develop quite slowly. This implies enthusiasm about the general contribution of new techniques and skepticism about the specific contribution of any one technique. Such a stress on breakthroughs neglects the contribution of numerous small but steady improvements in existing techniques. In addition, the skepticism about major advances is one of degree. It is not denied that breakthroughs occur and make important contributions. The problems are that many promising ideas can never be translated into economic successes and that even those that prove viable take many years to develop.

These principles are clearly relevant to future energy market developments. The long construction lead times involved with building a typical facility for energy production, transformation, or use means that any experimental plant takes several years to design, build, and test. Since a series of facilities of successively greater complexity and size are required before a commercial technology is developed, many years elapse before major new energy technologies can be commercially exploited. Thus, while new technology could be a major contributor to energy market conditions in the late 1980s and beyond, major breakthroughs are unlikely before that time.

Nevertheless, a wide spectrum of new energy technologies are under consideration (see Hottel and Howard, 1971, and Schurr, et al., 1971 for detailed reviews). Until the early 1970s, primary stress of U.S. government activity was upon development of fast breeder reactors. These are a form of nuclear reactor that produces more fuel than it uses. Reactors use a fuel that is a mixture of various uranium isotopes, and only a part consists of the reactive form U235. However, the reaction converts some of the other isotopes to plutonium. The reactors in use in the seventies produce an amount of plutonium with less fuel value than the U235 that is consumed, but a fast breeder would cause plutonium output to exceed U235 use. Since breeders would lead to greater productivity of existing uranium supplies, the U.S. Atomic Energy Commission (AEC) has vigorously financed its development.

A number of criticisms have been raised against this strategy. The most widely held is that the breeder is not the only promising new technology. MacAvoy (1969) has suggested that the AEC did not select the most promising of several alternative breeder technologies. Others have contended that the case for the breeder is essentially another fallacious application of the argument that a threat of fuel exhaustion is imminent. The criticism takes the explicit form of assertions that uranium supplies are sufficiently ample, and that no pressing need arises to increase the amount of energy secured from a unit of uranium. The savings due to lower fuel requirements may be offset by the higher capital costs of breeders compared to existing reactors (see, e.g., Cochran, 1974).

While other techniques have not received the strong financial support provided the breeder, many have been studied. For example, research has been conducted on several new techniques for generating electricity from fossil fuels. Numerous studies also have been made of methods for manufacturing synthetic fuels from coal. These include techniques to duplicate the properties of crude oil and natural gas and to use coal to produce a clean industrial fuel that may be a gas, a liquid, or even a solid (see chapter 5). The pressure of new environmental regulations has similarly inspired extensive research on techniques for facilitating compliance.

It may be noted that none of these major projects is directed towards improvement in the extraction of fuels. It appears, moreover, that concern about the adequacy of technical progress in extraction is confined to coal mining. The need for new coal mining techniques is widely discussed but no clear direction has emerged.

All of these prospects are in fairly early stages of development, so the argument that no major breakthroughs are likely until, at the earliest, the middle eighties applies to all of them. Moreover, few have even progressed far enough to permit adequate forecasts of their costs. Thus, no firm predictions about which new technologies, if any, become important are possible. It is argued below that unless important advances occur in the technology of coal mining and coal use, the future of coal may be severely impaired.

THE IMPLICATIONS FOR THE STATUS OF COAL
IN THE ENERGY MARKET

The prior discussion suggests that a comprehensive study of the prospects for coal is far beyond the scope of a single study. Thus, much more modest goals are pursued here. The basic approach is to stress that the future of coal is by no means as clear as is often argued.[3] Massive growth in coal output is not guaranteed, but can occur only if rather substantial obstacles are overcome. Rather than make specific forecasts, I will discuss

---

[3] A typical example of the extravagant, optimistic statements about coal that are quite widely made can be found in the speeches, largely made by U.S. government officials, to the 1973 convention of the National Coal Association.

a number of plausible cases to show that the uncertainty about the prospects for coal is considerable. A fairly elaborate examination is provided of electric utility demand for coal, but only superficial attention is given the prospective major market for coal as the source of substitutes for crude oil and natural gas. These choices reflect the combined influence of the present importance of the markets, growth prospects, technological uncertainties, and data availability.

As the prior argument suggests, the general practice here is to limit severely the extent to which alternative views of the supply of rival fuels and the policies affecting them are considered. The basic principle is that the cases treated be interesting in the dual sense that they are plausible and that their implications are not obvious. Plausibility is defined as the existence of a reasoned justification. For example, the range of informed opinion on future oil and gas costs implies that many different price levels deserve consideration.

However, the implication of many of these forecasts is so clear that no detailed discussion is required. Oil could become so cheap that it rules out the use of any other fuel or so expensive that it could never compete with coal. However, the interesting cases are those in which oil prices remain at levels between the two extremes. In such situations, more detailed comparisons are necessary before the implications of the price projections can be deduced.

The case in which oil prices are at such an "intermediate" level, defined as one similar to that prevailing in 1972, is stressed here. No corresponding assumption is provided for natural gas. This expedient can be justified by accepting the widespread belief that natural gas prices are likely to rise well above levels that would permit continued natural gas use in electric power generation. However, a more general rationale is that the effect on *coal* of lower gas prices is similar to that of the oil price assumption. Thus, the oil price assumption suffices to handle the general case of fossil-fuel prices low enough to constitute a competitive challenge to coal. Of course, this "interesting" case looks much less plausible than when it was originally adopted. The sharp rises in oil prices in 1973 and 1974 may be difficult to reverse.

The emphasis on interesting cases also extends to treatment of environmental issues. It is more difficult to argue that any particular set of environmental regulations is too implausible to consider. The effects of some sort of ban on nuclear power or the failure to develop methods to control sulfur oxide emissions from coal burning facilities when such controls are required by law should be quite clear. This neglect, of course, does not imply that such difficulties as failure of scrubber technology will not arise.

In this study, the only environmental policy variations considered relate to sulfur oxide regulations. Four options are evaluated—the absence of sulfur regulations, the general imposition of the U.S. government's current standards for new plants on all plants, a sulfur tax, and regulations stricter than the U.S. rules for new plants. This by no means covers every interesting case but should suffice to characterize the situation adequately. It is likely that each region of the United States will adopt one of these four strategies. The overall effect can be deduced by applying the analysis for each strategy to the regions that employ it. Therefore, the present discussion provides the building blocks for treatment of the many different regional patterns that may emerge.

A final limitation imposed upon this study is a restriction on the time frame of the projections. The basic goal is to describe possible developments in the 1980s. However, costs are only projected up to 1980 and analysis proceeds on the assumption of no radical changes in *relative* cost positions after 1980. No effort is made to incorporate inflationary trends; prices are set in 1973 dollars.

Only one aspect of new fuel technology is considered here—the development of an improved method of generating electricity from fossil fuels. Here, there exists an option (see chapter 7) that has been developed sufficiently for fairly reasonable estimates of performance and costs to be made. While it is not argued that this particular method will in fact be the one adopted, it can serve as an example of the possible impact of better generation techniques.

2

Fuel Cost and Consumption—
1946–1972

INTRODUCTION

Since electric power use of coal is the focus of the present study, it is appropriate to begin with review of past fuel use in the industry. This chapter starts with a brief note on electric power output trends. Then an overview of fuel use patterns is provided. Two further sections discuss critical details; the first deals with the East Coast market, and the following section treats important points about other parts of the country. Appendix A to the chapter relates the regional patterns of fuel use by individual companies, and Appendix B discusses conceptual problems related to the data.

Much of the requisite information is best presented in tabular form, and the text concentrates on discussing points of particular interest. Several other limitations of this chapter may be noted. The discussion does not pretend to handle all the forces affecting market prices; only those most relevant to the present chapter are noted. Later chapters deal more fully with many of these issues. The data are deliberately presented without any more aggregation or deflation than the sources provide. Disaggregation provides a better view of the situation than a complex synthetic index; deflation is avoided mainly as a burdensome refinement not essential to the purposes of this study.

A NOTE ON THE REGIONAL PATTERNS OF
ELECTRIC POWER OUTPUT GROWTH

Since fuels differ in their competitive position from region to region, interregional differences in demand growth should affect the relative national position of fuels. Therefore, table 2.1 shows the growth rates of electric power output in different parts of the country. The only striking development revealed by the data is that the highest electric power output growth occurred in the gas using West South Central region. Otherwise differential regional electric power growth was not a predominant influence on the evolution of the share of each fuel in the national totals.

TABLE 2.1
Regional Patterns of Electric Power Use in the United States

Region	Electric power output						Average annual % increase		
	million kwh			% of total					
	1946	1959	1971	1946	1959	1971	1946–1959	1959–1971	1946–1971
New England	12,307	27,719	63,937	5.5	3.9	4.0	6.5	7.6	6.6
Middle Atlantic	47,349	107,201	222,373	21.2	15.1	13.8	6.1	6.3	6.2
East North Central	50,069	158,523	302,754	22.4	22.3	18.8	9.4	5.9	7.2
West North Central	13,187	41,001	103,012	5.9	5.8	6.4	8.9	8.1	8.4
South Atlantic	28,551	98,131	265,227	12.8	13.8	16.4	9.9	9.1	9.0
East South Central	16,486	82,077	151,112	7.4	11.6	9.4	14.9	5.4	9.5
West South Central	13,069	59,315	188,741	5.9	8.4	11.7	12.4	10.3	10.7
Mountain	11,659	34,047	80,034	5.2	4.8	5.0	5.4	7.5	7.5
Pacific	30,501	101,992	230,925	13.7	14.4	14.3	9.6	7.4	8.3
Alaska and Hawaii[a]	—	—	5,821	—	—	0.4	—	—	—
Total public utility sector	223,178	710,006	1,613,936	100.0	100.0	100.0	9.4	7.4	8.0
Total generation	269,609	795,251	1,717,521				8.8	6.9	7.5
Total availability	272,000	798,858	1,720,770				8.8	6.9	7.5

Sources: FPC data as tabulated by the National Coal Association (1960) and the Edison Electric Institute, *Statistical Yearbook*, 1972. *Note:* Total generation includes electric utilities, industrial, mine, and railroad plants only; total availability is generation plus net imports. [a] Alaska and Hawaii only included starting in 1960.

REGIONAL PATTERNS OF ELECTRIC UTILITY FUEL USE—
THE RECORD SINCE 1946

Before discussing fuel use patterns, it is necessary to note a few points affecting fuel choice. Given the high levels of transportation costs relative to mine or well head prices (see chapter 5), fuels compete most effectively near centers of production. The concentration of coal production centers is discussed more fully elsewhere, so this section can proceed directly to evaluation of fuel use patterns after briefly noting some critical points about gas and oil.

Gas production is centered in the West South Central States and California. In these regions, it has long been quite a cheap fuel. Moreover, the provisions of government regulation of natural gas field prices encourage greater gas availability for consumers within a producing state. Sales to interstate pipelines are subject to Federal Power Commission price controls, but intrastate sales are not. Local customers can, therefore, offer higher prices.

In viewing gas use in areas distant from the gas fields, a critical consideration is that a significant portion of gas use is for space heating and is, therefore, highly seasonal. Pipeline capacity must suffice to provide the gas needed throughout the year. The pipeline company has a choice between shipping the gas to market during low demand periods for storage and providing enough transmission capacity to meet the peak demands. In the latter case, the theory of peak load pricing suggests that reduced prices be given those who would use this extra capacity in offpeak periods.

Gas storage is practiced, but costs are such that it does not pay to offset demand fluctuations entirely through inventories. Extra capacity is provided, and interruptible sales contracts are made. These involve selling gas to industrial users, including electric power utilities, at prices competitive with residual fuel oil or coal. Sales may be limited to summer months when heating demands are absent, but in any case the buyers agree to accept cutoff of deliveries on short notice if the need arises. Such cutoffs were rare until the growing gas shortage of the seventies.

The main utility petroleum product has long been residual fuel oil. The traditional residual oils such as number 6 or bunker C are quite viscous and have high pour points—i.e., they flow only at elevated temperatures. This has meant that only tanker or barge deliveries were economical so that oil use was limited to coastal areas. Pipelining was considered impractical except for a few intracity lines.

Oil economics have long been unfavorable to domestic production of residual oil in the United States. Residual oil prices have had to match those of rival fuels. At the low prices prevailing for such substitutes, it has been more profitable to employ refining processes that produced little or no residuum.

However, elsewhere in the world, demand conditions and the nature of the crude oils used are more favorable for residual oil production. Foreign refineries—particularly in the Caribbean—still produce substantial amounts of residual oil. Since 1966 when import controls were effectively removed on the East Coast, electric utilities in the area have rapidly shifted to residual oil. Air pollution regulations restricting the use of high-sulfur fuel accelerated the process.

The only other area of substantial use of residual oil is in California; the refineries in the area produce proportionally more residual fuel than those in other regions. Provisions in the old oil import program for the West Coast that provide larger crude oil import quotas to West Coast refineries producing low-sulfur residual oil were designed to encourage more refining of residual oil. However, this was offset by exemptions from import control applied to low-sulfur residual oil. Electric utility use of residual oil away from the two coasts was limited to a few plants located near refineries.

A variety of forces could alter the situation during the 1970s. Among the most critical are the effects of sulfur regulations discussed in chapter 6. A movement to oils with lower pour points and direct burning of crude oil has been encouraged by the new fuel cost economics that result from the sulfur regulations. This development and the problems of meeting emission standards with coal may produce substantial inland pipelining of oil to power plants. The prospects are fully reviewed later, and it suffices to note here that the first sign of some radical shifts are already represented by inland shipments of oil to such companies as Commonwealth Edison in Chicago. Use was initially limited largely to small, old plants for which other alternatives for meeting air quality standards are extremely expensive. The oil can in some cases be barged up the Mississippi but in others must go through the St. Lawrence Seaway (which is closed during the winter). In either case extra transportation costs are involved. Plans for base load plants using oil have been announced for the Middle West although sharply rising oil prices may reverse the trend.

Waterpower resources are scattered about the United States but, because the most economic sites have already been exploited, hydropower expansion has been much slower than that of electric power generation. Table 2.2 lists the distribution of U.S. hydropower output in the states most heavily reliant on it, and the role of hydropower in the electric power generation of each state. Only 1946 and 1971 figures are shown. The importance of waterpower differs widely among states. In particular, we can identify states such as Oregon and Idaho almost totally supplied by hydropower in 1971, and states such as Washington, South Dakota, Montana, and Vermont which use a high proportion of waterpower. While a national trend to reduced relative reliance on waterpower is seen to predominate— particularly in the East South Central States served by the Tennessee

TABLE 2.2

Leading Hydroelectric Power Producing States, 1946 and 1971

	Hydroelectric generation					
	million kwh		% of state total		% of U.S. total	
State[a]	1946	1971	1946	1971	1946	1971
Washington	8,862	71,429	98.0	96.6	11.3	26.8
California	12,650	39,045	73.1	31.8	16.1	14.7
Oregon	3,994	34,305	96.3	99.9	5.1	12.9
New York	7,549	25,178	33.0	25.6	9.6	9.5
Alabama	6,044	9,912	82.8	21.1	7.7	3.7
Montana	2,432	9,595	98.6	90.1	3.1	3.6
Tennessee	6,158	9,420	93.6	21.5	7.9	3.5
South Dakota	17	7,742	5.4	92.3	0.0	2.9
Idaho	1,333	7,469	99.8	100.0	1.7	2.8
Arizona	2,438	6,621	86.3	45.1	3.1	2.5
North Carolina	2,862	5,910	50.4	11.0	3.7	2.2
Kentucky	1,517	3,536	63.7	7.2	1.9	1.3
South Carolina	2,329	3,440	90.2	16.0	3.0	1.3
Georgia	1,470	3,247	48.3	11.0	1.9	1.2
North Dakota	0.0	3,235	0.0	39.1	0.0	1.2
Total above	59,655	240,084	67.6	38.5	76.1	90.1
Nevada	2,482	1,678	99.8	20.0	3.2	0.6
Maine	1,220	1,651	89.0	38.0	1.6	0.6
Utah	354	979	77.4	31.9	0.5	0.4
New Hampshire	793	929	78.2	19.6	1.0	0.3
Vermont	747	683	98.4	80.4	1.0	0.3
Total all above	65,251	246,004	69.2	38.1	83.2	92.4
Total U.S.	78,404	266,320	35.1	16.5	100.0	100.0

Sources: 1946 from National Coal Association, 1960; 1971 from Edison Electric Institute, *Statistical Yearbook*, 1972.
[a] States included consist of states producing more than three billion kilowatt hours from hydroelectric plants in 1971 and five others that secured the majority of their 1946 power from hydroelectric sources.

Valley Authority (TVA)—the table suppresses many complexities. Since waterpower output varies with climatic conditions, significant year to year fluctuations can occur in waterpower's share. More critically, most states did not show a regular downward trend in the role of hydroelectric power. Quite the contrary, sometime between 1946 and 1971, the majority of the water-using states recorded periods of temporarily rising reliance on hydroelectric power. This undoubtedly reflects availability of power from new projects.

Over the entire 1946–1971 period, the main changes in the national importance of different prime movers in generating electricity were a growth of natural gas's role and a decline in waterpower's importance (see table

2.3). The main growth in gas markets has been in the West South Central States and California. About 63 percent of the gas-generated electricity in 1971 was produced in these states. The roles of coal and oil have been more variable. Until 1966, coal was able to maintain a good share of the East Coast market but subsequently has been pushed inland.

In contrast, some evidence suggests that at least with the natural gas policy prevailing up to 1973, coal was improving its position in areas where it competes directly with gas. The market share of coal in the late sixties was somewhat below that of its share in both the early sixties and the late forties. The early fifties, however, represent the low point in the relative position of coal. Nevertheless, coal was by far the most important fuel for the industry throughout this period.

The importance of oil mounted rapidly up to 1950 and then began a steady decline. The liberalization of import controls in 1966 reversed this trend and, as shown below, helped start a substantial extension of its use. Nuclear power will not become a significant force until well into the seventies.

As is shown in more detail below, considerable regional differences prevailed in coal use. Direct coal use in the Northeast (except for inland Pennsylvania and upstate New York) has virtually disappeared. Largely because of reduced relative reliance on water power, the South Atlantic and East South Central regions became more heavily dependent on coal.

In sum, no more than two fossil fuels have been major potential suppliers in any one region. On the East Coast, coal competed with oil. In various inland states, coal and natural gas have competed. This has been mainly in certain West North Central and Mountain States. Earlier in the post-World War II period, gas competition was also significant elsewhere—notably in the Southeast. California has had some gas-oil competition. Some areas relied almost entirely on a single fuel: gas in the South Central region, oil in certain East Coast regions far from the coal fields, and coal in regions best described as having much easier access to it than to the other fuels.

In some cases, the consuming area is quite close to coal fields. Other regions, notably the Upper Midwest, are distant from all fuel production points.

The principal region-by-region effects of these historical trends are as follows:

1. New England. In 1946 Maine and Vermont both secured substantial portions of their power from water. The role of hydro resources declined in both states but more sharply in Maine. It has relied heavily on oil for its fossil-generated power. The other states were areas of oil-coal competition until 1966. Subsequently, coal use has sharply declined (see below).

TABLE 2.3
Distribution of Electric Power Generation by Energy Source, 1946–1971

Energy source	Electric power output			% of total			Average annual % increase		
	million kwh								
	1946	1959	1971	1946	1959	1971	1946–1959	1959–1971	1946–1971
Hydroelectric	78,404	137,782	266,320	35.1	19.4	16.5	4.7	5.7	5.0
Coal	111,654	378,424	714,756	50.0	53.3	44.3	10.2	6.0	7.9
Oil	14,082	46,840	218,162	6.3	6.6	13.5	8.2	14.2	8.8
Gas	18,820	146,619	375,939	8.4	20.6	23.3	16.5	8.5	11.7
Nuclear	—	188	37,899	—	0.0	2.3	—	44.0	—
Total	223,178	710,006	1,613,936	100.0	100.0	100.0	9.4	7.4	8.0

Source: Same as table 2.1.

TABLE 2.4
Role of Individual Fuels in Fossil Generation Electricity by States, 1946 and 1971

State and region	1946 Percent of electricity generated—all fossil plants			1971 Percent of fuel input to steam plant		
	Coal	Oil	Gas	Coal	Oil	Gas
Connecticut	68.5	31.5	—	21	79	—
Maine	12.7	87.0	—	—	100	—
Massachusetts	93.7	6.3	—	2	95	3
New Hampshire	82.6	17.4	—	60	40	—
Rhode Island	31.1	68.9	—	—	84	16
Vermont[a]	39.0	59.4	—	92	8	—
New England	75.7	24.3	—	13	85	2
New Jersey	84.3	15.7	—	26	65	9
New York	94.2	5.6	0.2	28	60	12
Pennsylvania	95.1	4.9	—	83	16	1
Middle Atlantic	92.6	7.3	0.1	54	40	6
Illinois	97.9	1.6	0.5	79	6	15
Indiana	96.7	1.6	1.7	94	1	5
Michigan	98.4	1.6	—	83	8	9
Ohio	98.8	0.7	0.5	98	—	2
Wisconsin	97.6	2.3	—	88	2	10
East North Central	98.1	1.4	0.5	89	3	8
Iowa	67.2	12.6	19.9	58	—	42
Kansas	24.1	10.6	65.3	5	1	94
Minnesota	68.7	7.4	23.6	67	2	31
Missouri	53.0	10.9	36.1	80	—	20
Nebraska	43.7	11.0	45.3	32	1	67
North Dakota	91.0	7.2	1.8	100	—	—
South Dakota	35.6	25.7	38.7	57	12	31
West North Central	52.7	10.8	36.4	58	1	41
Delaware	72.3	27.7	—	72	20	8
District of Columbia	98.9	1.1	—	28	72	—
Florida	—	93.3	6.7	17	45	38
Georgia	33.1	6.9	60.0	75	3	22
Maryland	97.9	2.1	—	62	38	—
North Carolina	98.8	1.2	—	98	—	2
South Carolina	95.7	4.3	—	72	5	23
Virginia	95.9	4.1	—	52	47	1
West Virginia	99.5	—	0.5	99	1	—
South Atlantic	79.8	14.3	5.9	62	23	15
Alabama	58.5	0.3	41.3	97	—	3
Kentucky	99.2	0.8	—	98	—	2
Mississippi	1.3	7.1	91.6	11	5	84
Tennessee	64.9	1.0	34.1	95	—	5
East South Central	67.5	1.1	31.4	89	1	10

TABLE 2.4. *Continued*

State and region	1946 Percent of electricity generated—all fossil plants			1971 Percent of fuel input to steam plant		
	Coal	Oil	Gas	Coal	Oil	Gas
Arkansas	4.6	8.8	86.6	—	16	84
Louisiana	—	4.4	95.6	—	1	99
Oklahoma	15.8	6.3	77.9	—	—	100
Texas	—	2.4	97.6	—	—	100
West South Central	2.6	3.7	93.7	—	1	99
Arizona[a]	0.1	39.1	60.6	10	3	87
Colorado	62.2	7.5	30.3	55	2	43
Montana	—	8.0	92.0	89	—	11
Nevada	—	100.0	—	44	1	55
New Mexico[a]	8.8	10.8	78.7	70	1	29
Utah	81.8	17.3	0.9	43	49	8
Wyoming	62.4	17.7	19.9	95	1	4
Mountain[a]	35.6	15.9	48.1	56	4	40
California[a]	—	78.9	20.2	—	26	74
Oregon[a]	—	26.0	—	—	29	71
Washington[a]	1.4	78.9	—	—	100	—
Pacific[a]	0.1	77.3	18.9	—	26	74
Total Contiguous Forty-eight States[a]	77.1	9.7	13.0	54	16	30

Sources: National Coal Association (1960) and National Coal Association, *Steam Electric Plant Factors,* 1972.

[a] Wood and waste used in 1946.

2. The Middle Atlantic States. The New York City area, Philadelphia, and New Jersey were regions of coal-oil competition, but coal's position sharply deteriorated after 1966. The rest of Pennsylvania and New York relied almost entirely on coal for fossil-fuel generated power, but oil use started in upstate New York in the early seventies and is planned for in-land Pennsylvania. New York also has significant waterpower resources.
3. The East North Central States. Coal has dominated because three states are major producers and the other two have better access to coal than to other fuels.
4. The South Atlantic States. Water power, most important in the Carolinas, has declined sharply in importance. Coal dominated fossil-fuel generation everywhere but in Florida. The east coast of Florida re-lied heavily on oil but the west coast was a center of oil-coal competition. Oil use has become more important in parts of the region—particularly Virginia.
5. The West North Central States. South Dakota has greatly increased its

TABLE 2.5
Importance of Coal and Oil in Electric Power Generation: Eastern United States
in Selected Years
(percent)

	Coal						
	% of elec. generated—all fuel powered plants		% of Btu consumed in steam plants				
States and regions	1946	1951	1951	1956	1966	1969	1971
Connecticut	68.49	71.36	74	84	84	32	21
Maine	12.70	—	1	—	—	—	—
Massachusetts	93.74	43.84	45	58	45	19	2
New Hampshire	82.61	7.14	3	40	45	67	60
Rhode Island	31.12	59.37	45	74	62	—	—
Vermont	39.02	0.62	—	99	100	93	92
New England	75.72	52.18	51	65	56	25	13
New Jersey	84.31	61.27	58	73	61	32	26
New York City }	94.17 }	84.32	73[a]	73	35	23	7
Other New York State }			100[a]	99	99	92	67
Philadelphia }	95.12 }	95.02	85[b]	90	76	41	26
Other Pennsylvania }			100[b]	100	100	100	99
Middle Atlantic	92.58	85.02	85	88	73	60	54
Delaware	72.26	97.77	100	79	87	80	72
District of Columbia	98.88	99.58	100	100	98	63	28
Florida	—	—	—	4	20	21	17
Georgia	33.10	28.29	27	50	100	83	75
Maryland	97.86	98.55	100	100	99	88	62
North Carolina	98.78	98.97	100	100	99	99	98
South Carolina	95.74	84.29	85	30	79	73	72
Virginia	95.93	98.31	100	99	99	78	52
West Virginia	99.48	99.85	100	99	100	100	99
South Atlantic	79.82	76.53	77[c]	73	80	73	62

Source: Same as table 2.4.

[a] Total New York State figures on a percent of Btu consumed basis (83) provide a comparison between columns 2 and 3.

[b] Total Pennsylvania figures on a percent of Btu consumed basis (96) provide a comparison between columns 2 and 3.

dependence on waterpower. The fossil-fuel situation differs substantially among states. The Dakotas possess the only substantial coal reserves, but other states, notably Missouri and Minnesota, are favorably located to secure Illinois coal. In other states, such as Kansas and Nebraska, gas has been the main fossil fuel.

6. The East South Central States. This area is dominated by TVA and, therefore, its electric generating pattern largely follows that of TVA—a shift from reliance on waterpower to the dominance of coal-fired plants. Mississippi, however, is largely a gas-using state with one major plant burning coal.

	% of elec. generated—all fuel powered plants		% of Btu consumed in steam plants				
States and regions	1946	1951	1951	1956	1966	1969	1971
Connecticut	31.50	28.64	26	14	16	68	79
Maine	87.04	100.00	99	100	100	100	100
Massachusetts	6.33	56.17	55	36	50	79	95
New Hampshire	17.39	92.87	97	60	55	33	40
Rhode Island	68.87	40.64	55	26	37	94	84
Vermont	59.35	99.38	100	1	—	7	8
New England	24.30	47.82	49	31	42	74	85
New Jersey	15.68	32.67	37	21	32	57	65
New York City	5.63 }	9.74 }	17[d]	15	46	57	77
Other New York State			—	—	—	1	28
Philadelphia	4.88 }	1.67 }	6[e]	10	24	57	70
Other Pennsylvania			—	—	—	—	1
Middle Atlantic	7.33	10.13	10	8	21	32	40
Delaware	27.74	2.22	—	4	1	13	20
District of Columbia	1.11	0.42	—	—	2	37	72
Florida	93.32	92.35	91[c]	86	53	44	45
Georgia	6.87	6.07	8	3	—	1	3
Maryland	2.13	1.45	—	—	1	12	38
North Carolina	1.19	1.04	—	—	—	—	—
South Carolina	4.27	15.72	15	1	1	4	5
Virginia	4.07	1.53	—	—	—	21	47
West Virginia	0.04	0.11	—	—	—	—	1
South Atlantic	14.33	14.38	13[c]	15	12	15	23

c 1952 source did not tabulate 1951.

d Total New York State figures on a percent of Btu consumed basis (11) provide a comparison between columns 2 and 3.

e Total Pennsylvania figures on a percent of Btu consumed basis (2) provide a comparison between columns 2 and 3.

7. The West South Central States. Gas dominates.

8. The Mountain States. The role of water power has declined sharply except in Idaho. Coal–gas competition has prevailed in the fossil fuel sector, but the large coal resources of the region are expected to meet much of the future growth of fossil-fuel generation.

9. The Pacific States. The heavy dependence on water power in Washington and Oregon is expected to decline in the 1970s. California's pattern has been particularly complex. It reduced its dependence on water power and turned primarily to gas use supplemented by oil. The Southwestern coal-fired mine mouth plants now supply California.

TABLE 2.6
Role of Coal in Electric Power Generation: Selected States in Selected Years
(percent)

State and region	Based on % of electricity generated		Based on % of Btu consumed				
	1946	1951	1951	1956	1966	1969	1971
Illinois	97.87	89.33	90	87	93	90	79
Indiana	96.69	98.74	99	97	96	96	94
Michigan	98.38	98.10	100	100	100	94	83
Ohio	98.82	99.24	100	99	100	99	98
Wisconsin	97.59	98.42	100	100	92	89	88
East North Central[a]	98.05	96.11	97	95	97	94	89
Iowa	67.20	58.93	65	52	50	55	58
Kansas	24.10	16.89	21	10	8	5	5
Minnesota	68.66	51.02	57	59	67	64	67
Missouri	52.97	59.73	67	65	74	78	80
Nebraska	43.73	29.87	31	20	22	34	32
North Dakota	90.98	95.55	100	99	100	100	100
South Dakota	35.60	46.96	63	61	56	59	57
West North Central[b]	52.73	46.91	55	48	51	54	58
Alabama	58.47	60.20	63	90	98	96	97
Kentucky	99.22	95.51	95	97	100	98	98
Mississippi	1.33	0.23	—	—	—	13	11
Tennessee	64.88	86.18	99	100	93	94	95
East South Central[b]	67.53	66.45	70[c]	90	91	89	89
Arkansas	4.56	0.04	1	—	—	—	—
Louisiana	0.01	0.01	—	—	—	—	—
Oklahoma	15.81	2.22	1	—	—	—	—
Texas	—	—	—	—	—	—	—
West South Central[b]	2.56	0.27	1[c]	—	—	—	—
Arizona	0.13	—	—	—	14	12	10
Colorado	62.18	29.27	43	32	65	59	55
Montana	—	—	—	—	52	78	89
Nevada	—	—	—	—	31	43	44
New Mexico	8.82	5.42	6	3	45	47	70
Utah	81.78	61.47	81	32	40	41	43
Wyoming	62.43	85.95	86	87	100	95	95
Mountain[d]	35.59	20.83	29[c]	22	51	51	56
California	—	—	—	—	—	—	—
Oregon	—	—	3[c]	—	—	—	—
Washington	1.36	—	—	—	—	—	—
Pacific[e]	0.05	—	—	—	—	—	—
U.S.A. total	77.12	68.36	67[c]	70	65	59	54

Source: Same as table 2.4.
[a] Otherwise gas.
[b] Otherwise predominantly gas.
[c] 1952 since source did not tabulate 1951.
[d] Otherwise predominantly gas except large amounts of pitch in Utah.
[e] Mainly gas but significant proportion of oil.

TABLE 2.7

Role of Oil in Electric Power Generation: Selected States in Selected Years
(percent of total)

	% of elec. generated in all fossil fuel powered plants		% of Btu used in steam plants				
	1946	1951	1952[a]	1956	1966	1969	1971
Utah	17.34	37.74	46	24	33	46	49
California	78.93	52.81	51	47	18	17	26
Oregon	26.02	18.61	97	—	74	20	29
Washington	78.89	62.45	100	100	100	100	100
Pacific	77.29	52.21	55	48	18	17	26
U.S.A.	9.72	10.59	10	8	8	12	16

Source: Same as table 2.4.
[a] 1952 used because source did not tabulate prior years.

The critical elements of the fossil fuel portion of this pattern are summarized in tables 2.4–2.8. The first shows the 1946 and 1971 shares of all fuels in each state. Table 2.5 compares the shares of coal and oil in East Coast electric power fossil fuel use. Table 2.6 then shows the share of coal elsewhere in the United States. In tables 2.7 and 2.8, the corresponding figures for oil and gas are shown. In all but table 2.4, only those states in which significant proportions of the energy was supplied by a given fuel are included.

ENERGY MARKET CONDITIONS ON THE EAST COAST

As already noted, the East Coast was the center of coal–oil competition. Until the late sixties, however, the bulk of the rivalry centered on the area extending from Philadelphia to Portsmouth, New Hampshire, and on western Florida. Since the removal of import control on residual fuel oil and the rise of stringent air pollution regulations, oil has become markedly more important in other coastal areas.

It may be seen from table 2.5 that the fuel use patterns differ quite considerably among states. At one extreme, in Maine and on the East Coast of Florida, oil is the predominant fuel. Conversely, coal was long the dominant fuel in New York (outside of the New York City area), Pennsylvania (outside of Philadelphia), and West Virginia.[1] However, shifts to oil have been made or planned to meet environmental regulations in upstate New York and parts of Pennsylvania outside Philadelphia.

[1] The National Coal Association defines the New York City area as the plants of Consolidated Edison and Long Island Lighting. However, two other nearby companies, Central Hudson Gas and Electric and Orange-Rockland Utilities, are also heavy oil users. The first has stopped and the second has greatly curtailed coal use.

TABLE 2.8
Role of Natural Gas in Electric Power Generation: Selected States in Selected Years

	% of electricity generated in all fossil fuel powered plants		% of Btu used in steam plants				
	1946	1951	1951	1956	1966	1969	1971
Georgia	60.00	65.62	65	47	—	16	22
South Carolina	—	—	—	69	20	23	23
Florida	6.68	7.65	9[b]	10	27	35	38
Alabama	41.26	39.80	37	10	2	4	3
Mississippi	91.61	99.10	100	99	100	85	84
Tennessee	34.10	12.65	1	—	7	6	5
Iowa	19.92	31.53	34	48	50	45	42
Kansas	65.35	74.29	73	89	92	94	94
Minnesota	23.59	42.05	42	40	32	34	31
Missouri	36.13	29.16	30	34	26	22	20
Nebraska	45.25	61.11	68	80	78	65	67
South Dakota	38.70	33.91	36	39	44	37	31
West North Central	36.38	43.94	43	51	49	45	41
Arkansas	86.62	95.70	95	99	100	98	84
Louisiana	95.58	98.30	100	100	100	100	99
Oklahoma	77.86	95.89	99	100	100	100	100
Texas	97.61	99.24	100	100	100	100	100
West South Central	93.71	98.23	99[b]	100	100	100	99
Arizona	60.58	96.24	99[b]	100	86	87	87
Colorado	30.28	66.93	54	67	35	40	43
Montana	92.08	62.16	79	100	42	16	11
Nevada[a]	—	—	—	—	69	56	55
New Mexico	78.70	90.11	92	97	55	53	29
Utah	0.87	0.79	—	44	27	13	8
Wyoming	19.92	11.53	14	13	—	5	4
Mountain	48.06	72.15	60[b]	73	46	46	40
California	20.20	47.04	49[b]	53	82	83	74
Washington	—	—	—	—	26	80	71
Oregon	—	—	—	100	—	—	—
Pacific	18.87	45.54	45[b]	52	82	83	74
U.S.A.	13.00	20.90	23[b]	22	27	29	30

Source: Same as table 2.4.

[a] First fossil plant 1957.

[b] 1952 data since source did not tabulate 1951 data.

This review concentrates upon developments in the area of long-standing use of both coal and oil, the regions in which this began after 1966, and the areas into which oil has not penetrated. Developments are updated to 1972 from figures secured from individual companies and data available from the National Coal Association.

By the end of 1972, only one major coal-using plant remained in New England—a plant in New Hampshire, which, being inland, lacks easy access by water to oil. Elsewhere in New England, coal use was limited to a few small plants. Similar sharp declines in coal use have occurred in the portion of the East Coast from New York to Virginia. Consolidated Edison and Long Island Lighting in the New York City area have completed total conversion to oil. Coal use has been sharply reduced in the rest of the region, and the reliance on mine mouth plants has failed to offset this trend. (A partial, possibly temporary resumption of coal use was inspired by the 1973 Arab oil boycott).

Oil use was still negligible in Georgia and the Carolinas until 1972 when a few small plants began using it. Apparently, this reflects the dominance of inland areas as electric power markets. The two largest firms in the Carolinas—Duke and Carolina Power—operate largely inland as does the main Georgia firm—Georgia Power of the Southern Company.[2]

Florida's west coast is a special case. Coal use began in 1953 and accounted for a growing share of the market. However, Florida Power, one of the three coal users, has completed a shift to oil.

These trends are the result of both price and regulatory developments. A mail survey of East Coast utilities contained a question about the main causes of shifts to oil. Only three companies indicated that pollution regulations were the dominant consideration. Six assigned the primary influence to prices, and the rest said their initial increase in oil use was based on prices, but regulatory pressures caused further conversion. Presumably, more recent replies would lean to this last view. However, interviews with the companies indicated that the earlier shifts would have been made even without the rise of environmental pressures. Therefore, statements that attribute the shift to oil wholly to environmental pressures exaggerate the influence of sulfur pollution regulations.

Tables 2.9–2.14 provide available price data to suggest some of the forces at work. The first of these shows coal prices for all the East Coast states with any significant amounts of coal consumption. In table 2.10, oil prices for all areas in which residual oil use was significant are compared to those for coal.

To provide an updating, figures for more recent years are provided for coal in tables 2.11 and 2.12 and for oil in tables 2.13 and 2.14. The first

---

[2] Duke is entirely inland; Carolina serves the lower two-thirds of the North Carolina coast.

TABLE 2.9
Coal Prices in Eastern States, 1951–1971
(area averages in cents per million Btu)

Year	Conn.	Maine	Mass.	N.H.	R.I.	N.J.	N.Y.C.	Other N.Y.	Phila.	Other Pa.	Delaware	D.C.	Fla.	Ga.	Md.	N.C.	S.C.	Va.	W.Va.
1951	36.3	39.1	37.0	40.4	34.1	32.4	35.2	30.4	32.3	20.8	31.5	33.4	—	31.2	31.3	30.7	30.5	27.4	17.7
1952	37.0	41.1	38.0	42.2	35.6	33.3	36.2	31.6	33.5	21.6	31.5	35.0	—	31.7	31.6	31.7	30.9	28.4	18.3
1953	36.3	41.1	37.2	44.7	34.3	33.4	36.9	32.5	34.3	22.3	31.8	35.4	28.5	32.8	33.4	32.6	31.8	29.0	17.9
1954	35.5	42.1	33.3	37.9	34.4	32.6	35.8	31.3	32.6	21.9	31.1	33.9	26.2	31.1	32.3	30.1	29.8	28.5	17.7
1955	35.5	38.8	35.3	42.1	35.5	32.0	35.3	30.7	32.0	21.3	30.3	33.3	26.0	27.3	31.3	29.0	29.8	28.8	17.1
1956	38.0	—	39.0	44.4	40.2	33.9	37.4	32.4	33.4	22.0	32.1	36.5	26.0	28.1	32.9	31.5	32.5	31.8	17.4
1957	40.0	—	40.7	45.4	44.7	35.9	39.5	34.9	35.9	23.6	34.4	37.7	31.8	29.1	35.3	32.4	32.8	32.7	18.3
1958	39.4	—	39.6	44.8	43.2	36.2	39.7	35.1	36.8	24.3	35.6	36.5	31.8	29.5	35.5	30.7	31.4	31.1	18.6
1959	38.0	—	37.1	46.0	37.0	35.8	37.7	34.2	36.1	23.0	34.4	35.0	31.5	29.6	34.0	28.5	29.7	27.8	19.1
1960	36.6	41.1	36.2	43.5	36.2	35.0	36.4	33.2	35.0	22.3	33.1	34.3	30.1	29.3	31.7	27.6	27.8	26.5	18.9
1961	35.9	—	35.8	40.5	36.1	34.6	36.4	32.7	35.0	22.0	33.7	34.6	30.4	28.7	31.9	26.9	27.3	26.3	18.4
1962	35.4	—	35.2	37.9	36.0	34.0	35.7	32.0	34.4	21.7	33.1	34.8	29.8	29.2	30.6	26.8	27.3	25.6	18.2
1963	32.8	—	34.9	35.8	36.2	31.7	32.5	30.8	31.4	21.1	30.4	34.8	29.6	28.8	28.4	27.1	27.9	25.9	17.9
1964	31.4	—	34.4	34.8	36.6	29.4	30.9	29.3	29.5	20.6	27.9	34.9	29.4	28.7	27.0	27.1	27.7	26.6	17.6
1965	31.7	—	34.6	35.3	37.5	29.6	30.9	28.7	29.3	21.0	27.9	32.3	27.4	28.3	27.0	26.6	28.2	25.4	17.7
1966	32.0	—	35.1	35.3	36.1	30.2	32.1	28.8	29.9	21.5	28.5	34.1	26.5	28.8	27.8	27.5	29.2	25.5	17.8
1967	32.6	—	35.8	34.5	38.1	31.9	35.9	30.5	31.5	21.8	30.2	35.9	26.7	28.7	29.9	28.2	30.4	27.1	18.7
1968	32.5	—	36.7	31.0	41.0	33.0	38.0	31.3	32.4	22.3	31.2	37.8	26.9	29.3	30.8	28.2	29.9	28.0	19.2
1969	35.2	—	41.2	32.6	—	36.1	39.7	34.2	34.0	24.6	33.7	41.1	29.0	31.3	32.6	29.8	32.0	29.5	20.2
1970	44.8	—	43.8	36.1	—	47.4	50.3	45.3	39.0	29.5	43.9	57.9	30.6	37.9	41.7	40.6	43.4	38.5	24.5
1971	53.5	—	42.3	43.9	—	59.3	66.1	50.3	46.0	35.1	51.0	69.6	33.6	43.5	51.6	45.3	49.2	44.6	31.4

Source: Same as table 2.4.

TABLE 2.10

Comparative Prices of Coal and Oil, Selected East Coast Markets, 1951–1971

(area averages in cents per million Btu)

Year	Connecticut Coal	Connecticut Oil	Massachusetts Coal	Massachusetts Oil	New Hampshire Coal	New Hampshire Oil	Rhode Island Coal	Rhode Island Oil	Maine Oil	New York City Coal	New York City Oil	New Jersey Coal	New Jersey Oil	Philadelphia Coal	Philadelphia Oil	Florida Coal	Florida Oil
1951	36.3	36.6	37.0	35.1	40.4	36.2	34.1	34.3	39.4	35.2	37.0	32.4	34.8	32.3	36.7	—	—
1952	37.0	37.8	38.0	35.1	42.2	36.1	35.6	36.6	37.5	36.2	36.9	33.3	34.4	33.5	34.4	—	33.0
1953	36.3	36.6	37.2	33.4	44.7	34.1	34.3	34.4	35.6	36.9	34.2	33.4	32.4	34.3	33.8	28.5	31.4
1954	35.5	37.2	35.3	33.8	37.9	35.2	34.4	34.6	35.9	35.8	34.8	32.6	32.9	32.6	34.0	26.2	33.6
1955	35.5	39.8	35.3	34.8	42.1	39.3	35.5	35.6	41.2	35.3	38.0	32.0	33.4	32.0	35.7	26.0	35.7
1956	38.0	43.8	39.0	39.6	44.4	43.1	40.2	41.1	44.8	37.4	42.9	33.9	37.1	33.4	38.6	26.0	39.2
1957	40.0	49.7	40.7	45.1	45.4	49.0	44.7	45.7	50.5	39.5	49.0	35.9	43.3	35.9	43.1	31.8	45.8
1958	39.4	43.2	39.6	39.9	44.8	38.7	43.2	41.7	43.1	39.7	39.1	36.2	37.5	36.8	38.6	33.3	39.2
1959	38.0	37.1	37.1	35.1	46.0	34.9	37.0	37.7	38.0	37.7	34.9	35.8	35.2	36.1	37.3	31.5	35.2
1960	36.6	37.2	36.2	35.1	43.5	36.5	36.2	37.7	39.8	36.4	34.6	35.0	34.5	35.0	37.1	30.1	35.4
1961	35.9	39.7	35.8	36.8	40.5	37.7	36.1	38.9	40.3	36.4	36.3	34.6	35.0	35.0	37.6	30.4	34.9
1962	35.4	37.7	35.2	35.5	37.9	35.6	36.0	37.6	37.6	35.7	33.5	34.0	33.9	34.4	36.5	29.8	34.3
1963	32.8	34.4	34.9	34.4	35.8	34.5	36.2	35.0	36.2	32.5	32.5	31.7	30.9	31.4	32.3	29.6	34.2
1964	31.4	34.3	34.9	33.7	34.4	34.4	36.6	35.1	36.7	30.9	32.9	29.4	29.7	29.5	31.3	29.4	33.6
1965	31.7	34.4	34.6	33.5	34.8	34.4	37.5	35.5	36.5	30.9	33.1	29.6	30.6	29.3	31.9	27.4	33.5
1966	32.0	33.5	35.1	32.4	35.3	32.2	36.1	34.5	33.9	32.1	32.1	30.2	31.1	29.9	31.5	26.5	33.3
1967	32.6	30.6	35.8	30.3	34.5	29.9	38.1	31.0	31.5	35.9	32.8	31.9	33.5	31.5	32.5	26.7	32.3
1968	32.5	29.3	36.7	29.1	31.0	28.5	41.0	30.8	30.4	38.0	34.9	33.0	35.4	32.4	33.3	26.9	31.7
1969	35.2	28.3	41.2	28.2	32.6	28.0	—	29.1	30.3	39.7	40.0	36.1	34.5	34.0	30.3	29.0	30.1
1970	44.8	32.8	43.8	33.6	36.1	27.1	—	28.3	30.4	50.3	37.6	47.4	42.2	39.0	40.1	30.6	30.6
1971	53.5	49.1	42.3	50.4	43.9	27.0	—	32.9	32.6	66.1	49.8	59.3	67.2	46.0	67.1	33.6	38.8

Source: Same as table 2.4.

TABLE 2.11
Behavior of Delivered Coal Prices, 1969–1972: Selected Company Reports
(cents per million Btu)

	1969	1972	Increase 1969–1972
Public Service Co. of New Hampshire	32.6	47.9	15.3
Northeast Utilities Connecticut	35.2	46.7	11.5
Consolidated Edison Co.	39.7	68.4	28.7
New York State Electric and Gas Corp.[a]	33.1	45.1	12.0
Niagara Mohawk Power Corp.	33.4	53.4	20.0
Rochester Gas and Electric Corp.	37.2	55.1	17.9
Atlantic City Electric Co.[b]	36.1	56.7	20.6
Public Service Electric and Gas (N.J.)[c]	32.2	47.7	15.5
Metropolitan Edison[d]	35.3	53.1	17.8
Pennsylvania Electric[d]	24.0	36.8	12.8
Philadelphia Electric Co.[a]	34.0	53.4	19.4
Pennsylvania Power and Light Co.[b]	28.4	44.8	16.4
Delmarva Power and Light Co.[a]	34.0	53.5	19.5
Baltimore Gas and Electric Co.[b]	33.3	45.8	12.5
Potomac Electric Power Co.[b]	35.7	54.9	19.2
American Electric Power			
Appalachian Power	21.7	36.6	14.9
Ohio Power	20.0	35.9	15.9
Indiana and Michigan	22.9	34.0	11.1
Kentucky Power	19.0	36.6	17.6
Allegheny Power System	19.5	30.8	11.3
West Penn Power Co.	20.8	31.9	11.1
Monongahela Power Co.	18.0	29.0	11.0
Potomac Edison Co.	23.1	31.0	7.9
Ohio Edison Co.	21.9	35.8	13.9
Duquesne Light Co.	22.2	36.5	14.3
Cleveland Electric Illuminating Co.	29.2	42.5	13.3
Toledo Edison Co.	29.9	44.8	14.9
Cincinnati Gas and Electric Co.	23.6	36.6	13.0
Dayton Power and Light Co.	31.5	41.5	10.0
Columbus and Southern Ohio Electric Co.	22.6	34.0	11.4
Public Service Co. of Indiana	21.6	28.4	6.8
Indianapolis Power and Light Co.	23.1	30.5	7.4
Northern Indiana Public Service Co.	27.8	35.7	7.9
Detroit Edison Co.	29.1	43.7	14.6
Consumers Power Co.	31.8	44.8	13.0
Kentucky Utilities Co.	21.8	37.0	15.2
Louisville Gas and Electric Co.	21.8	31.3	9.5
Tennessee Valley Authority[e]	19.2	29.9	10.7
Virginia Electric and Power Co.	28.8	44.4	15.6
Carolina Power and Light Co.	31.2	45.7	14.5
Duke Power Co.	29.3	43.9	14.6
South Carolina Electric and Gas Co.	31.7	46.7	15.0

TABLE 2.11. *Continued*

	1969	1972	Increase 1969–1972
Southern Co.			
Alabama Power Co.	25.8	38.9	13.1
Gulf Power Co.	28.1	46.9	18.8
Mississippi Power Co.	25.9	34.6	8.7
Georgia Power Co.	30.3	44.7	14.4
Tampa Electric Co.	29.3	39.6	10.3
Commonwealth Edison Co.	28.2	43.2	15.0
Illinois Power Co.	23.2	28.1	4.9
Central Illinois Public Service Co.	23.8	36.5	12.7
Central Illinois Light Co.	25.5	33.9	8.4
Union Electric Co.	22.5	33.4	10.9
Wisconsin Electric Co.	32.7	44.4	11.7
Wisconsin Power and Light Co.	32.8	44.4	11.6
Wisconsin Public Service Corp.	35.0	50.7	15.7
Northern States Power Co.	30.4	41.1	10.7
Minnesota Power and Light Co.	37.2	40.3	3.1
Iowa Electric Light and Power Co.	33.8	46.9	13.1
Iowa Power and Light Co.	28.7	37.8	9.1
Interstate Power Co.	27.3	38.7	11.4
Kansas City Power and Light Co.	22.3	31.2	8.9
Public Service Co. of Colorado	25.6	29.1	3.5
Utah Power and Light Co.	20.7	25.5	4.8
Arizona Public Service Co.	15.9	17.7	1.8
Nevada Power Co.	28.3	35.3	7.0

Sources: The 1972 company figures with the exception of those for General Public Utilities and TVA come from company "Uniform Statistical Reports." These reports are generally only issued by private companies and sometimes fail to report the cost of individual fuels. TVA and GPU figures come from annual reports.

The 1969 figures except for Public Service Electric and Gas were compiled from *Steam Electric Plant Factors.* A weighted average of as-burned costs was used; the weights were the proportions of coal tonnage represented by each plant. The "Uniform Statistical Report" was obtained from Public Service. A minor consistency problem arises with the data; the 1969 figures relate to the plants operated by the company; in some cases, the 1972 numbers also include shares of joint ventures. Treatment in particular cases includes:

[a] Exclusion of joint ventures possible for 1972.

[b] Joint ventures included only for 1972.

[c] Joint ventures included in both 1969 and 1972.

[d] These are fuel costs for all fuels but these companies predominantly burn coal.

[e] Data apply to fiscal year ending June 30 of year listed; in fiscal year ending June 30, 1973, cost was 34.6 cents.

coal table compares 1972 to 1969—the year the Health and Safety Act was passed—while the first oil table shows 1970 and 1972. The second table for each fuel tabulates data from a Federal Power Commission (FPC) survey of fuel prices.

The comparability of these data is limited by differences in the characteristics of the companies and their fuel use (see Appendix B). Thus, both distance from suppliers and the type of transportation used affect the price pattern. Differences even arise within given modes of transportation. This is particularly true of rail shipments. The extent of unit train use can greatly affect costs, as can be seen by noting that, in the last few years reported, costs to New Hampshire, where all deliveries are by unit train, are below those in many areas nearer to coal fields. Regulatory pressures are another major influence, particularly in explaining the differences among oil prices in the early seventies. Sulfur emission regulations differ in

TABLE 2.12

Delivered Prices of Coal in Selected States, Second Half 1972
(cents per million Btu)

State	1 % sulfur or less		1.01 to 3 % sulfur		3.01 % or more sulfur	
	July	December	July	December	July	December
New Jersey	63.01	69.19	59.36	59.62	—	—
New York	57.84	61.68	47.49	47.47	—	52.80
Pennsylvania	43.17	38.04	39.71	41.06	40.73	41.74
Illinois	61.05	62.76	33.74	36.33	31.50	31.57
Indiana	52.55	59.83	31.32	31.38	28.70	31.96
Michigan	56.75	56.50	41.61	40.69	40.05	40.49
Ohio	39.91	43.68	36.18	39.32	38.50	40.23
Wisconsin	52.92	52.90	45.93	45.87	46.52	48.31
Minnesota	36.32	41.38	42.08	35.99	38.34	55.80
Missouri	41.26	42.49	27.96	32.38	30.67	28.68
Delaware	52.87	50.04	53.13	54.40	—	50.30
District of Columbia	59.56	59.56	—	—	—	—
Florida	—	—	43.77	49.24	37.65	40.89
Georgia	33.69	40.12	43.28	46.93	48.00	41.59
Maryland	54.07	52.10	50.60	50.20	—	—
North Carolina	46.17	46.40	43.34	42.37	44.10	43.20
South Carolina	46.18	46.84	46.54	47.51	—	43.20
Virginia	39.16	40.67	53.84	38.88	33.50	—
West Virginia	36.72	39.48	33.10	33.49	27.90	27.12
Alabama	38.72	37.28	34.06	36.75	39.77	38.75
Kentucky	35.94	34.90	36.31	30.76	29.37	25.60
Tennessee	35.17	32.98	32.21	35.90	26.74	33.85
New Mexico	13.80	14.70	—	—	—	—
Colorado	24.86	28.41	26.60	—	—	—

Source: Federal Power Commission (1973).

TABLE 2.13

Price per Barrel of Oil Delivered to Selected Utilities: Selected Company Reports
(dollars)

Company	1970	1972	Increase 1970–1972
Central Maine Power Co.	1.82	1.85	0.03
Public Service Co. of New Hampshire	1.77	2.06	0.29
Boston Edison Co.	1.95	4.27	2.32
New England Electric and Gas Assoc.	2.01	3.40	1.39
Northeast Utilities	2.52	3.78	1.26
United Illuminating Co.	1.75	3.63	1.88
Consolidated Edison Co.	2.49	3.95	1.46
Orange and Rockland Utilities, Inc. (#6)	2.57	2.50	(0.07)
Central Hudson Gas and Electric Co. (#6)	3.53	1.89	(1.64)
Niagara Mohawk Power Corp.	2.10	2.94	0.84
Public Service Electric and Gas Co.	2.58	4.08	1.50
Atlantic City Electric Co.	2.89	4.40	1.51
Philadelphia Electric Co.	2.47	4.16	1.69
Baltimore Gas and Electric Co.	2.12	3.97	1.85
Delmarva Power and Light Co.	2.15	3.99	1.84
Potomac Electric Power Co.	2.35	3.04	0.69
Virginia Electric and Power Co.	1.77	2.62	0.85
South Carolina Electric and Gas Co.	1.84	3.12	1.28
Florida Power and Light Co.	1.96	3.40	1.44
Florida Power Corp.	1.81	1.90	0.09
Tampa Electric Co.	1.76	2.93	1.17
Commonwealth Edison Co.	2.93	3.76	0.83
Detroit Edison Co. (#6)	3.21	4.12	0.91
Pacific Gas and Electric Co.	2.14	4.04	1.90
Southern California Edison Co.	2.45	4.80	2.35

Source: Same as table 2.11.
Note: #6 indicates price is for number 6—i.e., residual fuel oil—only.

stringency, so firms facing severe controls must pay a premium price for low-sulfur oil. In addition, it appears that the companies differed considerably in the extent to which contracts protected them from the impacts of world oil market developments in 1971 and rising coal prices.

With these caveats in mind, the data clearly indicate that oil became significantly cheaper than coal in the Northeast starting with liberalization of import controls in 1966. However, sharp price rises for both fuels have occured in the last years covered.

INTERFUEL COMPETITION ELSEWHERE IN THE UNITED STATES

Elsewhere, patterns of fuel use lack the neatness of the straightforward coal–oil competition in the East. In some senses, each state is a unique entity. Some idea of the role of other fuels is provided by tables 2.7 and 2.8.

TABLE 2.14

Delivered Prices of Fuel Oil to Selected States, Second Half 1972

(dollars per barrel)

State	Low sulfur oil (0.5% or less)		Medium sulfur oil (0.5 to 2.00%)		High sulfur oil (2.01% or more)	
	July	December	July	December	July	December
Connecticut	—	4.16	3.53	—	—	—
Maine	—	—	2.90	1.82	1.82	2.01
Massachusetts	3.81	3.90	2.98	3.11	2.58	—
New Hampshire	—	—	—	—	1.67	—
Rhode Island	—	—	3.40	3.40	—	—
New Jersey	3.96	4.18	4.08	4.21	3.09	—
New York	3.93	4.35	2.97	2.93	2.81	2.69
Pennsylvania	4.25	4.40	4.30	—	—	—
Illinois	—	—	4.04	4.22	—	3.19
Michigan	—	—	4.09	4.33	3.90	—
Delaware	—	—	4.15	4.11	2.63	2.53
District of Columbia	—	—	3.97	3.99	—	—
Florida	—	—	3.41	3.65	2.00	2.21
Georgia	—	—	—	—	2.68	2.83
Maryland	—	3.99	3.30	3.54	—	—
North Carolina	—	—	—	—	2.92	2.90
South Carolina	—	—	3.32	3.39	—	2.91
Virginia	—	—	—	—	2.86	2.87
California	4.88	4.81	5.37	3.25	—	—

Source: Federal Power Commission reports converted from cents per million Btu by fuel contents reported by FPC.

The West South Central States are the easiest to treat since they have relied almost entirely on local natural gas supplies. Until 1968, Mississippi had a similar pattern. However, one plant then added a coal-fired unit and the state began to consume modest amounts of coal. At least since the late fifties, gas use has receded in all other southeastern states listed except Florida. Florida has raised its reliance on gas; its use is fairly evenly distributed around the state.

On an overall basis, both the West North Central and Mountain States are areas in which coal and gas compete vigorously. However, the patterns differ considerably from state to state and even within states. Moreover, the importance of individual states in the region is quite disparate.

Idaho and South Dakota may be ignored because of their dominant use of hydropower (table 2.2). Minor amounts of gas were consumed in Utah (for most of the period) and Wyoming. However, in Utah "oil"—actually locally produced pitch—had about the same market share as coal until its availability ended in 1972. Gas use in Montana has become relatively small. In all cases, local coals are the dominant source of coal supply.

In contrast, gas was long the dominant fuel source in Kansas, Arizona, Nevada, and New Mexico. U.S. Bureau of Mines' data on gas distribution suggest that Kansas and New Mexico secure most of their gas from wells within the state; most of the gas for Arizona and Nevada comes from surrounding states (see the gas chapter in the *Minerals Yearbook*).

Patterns of fuel use are changing radically, however, in the last three states. Coal-fired plants are already operating, and considerable expansion is expected. Since 1963, the Four Corners plant in New Mexico (initially serving Arizona) has been a large coal consumer. Coal burning began in Nevada in 1965—again at a single plant. In both cases, the plants were large enough so that their coal use is a significant fraction of the state total utility fuel consumption. Persistent coal–gas competition, however, prevails in Missouri, Minnesota, Iowa, Nebraska, and Colorado. Each state has peculiarities that necessitate separate discussions.

Significant variations in patterns prevail in different parts of Missouri. In particular, the Saint Louis area served by Union Electric relies heavily on coal. In the rest of the state, coal still competes but gas has a large share of the market. Coal's strength in the Saint Louis area is aided by proximity to Illinois coal across the Mississippi River. This situation has a great influence on the state averages, since Union Electric produced about 45 percent of Missouri's 1971 thermal electric generation. Another 24 percent was generated in the Kansas City area. Here, considerable amounts of both coal and gas are used.

While Minnesota has no significant energy resources, it has long been an area of intense coal–gas competition. Largely because most of the state's electricity is generated in the Minneapolis-Saint Paul area, this is the center of the interfuel rivalry. Northern States Power, most of whose plants are in this area, produced 70 percent of 1971 thermal electric output.

Iowa has only slightly more local energy production than Minnesota and is another area of intense interfuel competition. While several states supply gas, most of the coal comes from Illinois. Not surprisingly, therefore, coal's strongest position has been in the eastern part of Iowa.

Gas has been the principal fuel source in Nebraska. Since the state's local production is quite small, out-of-state gas, mainly from Kansas, has met the vast majority of the needs. The heaviest use of coal has been in the Omaha area.

Colorado produced both coal and gas, with the latter tending to lose position. Again, there is an intense localization of electric power output—about 70 percent in the Denver area. Coal's position in Denver is somewhat stronger than in the rest of the state.

California had become predominantly a gas consuming state but the share of oil in electric utility fuel use is high enough to make the state a major part of the electric utility market for fuel oil.

TABLE 2.15
Cost of Coal in Electric Power Generation, 1951–1971
(cents per million Btu)

Year	East North Central					West North Central						
	Illinois	Indiana	Michigan	Ohio	Wisconsin	Iowa	Kansas	Minnesota	Missouri	Nebraska	North Dakota	South Dakota
1951	25.6	24.6	30.6	22.9	31.8	29.4	22.3	34.7	23.1	30.9	26.6	36.1
1952	25.5	24.1	30.7	22.8	32.1	30.1	23.1	34.8	23.6	30.2	27.8	36.9
1953	25.6	24.3	30.7	23.2	32.0	30.6	25.9	34.2	23.7	31.5	27.7	36.9
1954	24.7	22.8	29.3	22.4	30.0	29.4	24.8	32.6	22.8	30.3	27.5	36.8
1955	23.8	21.4	28.6	21.2	28.8	26.7	24.8	30.8	22.6	29.6	27.0	33.3
1956	24.1	21.6	30.7	22.3	30.8	26.4	26.3	31.5	22.8	28.4	27.2	33.1
1957	25.0	21.9	32.1	23.2	33.1	27.9	26.8	33.6	24.6	29.4	26.1	32.4
1958	24.9	22.8	31.7	23.5	33.1	27.8	27.2	33.4	24.2	29.3	26.5	31.0
1959	25.0	22.9	31.9	22.9	32.7	27.8	28.0	32.8	23.4	32.2	27.7	30.1
1960	24.9	22.8	31.0	22.6	32.3	27.8	27.9	31.6	23.3	29.9	27.0	30.9
1961	24.8	22.0	30.8	22.4	31.6	27.1	28.5	29.9	22.4	n.a.	27.3	30.0
1962	24.8	22.2	30.0	22.3	31.7	27.3	27.2	30.8	22.3	31.4	28.0	32.1
1963	24.7	22.1	29.9	22.0	30.6	27.1	27.2	31.1	21.9	30.6	27.8	31.5
1964	24.4	21.8	29.4	21.8	30.2	27.0	26.8	29.9	21.8	29.3	26.8	31.5
1965	23.9	21.6	28.9	21.9	29.2	26.8	27.1	30.7	21.8	29.8	26.9	32.6
1966	23.6	21.5	29.1	22.4	29.7	27.1	26.1	30.9	22.0	30.2	21.6	30.3
1967	23.7	21.8	29.3	22.5	30.3	27.6	25.3	31.2	21.9	30.9	15.5	29.4
1968	24.5	22.2	29.7	23.0	31.4	27.4	25.2	31.1	22.1	31.1	14.2	28.6
1969	26.0	23.1	30.4	24.3	33.2	28.7	27.2	32.4	22.8	31.9	15.5	31.0
1970	29.5	25.1	35.4	29.1	38.6	31.5	28.0	35.0	24.8	34.9	15.8	31.0
1971	34.0	29.0	41.5	34.9	43.5	36.9	29.3	40.8	28.2	40.2	15.3	37.6

TABLE 2.15

Year	East South Central				Mountain						
	Alabama	Kentucky	Mississippi	Tennessee	Arizona	Colorado	Montana	Nevada	New Mexico	Utah	Wyoming
1951	18.8	20.4	—	21.9	—	23.3	—	—	25.4	26.9	17.7
1952	19.1	20.4	33.3	20.6	—	23.4	—	—	23.6	26.8	17.1
1953	20.8	20.1	33.5	20.3	—	23.8	—	—	26.9	25.7	17.1
1954	19.3	18.7	33.5	19.6	—	24.2	—	—	27.6	24.8	17.0
1955	18.6	18.0	33.5	18.6	—	25.6	—	—	24.0	22.1	15.6
1956	18.9	17.9	29.8	19.1	—	25.0	—	—	24.3	21.9	15.7
1957	19.5	18.4	34.0	20.1	—	25.6	—	—	23.7	21.6	16.6
1958	20.0	18.1	—	19.8	—	25.5	21.4	—	24.9	21.0	16.3
1959	20.1	17.6	—	19.4	—	25.6	20.4	—	26.1	21.7	12.9
1960	21.6	17.5	38.2	19.6	—	24.0	21.4	—	26.9	21.8	11.7
1961	22.3	17.5	—	19.1	22.7	23.4	21.6	—	n.a.	21.7	11.4
1962	22.6	17.3	41.1	19.1	23.4	23.5	21.9	—	25.6	21.9	19.0
1963	23.1	17.3	36.1	19.1	23.5	23.1	22.1	—	11.9	22.1	18.0
1964	22.5	16.4	37.4	18.9	23.2	23.5	22.3	—	12.4	21.8	18.5
1965	21.7	16.2	34.8	18.5	23.9	23.2	22.6	30.2	13.1	22.6	18.8
1966	22.1	16.3	n.a.	18.8	24.0	23.3	20.4	29.8	14.0	22.9	19.1
1967	22.8	17.2	—	19.7	24.6	22.1	21.1	30.1	14.5	22.1	19.4
1968	22.9	17.5	25.6	19.6	25.9	22.1	20.1	29.0	15.0	18.9	19.4
1969	23.5	18.5	25.9	20.6	26.8	23.5	20.0	28.3	14.4	20.7	19.6
1970	25.6	22.1	27.6	22.9	29.4	24.1	19.4	30.0	14.3	23.3	20.0
1971	32.9	25.3	31.6	30.3		25.5	20.4	30.7	15.0	28.5	19.9

Source: Same as table 2.4.

Table 2.15 shows coal costs in the rest of the United States. Two key points may be noted. First, most costs in the Mountain States are well below those elsewhere. This reflects the prevalence of ample strip reserves and the dominance of mine mouth plants. Second, this area and the Middle West seem to have experienced much less of a cost rise since 1969 than eastern electric utilities (including those heavily reliant on long-term contracts). The key difference probably lies in the heavy dependence on supplies from existing strip mines.

SUMMARY

This chapter indicates that while coal use in electric power generation has grown substantially since 1946, consumption of other fuels has grown more rapidly. While many forces have affected this, a particularly critical force in the late sixties was liberalization of oil import controls on residual fuel oil. This produced significant increases in oil use by formerly coal-using utilities. The switch to oil was further encouraged by imposition of air pollution regulations.

Appendix A

ELECTRIC UTILITIES AS POWER PRODUCERS
AND FUEL CONSUMERS

Not surprisingly, individual companies tend to show larger shares of consumption of individual fuels than of power generation. The reason for this is that use of specific fuels is concentrated in a few regions while power production is nationwide, and at least in a statistical sense, joint ventures can cause some companies to purchase more coal than they use for their own power production. Statistical reports of power output usually credit each participant in a joint venture with its share of the venture's output. However, the 1969 company fuel consumption totals shown here were computed by summing figures on individual plants. It was preferable to assign the fuel purchases to the company managing the plant. Not only does this simplify the calculation, but the treatment is more logical since the manager is responsible for fuel procurement.[3]

It should be observed that at least three measures of electric power company size could be used—capacity, output, or dollar sales. The second is stressed here in preference to the others. The criterion of dollar volume

---

[3] Two joint ventures are exceptional cases in that their output is separately reported. One, Ohio Valley Electric, is managed by American Electric Power (AEP) and has its coal use shown with AEP. The second, Electric Energy Inc., is treated as an independent coal buyer.

seems to have several drawbacks for present purposes. Such factors as fuel costs and clientele greatly affect the unit income of individual utilities. Certain companies wholesale large amounts of their power to distribution companies; large scale industrial consumers enjoy lower rates than households, so revenues reflect the kinds of customers.

Since this study deals with power production, physical output and capacity data seem more convenient to use. However, variations in definition make it difficult to develop consistent capacity figures, so output is stressed for purposes of comparison.

Table 2.16 lists all the firms (except cooperatives) with 1969 output in excess of two billion kilowatt hours and shows 1969 output and capacity.[4] Those listed produce over 90 percent of the national total; indeed the largest twenty have about half the output.

COAL CONSUMPTION PATTERNS

While the data on power generation and coal use are not directly comparable because of the differences in treatment of joint ventures, it is still possible to conclude that coal use is more concentrated than power generation. The ten largest coal consumers accounted for about half the electric power industry's coal use (table 2.17); their share in power generation was probably below 30 percent.[5] The ten largest power producers generated 33 percent of the electric power. The fifty largest coal consumers used 89 percent of the coal but apparently generated less than 60 percent of the electricity.[6] The fifty largest power producers accounted for 75 percent of generation.

As noted in the body of the chapter, numerous important changes in coal use patterns have arisen since 1969. Several companies—all in the East—ceased to use coal, and others had greatly reduced their use by 1972. Table 2.17, therefore, notes the cases in which coal use was eliminated and table 2.18 lists some of the major declines.[7]

---

[4] At the time this chapter was first drafted, 1969 was the latest year for which complete data were available. Updatings were not attempted mainly because of the relevance of the data in this chapter to the survey of fuel purchasing in chapter 3.

[5] The data in table 2.16 show that the share of the ten companies and Ohio Valley Electric was about 28 percent of national output; these data exclude the power generated for other companies in plants operated by American Electric Power and General Public Utilities—another manager of joint ventures. Examination of data on the output of these plants suggests that the addition of the excluded output would not raise the total to 30 percent.

[6] The eleventh through forty-ninth largest consumers of coal generated about 28 percent of national electric output; the fiftieth largest consumer was a cooperative and, therefore, not reported in table 2.16. Its output was less than 0.5 percent of the national total.

[7] A few omissions may arise because companies omit fuel use details from the "Uniform Statistical Reports" used as the basis of the calculations.

TABLE 2.16

Capacity and Generation in 1969 by Firms Producing More Than 2 Billion Kilowatt Hours

Company[a]	Capacity			Generation		
	Million watts	% of total	Cumulative % of total	Million kwh	% of total	Cumulative % of total
Tennessee Valley Authority (Tenn., Ala., Ky., Ga., N.C.)[b]	13,976	4.47	4.47	90,589	6.28	6.28
American Electric Power, Inc. (Ohio, W.Va., Va., Ky., Tenn., Ind., Mich.)	10,091	3.23	7.70	55,070	3.82	10.10
The Southern Co. (Ga., Ala., Fla., Miss.)	11,188	3.59	11.28	54,996	3.81	13.92
Bonneville Power Administration (Suppliers) (Wash., Ore., Ida., Mont.)[bc]	8,001	2.56	13.84	51,125	3.55	17.46
Commonwealth Edison Co. (Ill., Ind.)	10,961	3.51	17.34	45,382	3.15	20.61
Southern California Edison Co. (Calif., Nev.)	9,023	2.89	20.23	42,475	2.95	23.55
Pacific Gas and Electric Co. (Calif.)	9,488	3.04	23.26	37,444	2.60	26.15
Duke Power Co. (N.C., S.C.)	6,258	2.00	25.27	33,018	2.29	28.44
Consolidated Edison Co. of New York	8,542	2.73	28.00	30,988	2.15	30.59
Texas Utilities Co.	7,438	2.38	30.38	30,654	2.13	32.72
The Detroit Edison Co. (Mich.)	5,968	1.91	32.29	30,561	2.12	34.84
Middle South Utilities, Inc. (Ark., La., Mo., Tenn., Miss.)	6,113	1.96	34.24	29,709	2.06	36.90
Public Service Electric & Gas Co. (N.J.)	6,136	1.96	36.21	27,087	1.88	38.77
Houston Lighting & Power Co. (Tex.)	5,802	1.86	38.06	25,919	1.80	40.57
Virginia Electric & Power Co. (Va., W.Va., N.C.)	5,463	1.75	39.81	22,897	1.59	42.16
Power Authority of the State of New York[c]	3,102	0.99	40.81	22,407	1.55	43.71
Central & South West Corp. (Tex., Okla., La., Ark.)	4,511	1.38	42.18	22,381	1.55	45.27
Florida Power and Light Co.	5,164	1.65	43.83	22,364	1.55	46.82
Philadelphia Electric Co. (Pa., Md.)	4,754	1.52	45.35	21,175	1.47	48.29
Allegheny Power System Inc. (Pa., Md., Va., W.Va., Ohio)	3,809	1.22	46.57	19,346	1.34	49.63
Consumers Power Co. (Mich.)	3,414	1.09	47.66	18,414	1.28	50.90
General Public Utilities Corp. (Pa., N.J., N.Y.)	4,110	1.31	48.98	18,067	1.25	52.16
Ohio Valley Electric Corp. (Ohio, Ind.)	2,390	0.76	49.74	17,721	1.23	53.39

Ohio Edison Co. (Ohio, Pa.)	2,952	0.94	50.69	17,334	1.20	54.59
Carolina Power & Light Co. (N.C., S.C.)	3,148	1.01	51.69	16,819	1.17	55.75
Gulf States Utilities Co. (Tex., La.)	2,967	0.95	52.64	15,955	1.11	56.86
Niagara Mohawk Power Corp. (N.Y.)	3,631	1.16	53.80	15,431	1.07	57.93
Union Electric Co. (Mo., Ill., Iowa)	3,527	1.13	54.93	14,658	1.02	58.95
Pennsylvania Power & Light Co.	3,122	1.00	55.93	14,572	1.01	59.96
Los Angeles Dept. of Water & Power (Calif.)[b]	3,074	0.98	56.91	13,847	0.96	60.92
Northeast Utilities (Mass., Conn.)	2,712	0.87	57.78	13,134	0.91	61.83
Wisconsin Electric Power Co. (Wisc., Mich.)	2,909	0.93	58.71	13,114	0.91	62.74
Baltimore Gas & Electric Co. (Md.)	2,046	0.65	59.37	13,055	0.91	63.64
Potomac Electric Power Co. (D.C., Md., Va.)	2,973	0.95	60.32	12,945	0.90	64.54
The Cleveland Electric Illuminating Co. (Ohio)	2,146	0.69	61.01	12,359	0.86	65.40
Northern States Power Co. (Minn., Wisc., N.D., S.D.)	2,889	0.92	61.93	12,131	0.84	66.24
Missouri River Basin Project (Suppliers) (Colo., Mont., S.D., Wyom.)[bc]	2,490	0.80	62.73	11,292	0.78	67.02
Public Service Co. of Indiana, Inc.	2,164	0.69	63.42	11,039	0.77	67.79
Long Island Lighting Co. (N.Y.)	2,270	0.73	64.15	10,710	0.74	68.53
Public Utility District No. 2 of Grant County (Wash.)[c]	1,620	0.52	64.67	10,162	0.70	69.23
Duquesne Light Co. (Pa.)	1,757	0.56	65.23	9,885	0.69	69.92
New England Electric System (N.H., Mass., R.I., Vt.)	2,389	0.76	65.99	9,387	0.65	70.57
Oklahoma Gas & Electric Co. (Okla., Ark.)	1,919	0.61	66.60	9,361	0.65	71.22
Boston Edison Co. (Mass.)	2,050	0.66	67.26	8,918	0.62	71.84
Florida Power Corp.	2,236	0.72	67.98	8,284	0.57	72.42
Electric Energy Inc. (Ill., Ky.)	1,100	0.35	68.33	8,140	0.56	72.98
The Cincinnati Gas & Electric Co. (Ohio, Ky.)	1,872	0.60	68.93	7,971	0.55	73.53
Idaho Power Co. (Ida., Nev., Ore.)	1,296	0.41	69.34	7,525	0.52	74.05
Illinois Power Co.	1,394	0.45	69.79	7,347	0.51	74.56
South Carolina Electric & Gas Co.	1,539	0.49	70.28	7,320	0.51	75.07
Public Service Co. of Colorado (Colo., Wyom.)	1,893	0.61	70.89	6,640	0.46	75.53
Northern Indiana Public Service Co.	1,349	0.43	71.32	6,639	0.46	75.99
Southwestern Public Service Co. (Tex., Okla., Kan., N.M.)	1,654	0.53	71.85	6,609	0.46	76.45
Public Utility District No. 1 of Chelan County (Wash.)[c]	975	0.31	72.16	6,353	0.44	76.89
Pacific Power & Light Co. (Ore., Wash., Mont., Calif., Ida.)	1,368	0.44	72.60	6,314	0.44	77.33
Arizona Public Service Co.	1,349	0.43	73.03	6,037	0.42	77.75

(Continued)

TABLE 2.16. (*Continued*)

Company[a]	Capacity			Generation		
	Million watts	% of total	Cumulative % of total	Million kwh	% of total	Cumulative % of total
Louisville Gas and Electric Co. (Ky.)	1,603	0.51	73.54	6,007	0.42	78.16
Tampa Electric Co. (Fla.)	1,599	0.51	74.05	5,914	0.41	78.57
Kansas City Power & Light Company (Mo., Kan.)	1,754	0.56	74.61	5,913	0.41	78.98
Seattle Department of Lighting (Wash.)	1,244	0.40	75.01	5,891	0.41	79.38
Aluminum Company of America (Ind., N.Y., N.C., Tenn.)	1,059	0.34	75.35	5,861	0.41	79.80
Kansas Gas & Electric Company	1,111	0.36	75.70	5,692	0.39	80.19
Central Illinois Public Service Company	1,074	0.34	76.05	5,600	0.39	80.58
Southwestern Power Administration (Suppliers)[bc] (Ark., Mo., Okla., Tex.)	1,425	0.46	76.50	5,534	0.38	80.97
San Diego Gas & Electric Company (Calif.)	1,481	0.47	76.98	5,431	0.38	81.34
Indianapolis Power & Light Company (Ind.)	1,572	0.50	77.48	5,310	0.37	81.71
Delmarva Power & Light Company (Del., Md., Va.)	868	0.28	77.76	5,282	0.37	82.08
Central Valley Project (U.S.B.R.) (Calif.)[bc]	1,141	0.36	78.12	5,211	0.36	82.44
The Dayton Power & Light Company (Ohio)	1,254	0.40	78.52	5,066	0.35	82.79
New York State Electric & Gas Corporation	1,548	0.50	79.02	4,909	0.34	83.13
Utah Power & Light Company (Utah, Ida., Wyom., Colo.)	1,102	0.35	79.37	4,840	0.34	83.47
The United Illuminating Company (Conn.)	1,002	0.32	79.69	4,799	0.33	83.80
The Toledo Edison Company (Ohio)	1,075	0.34	80.04	4,764	0.33	84.13
Columbus & Southern Ohio Electric	1,171	0.37	80.41	4,718	0.33	84.46
Atlantic City Electric Company (N.J.)	754	0.24	80.65	4,227	0.29	84.75
Southeastern Power Administration (Suppliers)[bc] (Fla., Ga., Ky., N.C., S.C.)	1,807	0.58	80.88	4,251	0.29	85.04
The Montana Power Company (Mont., Wyom.)	714	0.23	81.46	4,112	0.29	85.33
The Kansas Power & Light Co.	845	0.27	81.73	4,046	0.28	85.61
Colorado River Storage Project (Utah)[bc]	1,078	0.34	82.07	4,029	0.28	85.89
Public Utility District No. 1 of Douglas County (Wash.)[c]	774	0.25	82.32	4,015	0.28	86.17

Company	(left) No.	(left) %	(left) Cum. %	(right) No.	(right) %	(right) Cum. %
(… Vt.)			82.33	4,013	0.28	86.45
San Antonio City Public Service Board (Tex.)[bc]	1,459	0.47	83.06	3,930	0.27	86.72
Washington Public Power System (Wash.)[bc]	952	0.30	83.36	3,757	0.26	86.98
Wisconsin Power & Light Co. (Wisc., Ill.)	899	0.29	83.65	3,715	0.26	87.24
Jacksonville Electric Authority (Fla.)	977	0.31	83.96	3,682	0.26	87.49
Wisconsin Public Service Corp. (Wisc., Mich.)	733	0.23	84.19	3,653	0.25	87.74
Connecticut Yankee Atomic Power Co.	600	0.19	84.39	3,639	0.25	88.00
The Washington Water Power Co. (Wash., Ida., Wyom.)[c]	637	0.20	84.59	3,545	0.25	88.25
Hawaiian Electric Co., Inc.	821	0.26	84.85	3,524	0.24	88.49
Central Maine Power Co.	654	0.21	85.06	3,429	0.24	88.73
New England Gas & Electric Assoc. (Mass.)	761	0.24	85.31	3,362	0.23	88.96
Central Illinois Light Co.	879	0.28	85.59	3,354	0.23	89.19
Omaha Public Power District (Neb.)	838	0.27	85.85	3,080	0.21	89.41
Boulder Canyon Project (Ariz., Nev.)[b]	1,345	0.43	86.28	3,015	0.21	89.62
Central Hudson Gas & Electric Corp. (N.Y.)	617	0.20	86.48	2,948	0.20	89.82
Minnesota Power & Light Co. (Minn., Wisc.)	520	0.17	86.65	2,876	0.20	90.02
Kentucky Utilities Co. (Ky., Tenn., Va.)	762	0.24	86.89	2,712	0.19	90.21
Tacoma Light Division (Wash.)	719	0.23	87.12	2,603	0.18	90.39
Salt River Project (Ariz.)	598	0.19	87.31	2,589	0.18	90.57
Sacramento Municipal Utility District (Calif.)	523	0.17	87.48	2,546	0.18	90.74
Nevada Power Co.	534	0.17	87.65	2,490	0.17	90.92
El Paso Electric Co. (Tex., N.Mex.)	520	0.17	87.82	2,461	0.17	91.09
Interstate Power Co. (Ill., Iowa, Minn., S.D.)	549	0.18	87.99	2,410	0.17	91.25
Rochester Gas & Electric Co. (N.Y.)	557	0.18	88.17	2,403	0.17	91.42
Orange and Rockland Utilities, Inc. (N.J., N.Y.)	539	0.17	88.34	2,398	0.17	91.59
Central Louisiana Electric Co., Inc.	532	0.17	88.51	2,355	0.16	91.75
Portland General Electric Co. (Ore.)	610	0.20	88.71	2,354	0.16	91.91
Iowa Electric Light & Power Co.	496	0.16	88.87	2,302	0.16	92.07
The South Carolina Public Service Authority[b]	257	0.08	88.95	2,294	0.16	92.23
Iowa Power & Light Co.	579	0.19	89.13	2,268	0.16	92.39
Tuscon Gas & Electric Co. (Ariz.)	613	0.20	89.33	2,179	0.15	92.54
Lower Colorado River Authority (Tex.)[b]	452	0.14	89.48	2,022	0.14	92.68
San Francisco Hetch Hetchy Water Supply & Power Project[b] (Calif.)	293	0.09	89.57	2,009	0.14	92.82
National Totals	312,612	100.00	100.00	1,441,939	100.00	100.00

(*Continued*)

OIL USE PATTERNS

Oil use has traditionally been more concentrated than coal use—mainly on the East Coast northwards from Philadelphia, and in Florida and California. As later chapters show, radical changes in this pattern have begun and could continue throughout the 1970s. Table 2.19 shows that by 1969 the use of oil had spread down to Virginia.

At that time only twenty-eight companies consumed as much as a million barrels of oil a year and this accounted for 88 percent of electric power industry oil use. Seven companies accounted for over half the use. Incomplete data (table 2.20) for 1972 suggest that oil use by the companies listed in the table has generally risen—often quite sharply. Moreover, at least ten more companies have reached the million barrel level; the most notable newcomer is Commonwealth Edison with over 6 million barrels of 1972 oil consumption.

This oil is largely residual fuel oil. It has traditionally been the only economical fuel for large scale use. Further oil consumption was limited to small amounts of start-up oil and fuel for peaking units. However, as chapter 7 discusses, significant changes in this pattern may be emerging.

Notes to Table 2.16

Sources: These data are, except for those on the Tennessee Valley Authority, taken from Federal Power Commission Reports. TVA data are from its reports. The table only covers private and government operations—i.e., exclude cooperatives. The last are generally small. Private firm figures are on a calendar year basis, but government data cover whatever fiscal year is employed by the unit—e.g. ending on June 30 for Federal projects.

Private data as presented by the FPC were consolidated under the parent company; with the exception of one subsidiary of Hawaiian Electric identified from Moody's, the consolidation was based on information in the FPC report. Federal data may be presented in several ways, but it seemed best to combine all projects with a common marketing agency. Each forms an entity roughly comparable to a private power company. All but eight federal projects are associated with such agencies. Three of the eight are listed here as separate entities. Thus, five projects with an aggregate output of about 4 billion kilowatt hours are excluded. Coverage of captive facilities is limited to the Aluminum Company of America—the only operator of such facilities included in FPC reports. As rough measures of comparative importance such data are related to calendar year 1969 data from the Edison Electric Institute to determine percent shares.

Data on cooperatives are not reported by the Federal Power Commission, but the National Coal Association's reports on steam plants suggest that only two—Dairyland and Associated Electric Cooperative—belong on the list. Their steam plant output in 1969 was about 2.4 billion each.

[a] The states serviced are indicated in parentheses after any operation whose name does not completely describe its service area. In some cases, the area is served entirely from plants in other states—e.g. the various non-TVA suppliers of Tennessee do not generate in that state.

[b] Data relating to a fiscal year not ending on December 31.

[c] Hydropower operations.

TABLE 2.17
The Leading Coal Consuming Electric Utilities, 1969

	Coal consumption		
Company[a]	(thousand tons)	% of total	Cumulative % of total
1) Tennessee Valley Authority[b]	30,890	9.95	9.95
2) American Electric Power Co.	30,802	9.93	19.88
Wholly owned Plants	20,003	6.45	
Partially owned plants			
Ohio Valley Electric Co. (Ohio, Ind.)	7,174	2.31	
Beech Bottom Power Co. (W.Va.)	629	0.20	
Cardinal Operating Co. (Ohio)	2,996	0.97	
3) Commonwealth Edison Co.	18,905	6.09	25.97
4) The Southern Co.	17,409	5.61	31.58
5) Duke Power Co.	11,845	3.82	35.40
6) Detroit Edison Co.	11,745	3.78	39.19
7) General Public Utilities	9,901	3.19	42.38
8) Allegheny Power System, Inc.	8,979	2.89	45.27
9) Ohio Edison Co.	7,482	2.41	47.68
10) Consumers Power Co.	6,557	2.11	49.79
11) Virginia Electric & Power Co.	6,449	2.08	51.87
12) Carolina Power & Light Co.	5,880	1.89	53.77
13) Union Electric Co.	5,836	1.88	55.65
14) Cleveland Electric Illuminating Co.	5,593	1.80	57.45
15) Pennsylvania Power & Light Co.	5,432	1.75	59.20
16) Wisconsin Electric Power Co.	5,038	1.62	60.82
17) Public Service Co. of Indiana	5,008	1.61	62.44
18) Niagara Mohawk Power Corp.	4,712	1.52	63.96
19) Potomac Electric Power Co.	4,425	1.43	65.38
20) Duquesne Light Co.	4,230	1.36	66.75
21) Consolidated Edison Co.[c]	3,759	1.21	67.96
22) Cincinnati Gas & Electric Co.	3,575	1.15	69.11
23) Electric Energy, Inc.	3,511	1.13	70.24
24) Baltimore Gas & Electric Co.	3,451	1.11	71.35
25) Northern States Power Co.	3,402	1.10	72.45
26) Arizona Public Service Co.	3,175	1.02	73.47
27) Philadelphia Electric Co.	3,120	1.01	74.48
28) Northeast Utilities[c]	2,959	0.95	75.43
29) Illinois Power Co.	2,902	0.94	76.37
30) Central Illinois Public Service Co.	2,760	0.89	77.26
31) Indianapolis Power & Light Co.	2,471	0.80	78.05
32) Northern Indiana Public Service Co.	2,453	0.79	78.84
33) Tampa Electric Co.	2,286	0.74	79.58
34) Columbus & Southern Ohio Electric Co.	2,281	0.74	80.31
35) Louisville Gas & Electric Co.	2,210	0.71	81.03
36) Public Service Electric & Gas Co.	2,198	0.71	81.73
37) Kansas City Power & Light Co.	2,114	0.68	82.42
38) Public Service Co. of Colorado	2,032	0.65	83.07
39) New York State Electric & Gas Corp.	1,951	0.63	83.70
40) Dayton Power & Light Co.	1,878	0.61	84.30
41) Toledo Edison Co.	1,858	0.60	84.90

(*Continued*)

TABLE 2.17. *Continued*

Company[a]	Coal consumption		
	(thousand tons)	% of total	Cumulative % of total
42) Central Illinois Light Co.	1,611	0.52	85.42
43) Utah Power & Light Co.	1,567	0.50	85.93
44) South Carolina Electric & Gas Co.	1,528	0.49	86.42
45) Delmarva Power & Light Co.	1,527	0.49	86.91
46) Pacific Power & Light Co.	1,489	0.48	87.39
47) Wisconsin Power & Light Co.	1,476	0.48	87.87
48) Kentucky Utilities Co.	1,274	0.41	88.28
49) Wisconsin Public Service Co.	1,236	0.40	88.68
50) Basin Electric Coop.	1,184	0.38	89.06
51) Associated Electric Coop.	1,166	0.38	89.43
52) Dairyland Power Coop.	1,142	0.37	89.80
53) New England Electric[c]	1,036	0.33	90.14
54) Atlantic City Electric Co.	1,027	0.33	90.47
55) Minnesota Power & Light Co.	1,025	0.33	90.80
56) Central Hudson Gas & Electric Corp.[c]	995	0.32	91.12
57) Florida Power Corp.[c]	940	0.30	91.42
58) Public Service Co. of New Hampshire	934	0.30	91.72
59) Montana-Dakota Utilities Co.	886	0.29	92.01
60) Rochester Gas & Electric Co.	871	0.28	92.29
61) Otter Tail Power Co.	824	0.27	92.55
62) United Power Assoc.	807	0.26	92.81
63) Interstate Power Co.	754	0.24	93.06
64) So. Indiana Gas & Electric Co.	753	0.24	93.30
65) Iowa Southern Utilities Co.	746	0.24	93.54
66) East Kentucky Rural Electric Corp.	693	0.22	93.76
67) Iowa Electric Light & Power Co.	658	0.21	93.97
68) Lansing Board of Water & Light[b]	646	0.21	94.18
69) Nevada Power Co.	631	0.20	94.39
70) Upper Peninsula Power	611	0.20	94.58
71) Colorado-Ute Electric Assoc., Inc.	606	0.20	94.78
72) Omaha Public Power District	597	0.19	94.97
73) S. Carolina Public Service Authority[b]	590	0.19	95.16
74) Black Hills Power & Light Co.	526	0.17	95.33
75) Springfield (Ill.) Water Light & Power Dept.[b]	522	0.17	95.50
76) Iowa Power & Light Co.	519	0.17	95.67
77) Owensboro (Ky.) Municipal Utilities[b]	497	0.16	95.83
78) Missouri Public Service Co.	413	0.13	95.96
79) Orange & Rockland Utilities, Inc.[c]	367	0.12	96.08
80) United Gas Improvement Co.	356	0.11	96.19
81) Cleveland Dept. of Public Utilities	348	0.11	96.30
82) Iowa-Illinois Gas & Electric Co.	322	0.10	96.41
83) Big Rivers Electric Coop.	299	0.10	96.50
84) Iowa Public Service Co.	291	0.09	96.60
85) Montana Power Co.	283	0.09	96.69
86) Detroit Public Lighting Commission[b]	282	0.09	96.78
87) Nebraska Public Power District	267	0.09	96.87
88) Southern Illinois Power Coop.	207	0.07	96.93
89) Richmond (Ind.) Power & Light	194	0.06	96.99
Total Industry Consumption	310,312		

TABLE 2.18

Major Declines in Coal Use, 1972 Compared to 1969

Company	Coal Consumption (thousand tons)	
	1969	1972
Commonwealth Edison	18,905	17,062
Consumers Power	6,557	6,231
Virginia Electric & Power	6,449	3,740
Carolina Power and Light	5,880	5,732
Niagara Mohawk Power	4,712	3,138
Consolidated Edison	3,759	145
Baltimore Gas and Electric[a]	3,451	2,048
Philadelphia Electric[b]	3,120	1,841
Northeast Utilities	2,959	67
Public Service Electric and Gas[c]	2,970	2,562
New York State Electric and Gas[b]	1,951	1,915
Delmarva Power and Light[b]	1,527	883
Atlantic City Electric[a]	1,027	375
Rochester Gas and Electric	871	783
Orange and Rockland Utilities	367	1

Source: Company Uniform Statistical Reports.

[a] 1969 excludes, 1972 includes share of mine mouth power.

[b] Excludes share of mine mouth power.

[c] Includes share of mine mouth power.

Appendix B

THE DATA AND THEIR ANALYSIS

The basic source of data on electric power is the Federal Power Commission (FPC), which collects rather extensive information. However, it does not necessarily make all this information available in a convenient

---

Notes to Table 2.17

Source: Details from National Coal Association, *Steam Electric Plant Factors, 1970;* Total—Edison Electric Institute, *Statistical Yearbook,* 1970.

Notes: After this table was completed and used to prepare elaborate tabulations for chapter 3, additional data from the Federal Power Commission's reports showed that we had overlooked small subsidiaries of a few companies—Union Electric had one using 4,000 tons of coal; Utah Power and Light, 65,000; Wisconsin Power and Light, 24,000.

The source adjusts the data to exclude coal used to generate steam; moreover, we made a plant by plant comparison between these reports and the subsequent listing of coal use and other data by the Federal Power Commission. The only unexplained major discrepancy that we found is that the Coal Association systematically lists lower figures for Potomac Electric.

Upper Peninsula Power includes Upper Peninsula Generating, a joint venture of Upper Peninsula Power and Cleveland Cliffs Iron Ore Company.

The data as reported by the National Coal Association include figures on a fiscal year basis.

[a] For companies whose name does not describe its service area, refer to table 2.16.

[b] Data on fiscal year ending during 1969.

[c] Coal use ended since 1969.

TABLE 2.19

Consumption of Fuel Oil in Electric Power Generation, 1969

Company[a]	Thousand barrels consumed	% of total	Cumulative %
Public Service Electric & Gas Co.	27,776	11.07	11.07
Consolidated Edison Co.	27,262	10.86	21.93
Philadelphia Electric Co.	19,497	7.77	29.70
Florida Power & Light Co.	18,686	7.45	37.15
Boston Edison Co.	15,019	5.99	43.13
Long Island Lighting Co.	14,855	5.92	49.05
Southern California Edison Co.	9,685	3.86	52.91
Northeast Utilities	9,594	3.82	56.74
United Illuminating Co.	9,011	3.59	60.33
Virginia Electric & Power Co.	8,619	3.43	63.76
New England Electric Co.	8,088	3.22	66.99
Florida Power Corp.	6,470	2.58	69.56
Jacksonville Electric Authority	6,075	2.42	71.98
New England Electric & Gas Assoc.	5,067	2.02	74.00
Pacific Gas & Electric Co.	4,557	1.82	75.82
Los Angeles Dept. of Water and Power[b]	4,075	1.62	77.44
Central Maine Power Co.	3,807	1.52	78.96
Eastern Utilities Assoc.	3,725	1.48	80.45
Baltimore Gas and Electric Co.	3,601	1.44	81.88
Potomac Electric Power Co.	2,208	0.88	82.76
Atlantic City Electric Co.	2,093	0.83	83.59
Public Service Co. of New Hampshire	2,009	0.80	84.39
General Public Utilities	1,988	0.79	85.19
Tampa Electric Co.	1,981	0.79	85.98
San Diego Gas & Electric Co.	1,671	0.67	86.64
Utah Power & Light Co.	1,620	0.65	87.29
Detroit Edison Co.	1,159	0.46	87.75
Delmarva Power & Light Co.	1,012	0.40	88.15
Total	250,938		

Source: Same as table 2.17.

[a] For companies whose name does not describe its service area, refer to table 2.16.

[b] Los Angeles based on fiscal year ending June 30, 1969.

form. Therefore, the chapter relies heavily on the valuable tabulation by the Edison Electric Institute (EEI) of general industry data and the special compilations about power plant fuel use from the National Coal Association.[8]

In the course of the present study, about a half dozen different techniques of defining regions had to be reconciled. None of the regions correspond precisely with the marketing areas of the different fuels since this was not the basis by which the regions were defined. In this study, the standard grouping of states in regions which is widely employed for presenting general economic and social data is frequently used. In contrast, much

[8] Strictly speaking, the bulk of the data the second source provides also appear in an FPC report; however, the latter omits some material on smaller plants, provides few tabulations, and appears at a later date.

TABLE 2.20

Consumption of Fuel Oil in Electric Power Generation, 1972—Selected Companies

Company	Thousand barrels consumed	Company	Thousand barrels consumed
Consolidated Edison Co.	42,525	Niagara Mohawk Power Corp.	5,416
Florida Power & Light Co.	32,891	Delmarva Power & Light Co.	5,335
Public Service Electric & Gas Co.	27,766	Orange & Rockland Utilities, Inc.	5,164
Southern California Edison Co.	23,877	Central Hudson Gas & Electric Corp.	5,180
Virginia Electric & Power Co.	23,751	Atlantic City Electric Co.	5,092
Northeast Utilities	21,440	Central Maine Power Co.	4,752
Philadelphia Electric Co.	20,905	Detroit Edison Co.	4,209
Long Island Lighting Co.	19,792	Carolina Power & Light Co.	2,752
Florida Power Corp.	16,350	Pacific Gas & Electric Co.	2,634
Boston Edison Co.	14,678	Southern Co.	2,459
Potomac Electric Power Co.	12,273	Public Service Co. of New Hampshire	2,220
Baltimore Gas & Electric Co.	11,130		
United Illuminating Co.	9,681	Tampa Electric Co.	2,186
New England Electric & Gas Assoc.	7,046	Duke Power Co.	1,459
		Union Electric Co.	1,113
Middle South Utilities	6,699	Consumers Power Co.	1,057
Commonwealth Edison Co.	5,581		

Source: Uniform Statistical Reports.

energy data are organized on quite different bases that often ignore political boundaries.

Perhaps the most complex system is that used by the Federal Power Commission to divide the country into power supply areas. Basically, each region contains the territory of a homogeneous group of companies. This produces a wide variety of relationships to political borders. Many districts contain parts of several states. Many states, in turn, are part of several districts, some of which also include other states. Area seven, consisting primarily of the Allegheny Power System and Duquesne Light, is perhaps the extreme case. Allegheny serves portions of Pennsylvania, West Virginia, Maryland, and Ohio—including an isolated pocket in Central Pennsylvania surrounded by area five territory.[9]

The FPC regularly aggregates these areas into eight regions for statistical reporting purposes. However, for the *1970 National Power Survey,* only six regions were distinguished—i.e., a different aggregation process was employed. In neither case did the borders correspond to state lines, but the eight region aggregation more closely resembles the more conventional groupings.

[9] The case is of special personal interest since, coincidentally, this study was written in a town within this isolated service area. To complicate matters further, cases arise in other parts of the country of assigning portions of a few companies' territories to different areas.

A similarly complex districting of bituminous coal-producing areas is employed in some Bureau of Mines data. The system was devised for the depression aid program under the Bituminous Coal Act of 1937 and was apparently based on similarities of conditions prevailing at the time. Here we do have some major producing states, such as Illinois, treated as a single district. However, districts often include parts of several states, particularly in Appalachia.

Petroleum data are presented primarily on the basis of Petroleum Administration for Defense (PAD) districts, which aggregate states into five regions. In addition, the PAD districts are subdivided into refining districts, which do not necessarily follow state lines.

The main problem with using any of these systems is that they combine areas with significantly different supply conditions. FPC supply area five, for example, includes New Jersey and Philadelphia, in which oil is dominant, with parts of inland Pennsylvania, where oil has been traditionally difficult to transport economically. Area twenty-two consists of part of the Southern Company's territory—some coal using and some gas using.

The rough regional distinctions used here represent a compromise between realism and feasibility. It is possible in principle to disaggregate enough to handle all possible distinctions. However, such a process would be overly tedious for researchers and readers. The data generally are disaggregated no more finely than in the published sources. In practice, this means that each state is usually considered as an entity. The main exceptions are that the sources permit treating New York City and Philadelphia as distinct from New York State and Pennsylvania.

These considerations are particularly relevant to the interpretation of regional price data. All one can tell from these figures is that somewhere in the region in question someone could secure a particular fuel at a given price. Ideally the exact location of the purchaser and the quantities involved should be reviewed, but such extreme disaggregation is impractical. In FPC area five, for example (or in the similar case of the Middle Atlantic States), coal prices in the territory are the average of those available to firms close to coal fields and those at a considerable distance from them. The oil price primarily reflects the low price available only on the coast. Such gas as was available was probably bought on an interruptible basis, and the price of large regular supplies would have been much higher.

Further complications are introduced both by the nature of purchasing and the presentation of price data. As explained later, much of the fuel is bought on long-term contracts. The average price then reflects a combination of purchases on such contracts and spot buying. In contrast, the most relevant price for forecasting is what coal will cost on a new contract. The spot price can clearly diverge considerably from such a price. Even contract prices with escalation included may not be accurate measures for forecasting. Further distortions are produced by differences in transportation methods. In particular, lower volume shipments are significantly more expensive than high volume ones. In sum, it should be emphasized that the existence of lower actual delivered prices in a given region does not necessarily mean that this fuel is the lowest cost long-run alternative.

Moreover, a mechanical problem is introduced by utility accounting practices. Fuel is valued by adding the cost of purchases to the value of inventories and then computing a weighted average. This weighted average, then, is both the value of fuel used and of next month's inventories. Analysis of this approach shows that the accounting method makes reported prices a weighted average of prices paid in all past periods. The most recent month has the greatest weight, and the more distant months have progressively lower weights.

Inventory holding patterns differ considerably among regions and vary over time. The national average holding time has ranged from two to three months over the 1940–1970 period (*Minerals Yearbook*), but a spot check of the monthly data for 1969–1971 by states reported by the Federal Power Commission suggests that electric utilities in most major consuming states typically maintain one to three month's inventories. In this inventory holding rate range, the weights accorded purchases in given months (with the most recent month assigned the lowest number) are:

	Inventories of one month's consumption		Inventories of two month's consumption		Inventories of three month's consumption	
	Individual month	Cumulative	Individual month	Cumulative	Individual month	Cumulative
1	0.500	0.500	0.333	0.333	0.250	0.250
2	0.250	0.750	0.222	0.555	0.188	0.438
3	0.125	0.875	0.148	0.703	0.141	0.578
4	0.063	0.938	0.099	0.802	0.105	0.684
5	0.031	0.969	0.066	0.868	0.078	0.763
6	0.016	0.984	0.044	0.912	0.059	0.822
7	0.008	0.992	0.029	0.941	0.044	0.867
8	0.004	0.996	0.020	0.961	0.033	0.900
9	0.002	0.998	0.013	0.974	0.025	0.925
10	0.001	0.999	0.009	0.983	0.019	0.944
11	0.0005	0.9995	0.006	0.989	0.014	0.958

In all three cases, the average is clearly almost entirely based on no longer than a year's experience. Moreover, the most recent months contribute a preponderance of the value. Thus, the lag is, in practice, only a few months.

The final and most critical problem is that the detailed data are available only through 1971. The price rises in 1972 can only be handled indirectly.

3

Fuel Procurement

INTRODUCTION

In this chapter, some of the responses of the electric utility industry to its need for assured substantial fuel supplies are examined. The discussion begins with review of the problems related to fuel supply confronting the industry and proceeds to present results of an extensive sample survey of electric utilities about their purchasing practices. Then an evaluation of the material is provided. This evaluation suggests some conclusions about the structure of the coal market and, therefore, the chapter concludes by relating the data on procurement to information about the coal industry. This provides a tentative evaluation of how effective competition is in the market.[1]

FUEL PURCHASING PROBLEMS IN THE ELECTRIC POWER INDUSTRY

The fundamental consideration for evaluation of electric power fuel needs is the magnitude of a typical plant's fuel requirements. Large plants are becoming typical. Most new plants will require over a million tons of coal a year, and many will require three million tons. This latter requirement, incidentally, easily exceeds the output of all but a few mines, since in 1970 only fifteen mines produced more than three million tons. In 1969, the 100 or so plants using at least a million tons of coal accounted for 69 percent of electric industry coal use. This demand permits use of large scale methods of transportation since coal consumption is sufficient to absorb frequent trainload lot deliveries (see below).

It long seemed probable that these large requirements would persist over much of the twenty-five to thirty year life of the generating unit. Conversely, at present, fears that coal use will cease are considerable. Problems of the flexibility of boilers in accepting different coals are also relevant to fuel purchasing decisions. Changing suppliers can be costly; at the

---

[1] Much of the present analysis of contracts plus an effort to develop a theory of procurement appears in a separately printed article in the *Journal of Industrial Economics* (Gordon, 1974b).

very least, new coals must be tested for suitability for use in existing boilers.

Clearly many trade-offs might be made between boiler design and assurance that a coal of a particular type could be secured regularly. Another critical question, to be discussed more fully later, is whether the substantial extra capital cost of using coal-fired rather than oil- or gas-fired stations is justifiable by fuel cost savings. Particular problems are associated with the inflexibility of some of the special capital equipment required, particularly for coal loading, transfer, and unloading, if a mine mouth plant is built or unit trains are used.

Several institutional factors also are influential. Most arise from regulation and its variation among states. First, the utilities have a legal obligation to meet demand. Second, states differ markedly in their willingness to allow rapid adjustment to cost changes. Fuels are the largest variable costs for an existing power plant and their prices can change more substantially than other items. While a growing number of state regulatory commissions allow increases in fuel prices to be passed on to consumers, this was not always true. Therefore, protection against fuel price rises was desirable.

Apparently states differ markedly in their attitudes toward vertical integration. Many utilities visited insisted that their state regulatory agency looked askance at integration. The integrated companies east of the Mississippi that were interviewed noted that they were limited to production of coal for their own use. However, some western companies have become active in supplying coal to other utilities. Another important problem is a standard one for fuel users; only active buyers can obtain accurate price information.

DATA ON ELECTRIC UTILITY COAL PROCUREMENT

Given the shortage of published data, the reluctance of companies to disclose many details, and the general difficulty in measuring many of the influences, only a limited amount of quantitative analysis is possible. It proved convenient to subdivide the electric power industry into three groups. The first consists of the eleven largest coal consumers in 1969; these companies absorbed over half the industry's coal burn. The second group consists of other companies using at least a million tons of coal; the third, other users of at least 200,000 tons (see tables 2.17 and 2.19 for a list of the companies).[2]

The present sample is clearly biased; it provides complete coverage of the

[2] Actually, inadvertently the first company below this last cutoff was included in the mail survey. It chose to reply and was included.

TABLE 3.1

Method of Coal Purchasing by Electric Utilities in the United States

	Eleven largest coal users	Other consumers of at least one million tons	Surveyed consumers of less than one million tons	All companies included
a. Distribution by Number of Companies				
Use long-term contracts	10	29	6	45
Use shorter-term contracts	1	7	8	16
Captive coal	0	2	3	5
Buy only for a year or less	0	3	7	10
Total	11	41	24	76
b. Distribution Based on 1969 Coal Burn (included company coal burns as percent of total industry burn)				
Use long-term contracts	48.1	27.3	1.2	76.6
Use shorter-term contracts	3.8	5.2	1.5	10.5
Captive coal	0	1.8	0.6	2.4
Buy for a year or less	0	3.5	0.7	4.2
Omissions	0	1.1	2.2	3.3
Total	51.9	38.9	6.2	97.0

Sources: Coal burn by companies: National Coal Association (1970); Industry coal burn: Edison Electric Institute (1970); Method of purchasing: company reports to the author.

Notes: Use of long-term contracts does not preclude that other methods are also used. However, those listed as using shorter term contracts or captive coal do not also use any other alternative except buying for less than one year.

The percentages in part b. are derived by summing the coal burns of the particular companies in each category and dividing the total by reported total domestic coal use for electric power generation (the Edison Electric Institute's number was used since it is the largest available and thus lessens any exaggeration). The missing 3 percent consists of the difference between the burn of the sampled companies and the total.

first group, includes most of the second, but has substantial omissions in the third. To reduce the effects of this bias, comparisons are made to total industry coal use rather than to that of the sample. This means that the figures provide minimum estimates of contract use.[3]

Procurement methods can be divided into four broad types—long-term (ten or more years) contracts, short-term contracts (one to ten years), purchases for a year or less, and captive production.[4] Two breakdowns are

[3] The evidence from the sample suggests that few if any of the users of contracts were omitted; most of the omissions were the small companies that tend not to contract. The total omission because of nonresponse was under 3 percent of total coal use. Another 3 percent was accounted for by the very small users not surveyed.

[4] This definition was used in the questionnaire, and the results suggest that it was doubly unfortunate. First, the classification was too broad. It might have been better to subdivide further—say a-more-than-one-to-less-than-five-year and a-five-to-less-than-ten-year breakdown of the short-term category. Secondly, it appears that some respondents may have biased their answers by reporting the remaining rather than initial lives of some contracts.

possible. We may divide companies by the combination of methods employed or allocate coal consumption to each method.

Table 3.1 provides a breakdown showing the predominant method used by the companies. Only four categories are shown. This was done both to simplify and to reduce the possibility of disclosing company data. The long-term contract group includes all companies that use this method regardless of whatever other methods are used. The captive group only includes companies that use no contracts—long- or short-term. The users of short-term contracts may also buy for shorter terms. The table shows that over three-quarters of the market falls into the long-term contract category. This outcome is greatly influenced by the greater tendency of the larger companies to contract. Chi-square tests on the distributions in part (a) of the table show that the differences among each pair of groups are highly significant.[5] Thus, we can conclude that the eleven largest are more likely to contract than either of the other two groups, and that the second group is more likely to contract than the third.

Turning to table 3.2, we find that deliveries under long-term contracts

TABLE 3.2

Role of Alternative Methods of Coal Purchasing in 1969 Coal Burn by Electric Power Industry

(percent of total burn)

	Eleven largest consumers	Other consumers of 1,000,000 tons	Surveyed consumers of 1,000,000 tons	All companies included
Long-term contracts	24.6	14.4	0.9	39.9
Shorter-term contracts:				
of companies with long-term	—	3.6	—	14.4
of other companies	—	2.0	—	6.7
Total	14.1	5.6	1.4	21.1
Captive	2.5	1.4	0.5	4.4
Less than one year				
Companies with long-term or captive	—	7.0	—	17.4
Companies with shorter-term contracts	—	3.6	—	4.1
Other companies	—	3.5	—	4.2
Total	10.7	14.1	0.9	25.7
Total Coverage	51.9	35.5	3.7	91.1

Sources: Same as table 3.1.
Note: Certain data are omitted or combined to avoid disclosure of figures on individual companies.

[5] The respective chi-square values are 21.71 between groups one and two; 122.37 between two and three and 232.99 between one and three. These values are significant at the 99 percent level.

TABLE 3.3

Coal Mining by Electric Power Companies, 1969

Electric company and coal subsidiary[a]	Coal output (tons)	Company burn[b] (thousand tons)	Coal output as % of burn
American Electric Power			
Central Ohio Coal	3,125,323	n.a.[c]	n.a.
Central Appalachian Coal	1,193,339	n.a.	n.a.
Total of above	4,318,662	20,003	21.6
Windsor Power House Coal	644,526	629	103
Total	4,963,188	30,802	16.1
Southern Company			
Southern Electric Generating	1,980,511	3,273	60.5
Alabama Power	752,107	4,793	15.7
Total	2,732,618	17,409	15.7
Ohio Edison	279,470	7,482	3.7
Duquesne Light Company	2,850,092	4,230	67.4
Pacific Power & Light	1,498,664	1,489	101
Montana Dakota Utilities			
Knife River Coal Mining	1,825,148	886	206
Black Hills Power & Light			
Wyodak Resources Development	558,106	526	106
Montana Power			
Western Energy Company	521,000	283	184

Sources: Coal Burn: National Coal Association (1970); Coal Production: Keystone Coal Industry Manual (1970).

[a] Blank means the coal company operates under the name of its parent; the "coal" companies shown for the Southern Company are, in fact, different subsidiaries in the electric power business.

[b] The breakdown for American Electric Power takes partial account of its various joint ventures; the production by its wholly owned mines are related to coal consumption in wholly owned plants. Windsor Power House is a subsidiary of Beech Bottom Power—a joint venture with the Allegheny Electric System. The total burn includes also two other joint ventures of AEP in electric power.

[c] n.a. Not applicable.

amount to about 40 percent of 1969 coal use and shorter contracts cover another 21 percent.[6] By dividing the data in the first row in this table by the corresponding line in part (b) of table 3.1, we can quickly calculate that long-term contract users in each group get the majority of *their* needs in this fashion. The dependency on long-term contract purchases is slightly over half for the first two groups but 75 percent for the third.

Information on integration appears in table 3.3. It may be noted that the table only includes wholly owned ventures. Two distinct universes seem to

[6] The main difference between the coverage in this table and table 3.1 relates to a few companies that reported their pattern without sufficient details on the breakdown. A few companies reported in table 3.1 as contract users secured no deliveries until after 1969 and so were omitted from this table.

exist. The first four companies are large eastern utilities with long histories of integration—twenty to sixty years—but mine far less than they consume. The others are western companies that are more recent entrants into mining but mine more than they consume.

Table 3.4 provides another view of the situation by subdividing the users of contracts by the number of years of use. Again chi-square tests were used to show that the differences among groups were significant.[7] We can conclude the largest eleven started contracting sooner than the other groups; the second group, before the third. However, this relationship only applies in this broad sense. The correlation between timing and size of coal use is only 0.21.

The availability of oil, however, complicates the interpretation of the data. Fourteen companies in the sample—ten in the second group and two each in the other two groups—were present or prospective oil users. An obvious effect of oil use is to lower the ranking of some companies as coal users. A larger proportional reliance on coal would have put the two group three oil-using companies into group two, and perhaps two or three of the

TABLE 3.4

Distribution of Long-Term Contracts by Number of Years Employed

Number of years using long-term contracts	Eleven largest consumers	Other consumers of at least one million tons	Surveyed consumers of less than one million tons	All companies included
a. Percent of Reporting Companies using Long-Term Contracts				
16 or more	70.0	31.1	16.7	37.8
12–15	10.0	24.1	50.0	24.4
8–10	20.0	20.7	16.7	20.0
0–6	0.0	24.1	16.6	17.8
Total	100.0	100.0	100.0	100.0
b. Companies Coal Burn as Percent of Total Industry Consumptions				
16 or more	39.6		0.3	39.9
12–15	17.9		0.4	18.3
8–10	12.2		0.2	12.4
0–6	5.7		0.3	6.0
Total	75.4		1.2	76.6

Source: Same as table 3.1.

Note: Differences from other tables reflect variability in number of responses. All companies over a million tons combined in part b. to avoid disclosure of details for individual companies. 1971 is year zero.

[7] The respective values are 88.03, 36.61, and 219.37.

group two companies would have been in group one. More critically, much of the difference between groups one and two seems attributable primarily to the availability of oil. We would expect that companies that might want to shift from coal to oil would not want their options foreclosed by contracts. Two of the three companies in group two not using contracts also were oil users; the third terminated its coal purchase arrangements because of excessively increased contract administration problems. Similarly, six of the seven firms limiting themselves to shorter contracts were oil consumers. Two oil users in group two did use long-term contracts. The oil users in group one are both long-term contract users. In both cases, however, the companies have individual plants that cannot easily be shifted to oil. Of the two oil users in group three, one used long-term and the other used short-term contracts.

Finally, tables 3.5 and 3.6 present summary data on some characteristics of the contracts in use. Since the Btu content of the coal was traditionally the sole consideration in valuation, prices were designed to guarantee control over this content. The most direct approach would presumably be to buy at a specific price per million Btu, but, as table 3.5 shows, the predominant method does this indirectly. The bonus penalty method involves a base price per ton with a bonus paid for Btu content above specification and a penalty for a content below specification. A small fraction of the industry pays a flat price per ton, but the coal must meet specified quality standards.

The contracts include formulas on which automatic price adjustments are based. Many techniques are in use. External data largely consisting of various government price indexes and union wage rates are widely used. Sole reliance on national price and wage trends is the most widely used basis for adjustment, and the vast majority of contracts are at least partially reliant on such trends (table 3.6). The other adjustment factors in-

TABLE 3.5
The Role of Alternative Pricing Methods Among Companies

	Coal burn	
Method	As % of burn by reporting companies	As % of industry burn
Primarily flat prices	12.6	9.1
Primarily on bonus penalty basis	49.8	35.9
Primarily cents per Btu	8.8	6.3
Combination of bonus penalty and cents per Btu	28.8	20.8
Total reporting	100.0	72.1

Source: Same as table 3.1.

TABLE 3.6
Techniques of Escalation of Electric Utility Long-Term Contracts

Method	Coal burn tonnages of reporting companies	
	As % of burn by reporting companies	As % of industry burn
Predominately by national trends	39.6	27.3
Predominately by mine costs	20.3	14.0
Predominately by costs and national trends	18.6	12.8
Predominately by national trends and mine productivity	17.6	12.1
Use combination of national trends, mine costs, and mine productivity	3.8	2.6
Total reporting	100.0	68.8

Source: Same as table 3.1.

clude the costs or productivity of the supplying coal mine. These clauses are analyzed below.

CONTRACTS FOR THE PURCHASE OF RESIDUAL FUEL OIL

Another widely employed, but relatively unpublicized, use of contracts is for the purchase of residual fuel oil. Only one of nineteen companies on which data were obtained failed to use contracts. More critically, thirteen companies secured all their oil in this fashion; three others bought the vast majority of their oil on contracts; one company relied on contracts for only 30 percent of its needs, and one failed to supply details.

The breakdowns by proportion of oil use cannot be shown without disclosing company data. However, we may note that the seven largest companies surveyed accounted for over half the electric industry's 1969 oil use. Curiously, the noncontracting company and two of the three companies only predominantly reliant on contracts are among these seven largest. Eleven of the eighteen contract-using companies undertook contracting in 1967 or later. The timing of the other initial contracting decisions ranges from 1931 to the early sixties. Here large size has the expected broad effect; five of the seven firms adopting contracts in earlier periods are among the seven largest oil users.

In any case, the reported contracts cover an average of 85 percent of the total oil use by the included companies. These, in turn, represent 71 percent of total industry oil use, so that these companies' purchases under contracts amount to 60 percent of the *industry* total. However, another 8 percent of the industry's oil use is accounted for by other large East Coast companies—defined here as those whose oil use at least equalled that of the smallest user in the sample (see table 2.19). The large West Coast users should be excluded because in 1969 they were not buying on long-term contracts. Assuming that the unsurveyed eastern companies had the identical reliance (85 percent) on contracts as the sample, another 7 percent of the industry total could be covered by contracts. This suggests oil contracts may provide a larger proportion of needs than do contracts and vertical integration for coal.

Only limited data were obtained on the nature of these contracts. At least in terms of the number of companies involved, the contracts are about equally divided between those with firm prices and those with adjustment clauses. However, these clauses were heavily concentrated among the contracts of the largest users. To be precise, nine of the nineteen companies had such clauses and these included all six of the top seven that contract. The clauses, moreover, are a relatively new development. Of the companies adopting contracts through the early sixties, five had adjustment clauses but only two had had them for extended periods. Conversely, the practice is not universal with newer contracts; only four of the eleven contracts dating from 1967 involve adjustment clauses.

The questionnaire unfortunately failed to probe adequately into the nature of these clauses, but a combination of volunteered responses and information in the published literature suggests that the principal adjustment originally was for *declines* in open market prices for residual fuel oil.[8]

HISTORY AND EVALUATION OF PROCUREMENT METHODS

The methods examined here prove disparate in their history and impacts. The reliance on coal contracts seems to have begun in 1903 and gradually spread throughout the market. The critical forces in stimulating at least the developments in the years after World War II are reasonably evident. Use of oil contracts became widespread somewhat more recently but the adoption apparently has exceeded contract use for coal.

In contrast, a great deal of randomness prevails in the area of vertical integration. The ventures reported in table 3.3 were instituted over a long period of time and are supplemented by various more limited ventures with similarly varied bases.

Like so much of modern electric power industry practice, the reliance on contracts can be traced to Samuel Insull. As early as 1903, he had decided that long-term contracts provided a means to insure reliable fuel supply for his Commonwealth Edison Company. He therefore negotiated such ac-

[8] The issue surfaced as a result of the 1971 rises in world oil prices. A number of electric companies resisted efforts of oil companies to increase prices; the ensuing law suits were reported in security prospectuses. However, many utilities were forced to relinquish contracts because the oil had too high a sulfur content.

cords with Peabody Coal. During the complex process by which Insull later assembled a vast empire, Peabody became a captive company. It was jointly owned by electric power companies under Insull control. The companies signed thirty-year contracts for Peabody to provide coal at a price equal to cost plus $0.15 a ton. (Peabody later was made independent as part of the breakup of the Insull system under the Public Utility Holding Company Act.)

It appears that the contracting originally was quite beneficial to the power companies; McDonald (1962) in his biography of Insull points out that considerable savings were reaped during the post-World War I inflation. As conditions changed, this arrangement became less attractive. The old Insull utilities became somewhat disenchanted with the contracts. The lack of pressure for cost control and the failure to adapt to a weak coal market apparently made what was desirable in 1918 unsatisfactory for 1948. Nevertheless, several companies maintain what appear to be revisions of the original contracts with Peabody.

The practice of contracting, nevertheless, spread through the industry as other companies found it desirable to secure coal on a more systematic basis. The process came largely after World War II. By the late fifties, companies accounting for most of the market had begun contracting (table 3.4). This can be attributed primarily to concern over the logistics of supplying the ever larger plants that the electric power industry was installing. Companies wanted assurance of the availability of the required amounts of coal.

In the late fifties and early sixties, transportation problems became a major consideration. Both the mine mouth plant and the unit train involve commitments that encourage contracting. The unit train can be adopted only if all parties are confident that its utilization will persist long enough to justify the requisite investment. Whether contracts are truly necessary clearly depends upon particular cases; the ease with which either supplier or buyer could make other arrangements differs with both market and transportation alternatives available. In the case of the unit train, respondents clearly felt that the uncertainties were large enough to necessitate contracts. The source of the pressure apparently differed from case to case. Buyer, seller, or railroad may each have the greatest concern in a particular situation. Similarly, mine mouth plants demand contractual commitment, since the mine and plant construct specialized coal handling systems to take advantage of the fuel's proximity—conveyor belts and private short-haul railroads, for example. It is not surprising that contracts are employed to insure supplies.

Since the middle sixties, contracts have allegedly become the only practical way to secure large tonnages of coal. Growth of consumption and the pressure of various new mining regulations have removed the problem of unused capacity. Uncertainty about market conditions has made the coal industry unable to develop new mines unless someone contracted to buy the coal. Financing could not be secured without such guarantees. The industry's initial fears were generated by the impression that nuclear power might have such low costs that coal could no longer compete. Although it quickly became apparent that nuclear plants would be more expensive than expected, unfortunately indications also appeared that the cost of burning coal would rise sharply.

The tendency of larger companies to be early adopters of long-term contracts suggests that the arrangements become more attractive when the absolute levels of purchases reaches a critical size. The bigger companies were necessarily the first to reach this size. Presumably, the greater amount of the purchases allows the contract administration costs, which are likely not to vary significantly with purchase levels, to be spread over a larger total and thus be less per ton bought. Moreover, increasing costs of spot purchasing may also prevail as it becomes necessary to search more widely for eligible suppliers.

However, the relative attractiveness of contracts is also affected by utility location. It was shown earlier in this chapter that oil users, probably because of the greater possibility of shifting fuel, were less likely to contract for coal. Examination of the underlying data suggests that those companies operating in coal regions tended to contract at earlier dates and rely somewhat more heavily on contracts. An obvious consideration is that shifts in fuel use are less likely for such companies, which presumably makes it less risky to contract. Such companies may also be able to monitor contracts more efficiently because of their proximity to suppliers.

It may be further noted that some difficult legal questions arise on which it proved impossible to secure solid opinions about contracts. In field interviews, widely disparate views were elicited from the nonlawyer respondents on whether regulatory bans on coal use would be a valid reason for contract termination. Whatever the truth may be, it was evident that many suppliers were demanding explicit protection from such circumstances, which suggests that they feared that current contracts could be broken.

The reliance on formulas for price adjustment is a natural feature of contracts of such long duration. Clearly, neither participant would wish to commit himself on the basis of what could be forecast in advance. Thus, some technique that adjusts prices to reflect long-run cost changes but ignores the impact of short-term demand fluctuations is likely to be adopted. The brief summary of techniques in table 3.6 hardly does justice to the complexity of the situation. A few contracts base escalation on adjustments arising under other contracts. Thus, one major consumer allows its supplier to vary prices at the average rate prevailing for the supplier's utility contracts in the eastern United States. Another user permits its smaller suppliers to change prices at the same rate as prevails with the user's other contracts.

Some methods are at times supplemented by performance incentives. Certain cost based formulas provide that the profits of the supplier vary inversely with costs; some formulas based on productivity improvement allow the producer to keep a portion, usually half, of the gain.[9] Finally, a bewildering variety of components of the Bureau of Labor Statistics Wholesale Price Index is used in the escalation formulas.

The available data simply will not permit derivation of any detailed analysis of the formulas used for price adjustment, but a rough impression is that no clear pattern exists. Given the difficulties in developing good measures of price level trends, this variation is hardly startling. It may be added that these clauses apparently proved inadequate to provide an adequate adjustment to the post-1969 rises in coal mining costs, and many ad hoc adjustments were necessary.

The situation of partial integration similarly defies analysis. It was noted that only fully integrated operations were included here. Moreover, since the data relate to 1969, the subsequent decisions of such companies as Duke, Pennsylvania Power and Light, and Virginia Electric and Power to integrate are neglected. The main examples of partial integration consist of the lease of coal lands to operating companies by at least three utilities. Another jointly operates a mine with a coal company.

No single theory adequately explains the vertical integration patterns that prevail. Most eastern cases can be rationalized by assuming that electric companies cannot run coal mines as cheaply as companies specializing in coal mining, but that integration can provide valuable information to the former. The experience in mining might improve the utilities' ability to negotiate and enforce purchase agreements. Under these assumptions, the dominant eastern pattern of large coal users relying on integration for part of their needs would be expected to prevail. The management-inferiority-of-electric-company assumption is needed to justify failure to integrate totally. Operation of a few mines should suffice to secure adequate information, because with further integration, the production cost disadvantage would exceed the value of the information obtained. Since information is more valuable to larger companies, they are more likely to integrate to secure information. However, other forces may also have been at work, and Duquesne Light's high level of integration cannot be explained by the hypothesis just developed.

The western pattern can be explained by arguing that the relative disadvantage in mining abilities is smaller, if not nonexistent. The companies use

[9] In many cases the system involves first establishing cost standards subject to escalation on objective bases similar to those used to set prices in other contracts, and then basing the profit variation on deviations from the standards.

the simpler technique of strip mining and operate in an area in which the activity of coal mining companies has been limited (a hypothesis confirmed by discussions with two operators).

If special conditions are necessary for integration to be advantageous, the limited scope of such ventures into coal mining is hardly startling. However, it leaves the question unresolved as to why companies such as TVA and Commonwealth Edison, which were also large coal consumers, did not find AEP's approach desirable. In the TVA case, political pressures to limit the scope of its activities may have been a restraining factor. A more general possibility is that management is most effective when mining occurs near the company's other activities. In any case, coal supply was never a serious problem up to 1969. It may be more surprising that AEP integrated than that comparable companies did not. Nevertheless, it must be recognized that the decisions were all made under conditions of uncertainty. Therefore, the influence of differences among corporations in their appraisals of the available information cannot be ruled out as an influence on integration decisions.

The situation with land-holding is even more difficult to analyze. It is hard to conceive of either a marked disadvantage in buying coal reserves or a marked advantage in possessing them.

In contrast, the oil contracting situation seems quite rational. Large oil users have commonly adopted contracts to insulate themselves from the severe gyrations in the spot market. A long-term contract leads to a long-term charter of tankers, and a substantial proportion of demand is satisfied in this fashion. A change in demand is concentrated on the spot market and prices in this sector thus fluctuate quite substantially. Moreover, substantial economies apparently result from contracting since the prices apparently are well below spot prices even in "normal" times.

The newness of many contracts, of course, largely reflects the 1966 liberalization of import controls that made residual oil more competitive on the East Coast. Most of the earlier contractors were in regions quite distant from coal fields so that oil was more likely to remain a competitive fuel. The rest were somewhat nearer to coal fields and were very large fuel users likely to require at least limited amounts of oil.

The single case of noncontracting can be validly explained by subjective factors. Most oil using companies were convinced that the dangers of reliance on foreign supply have been exaggerated. As one man put it, OPEC and the oil companies seem more reliable than the United Mine Workers and the coal companies. The noncontracting company, however, disagreed with this assessment, and preferred not to contract.

The role of price adjustment clauses merits further investigation than provided here. The willingness of oil companies to protect consumers against price rises but give them the benefit of price declines is particularly interesting. It suggests that at least a significant portion of the oil industry did not believe the standard prediction of rising oil prices. This disbelief is hardly startling considering that foreign oil prices had been falling throughout the 1960s. The more difficult issue to resolve is why this particularly attractive pricing provision was not secured by all the electric utilities buying on contracts.

COMPETITION IN THE ELECTRIC UTILITY FUEL MARKET

Having viewed the structure of the buying side of the market in chapter 2, and purchasing practices here, it is now desirable to see whether any conclusions can be reached on competitive conditions. This requires that some facts on the structure of the coal industry be noted, and that some tentative hypotheses be stated.

As table 3.7 shows, only two coal companies each produced more than 10 percent of 1970 national coal output and the leading fifteen companies (a number selected by the source) accounted for only slightly more than half of output. The remainder of the market is served by numerous firms. This clearly would not be considered evidence of a highly concentrated industry nationally. Two objections might be raised about such statements.

TABLE 3.7

Role of Leading Companies in Coal Production, 1970

Coal company	Parent company[a]	Thousand tons produced	% of U.S. production
Peabody Coal	Kennecott	67,850	11.3
Consolidation Coal	Continental Oil	64,062	10.6
Island Creek Coal	Occidental Petroleum	29,722	4.9
Pittston Coal		20,540	3.4
United States Steel		19,631	3.3
Bethlehem Steel		14,605	2.4
Eastern Associated Coal	Eastern Gas & Fuel	14,539	2.4
Amax Coal	Amax	14,427	2.4
General Dynamics		14,092	2.3
Old Ben Coal	Standard Oil (Ohio)	11,687	1.9
Westmoreland Coal		11,347	1.9
North American		9,674	1.6
Pittsburg & Midway Coal	Gulf Oil	7,838	1.3
Utah International		6,021	1.0
Southwestern Illinois		5,715	0.9
Total above		311,751	51.7
Total U.S.		602,932	100.0

Sources: Coal production by companies from *Keystone Coal Industry Manual;* U.S. total from USBM.

[a] Only shown if not self-explanatory.

First, since coal markets are regional, it might be argued that in any specific area concentration could be much greater. Actually, examination of regional details suggests that this is true for the Middle West but not for Appalachia. Even here some qualifications must be made. Appalachia and the Middle West are not totally separate markets. The service areas of TVA and AEP are such that they can draw on coal from both producing regions. Moreover, Exxon's ability to secure substantial coal reserves in Illinois suggests that considerable freedom of entry prevails.

A second fear widely expressed in various government studies (e.g. U.S. Federal Trade Commission 1971, Duchesneau, 1972, and U.S. House of Representatives, Subcommittee on Small Business, 1970 and 1971), is about the creation of energy monopolies by the purchase of coal companies by oil companies. To suggest at least the most obvious drawbacks of this argument, table 3.7 lists the oil (and other) company ownership of leading coal companies and the role of the leading oil companies. The table makes clear that only four coal companies listed are owned by oil companies. In no case, moreover, are *both* the coal and the oil company large enough to be considered even possibly dominant firms (see table 3.8). Much of the so-called entry of oil companies has taken the form of land purchasing that may create independent sources of competition in coal. Moreover, an exami-

TABLE 3.8

Runs of Crude Oil in U.S. and Canadian Refineries by Leading Oil Companies, 1970

Company	Thousand barrels/ day	% of total	Company	Thousand barrels/ day	% of total
1. Exxon	1,391	11.4	15. Cities Service	247	2.0
2. Shell	1,113	9.2	16. Marathon	187	1.5
3. Texaco	1,088	9.0	17. Getty-Skelly	157	1.3
4. Gulf	907	7.5	18. Petrofina	156	1.3
5. Standard Oil (Ind.)	895	7.4	19. Amerada Hess	120	1.0
6. Mobil	818	6.7	20. Tenneco	86	0.7
7. Standard Oil of California	731	6.0	21. Murphy	76	0.6
			22. Signal	60	0.5
8. Atlantic Richfield	678	5.6	23. Kerr-McGee	48	0.4
9. Phillips	532	4.4	24. Pennzoil United	32	0.3
10. Standard Oil (Ohio)–British Petroleum	457	3.8	25. Compagnie Française des Pétroles	29	0.2
11. Sun	456	3.8			
12. Union Oil	388	3.2	Total above	11,229	92.4
13. Ashland	289	2.4	Total "refining	12,151	100.0
14. Continental	288	2.4	runs"		

Sources: Oil refinery crude oil consumption from First National City Bank of New York (1972); total derived as sum of U.S. figure reported by the American Petroleum Institute (1972) and Canadian government data on receipts of crude oil by Canadian refineries.

nation of regional details tends to reinforce the argument. The strongest center of coal-oil competition is the U.S. East Coast, and the only oil company—Continental—owning a major eastern coal producer—Consolidation—does not market oil in the East. Curiously, it was the Peabody-Kennicott merger and not the coal-oil cases that provoked antitrust action. Divestiture was indeed ordered, and as of early 1975 various holders including TVA and a separate consortium of other electric utilities are trying to purchase Peabody.

Thus, it would appear that in coal markets a fairly large group of coal producers into which entry is relatively free, face a more concentrated group of sophisticated buyers. Adelman's argument that alert buying is a major force in stimulating competition seems critical to an explanation of the coal market.[10] Such buyers can recognize and exploit the tensions inherent in any oligopoly situation that might have existed. This vigor in seeking and securing lower prices, moreover, benefits the consumer since regulation reinforced by the apparent desire of the electric power industry to attract business by cutting electric power prices caused the savings to be passed on to electric power consumers. The whole process of contracting was apparently designed to simulate a competitive industry in long-run equilibrium. The widespread willingness of both sides to accept cost based contract formulas suggests absence of potential for coal producer monopoly profits. This does not rule out the possibility of monopoly in mineral rights ownership, but such cost data as are available suggest that royalties are too modest an element of price to reflect significant monopoly gains.

The oil case is less straightforward. The oil companies operating abroad have faced growing competition and the intervention of producing country governments was necessary to force prices up in 1971. However, room probably remains for the companies to engage in price discrimination. The rush into oil contracts undoubtedly reflected electric utility recognition of the opportunities. Adelman has suggested that such vigorous efforts to secure favorable prices are often the first steps in the breakdown of monopolistic behavior. Unfortunately, these pressures were offset by other forces, and the situation remains in doubt.

[10] This argument has appeared throughout his writings, most recently in his study of the oil market (1972a).

4

Fuel Transportation and
Plant Location

INTRODUCTION

Having viewed the historic patterns of fuel use and procurement, it is appropriate to turn to consideration of how the fuels are transported to the power plant. This, in turn, requires a glance at the forces determining power plant location. The initial discussions in this chapter follow those in chapter 3 in stressing the past, but the review concludes with comments on prospective transportation cost patterns.

The discussion begins with examination of the problems of plant location and fuel transportation, proceeds to review the patterns of transporting coal to power plant, and then provides a summary view of the pattern of oil and coal transportation costs within the United States.

FUEL TRANSPORTATION AND ELECTRIC TRANSMISSION

Two transportation steps are required in the electric power industry—from fuel production point to power plant and from power plant to consumer. A complex optimization process is involved in determining the pattern adopted. Formerly, transmission of power was so much more expensive than fuel transportation that the plants were placed as near as possible to consumers. However, this situation has altered in recent years. Innovations in transmission technology involving use of extra high voltages (EHV) have significantly lowered transmission costs and make plant locations near fuel (in practice, coal) *more* attractive. In addition, the tendency to build long-distance transmission lines to permit pooling of power also makes such remote siting less costly, since the transmission lines can often be routed near fuel supplies. Moreover, it has become difficult to build plants near consumers because of air pollution, cooling water, and other problems. The intermediate approach is obviously to locate the plant between the coal field and the market.

The mine mouth technique is by no means new. Two plants located near captive mines have operated since 1917.[1] American Electric Power started

[1] These are the Gorgas Plant of Alabama Power of the Southern Company and Windsor, a plant owned by a joint venture of AEP and Allegheny. (The dates are listed in FPC, 1972.)

locating plants near mines in the early fifties and by 1959 had moved outside its service area to build plants. The next important move outside a
firm's service area to build such plants was Arizona Public Service's 1963
venture just over the border in New Mexico to build the Four Corners
plant. This was quickly followed in 1965 by Virginia Electric and Power's
Mt. Storm plant in West Virginia and many others in later years. The
largest eastern complex of mine mouth plants is located near Johnstown,
Pennsylvania. Two plants—Keystone and Conemaugh—are jointly owned
by a consortium of companies in the Pennsylvania–New Jersey–Maryland
pool. The third—Homer City—is owned by General Public Utilities and
New York State Electric and Gas Company.

Development of western coal resources has involved a particularly heavy
reliance upon mine mouth and intermediate location plants. There are
cases in which the installations are within the service area, but important
developments have occurred in which these plants serve distant markets. At
least two different cases can be distinguished.

First, one group of utilities has built or planned a series of jointly owned
plants in Nevada, Arizona, and New Mexico. The cooperation began with
the addition of units to the Four Corners facility, and several additional
new plants are in various stages ranging from operation to study. The participants and their shares differ from project to project. Leading companies
in Southern California, Nevada, Arizona, New Mexico, and West Texas
are involved.

Another series of developments is taking place further north. Pacific
Power and Light has been particularly aggressive in this area. It built a
mine mouth plant in Wyoming and has also been heavily engaged in mining
coal that it sells to other utilities. It will own another Wyoming plant
jointly with Idaho Power. In 1971, the first half of a 1,400 megawatt (mw)
mine mouth plant in Washington began operation. Pacific Power and Light
was joined by seven other northwestern utilities in this venture. Another
mine mouth plant in Wyoming is operated by Utah Power and Light.

Some doubt exists, however, about whether the mine mouth concept will
make a great contribution beyond that already planned. The West Coast
utilities participating in the mine mouth projects seem somewhat
disenchanted with the development. One company wrote me early in 1971
that it would prefer to build nuclear plants if it could do so. The flood of
attacks on the coal-fired plants seems to have lessened their attractiveness
greatly, and statements in securities prospectuses and other reports of
various participants suggests that they are pessimistic about further
developments (see U.S. Senate Interior and Insular Affairs Committee,
1971a and U.S. Department of the Interior, 1972). Indeed the Secretary of
the Interior decided in 1973 not to allow the construction of the last and

largest (4,000 mw) plant planned by the western utilities, a decision the participating utilities are seeking to reverse.

The projects were a way to meet rapidly the rigorous environmental standards in California. It was hoped that the relatively low levels of pollution would be tolerable in the remote regions in which the plants were located. Unfortunately, the plants are so large that even with fairly good particulate emission control, the emissions remain substantial and apparently spread their effects over a wide area. To make matters worse, controversies arose over the coal mining operations serving these plants. A general attack on stripping was combined with allegations by some of the Indians on whose tribal land the coal was mined that those signing the contracts were not proper representatives. The low-sulfur content in the coal, moreover, is being criticized as still excessive though it meets the 1971 U.S. government standards. In general, it has been argued that California's problems should not be solved by spoiling an unpolluted region.

In the East, environmental problems, combined with the economic problems of coal use, may imply similar limits to further reliance on mine mouth plants. Moreover, suitable combinations of large coal reserves and good transmission logistics may be difficult to find in both regions. Those utilities concerned about their ability to continue coal use would also find the difficulties of securing oil for a plant at a mine mouth location undesirable.

In sum, it would appear that a relatively rare combination of circumstances is required to encourage construction of plants outside a company's service area. All present and planned examples involve supply of areas in which land is expensive, environmental pressures are severe, extensive transmission facilities exist, and fuel transportation is fairly expensive. The flurry of mine mouth projects in the sixties and seventies, therefore, *may* prove a temporary phenomenon at least unless public policy shifts towards encouraging such plants. Whatever the merits of this conjecture, it is clearly true that transportation of fuels is a critical consideration in utility fuel choices. Mine mouth plants are still less important than plants to which fuel is transported and even in evaluating the mine mouth option, the fuel transportation alternative must be appraised to determine which is more economic.

The choice of transportation methods is constrained by both the nature of the fuel and the geography. It is axiomatic that water is the cheapest method of transportation. Two forces are generally at work. Nature often provides the roadway although man, of course, may intervene to improve conditions. Moreover, significant economies of scale exist in transportation (see e.g. Adelman, 1972a). Generally, waterways are better able to accommodate larger devices than land based methods. User, though not social, costs of inland transportation in the United States are lowered because the

U.S. government does not charge for use of the services, such as widening and canalization, which it provides.

Nevertheless, water transportation is decidedly a secondary factor in coal transportation. The reasons for this transportation pattern are largely geographic; the number of connections between coal fields and acceptable power plant sites is limited. Conversely, residual oil moves from the Caribbean to power plants on the East Coast, and thus water transportation is the major method for such oil. Gas transportation is cheapest by pipeline; water transportation requires liquefaction and expensive specially equipped vessels to carry the liquefied gas (LNG). However, ocean shipments of LNG are becoming increasingly important. Actually, three distinct types of water transportation prevail for coal—use of inland waterways, use of the Great Lakes, and coastal shipments. In the last case, this invariably follows an initial rail shipment to water; similarly, many lake shipments follow an initial rail shipment.

An examination of coal flows shows that water transportation is used where possible. One case worth special attention is that of Tampa Electric. It is on the southern fringe of the utility coal market and has devised an unusual method of economizing on transportation. A special transfer facility was built to shift coal from river to oceangoing barges. Moreover, a backhauling arrangement involving shipping of phosphates was established. Of course, economies of scale are important and the so-called unit barge concept has arisen in which a group of barges are tied together. The economies are limited by the restrictions of channel width and depth, and by lock capacity.

It is similarly axiomatic that railroads are superior to trucks for large-volume, fairly long hauls. It turns out that, as a result, the majority of coal shipments are by rail. Preserving this position, curiously, required practically bludgeoning the railroad industry to reform radically its coal handling practices. Railroads have traditionally made the carload the basic unit of shipping. Freight transportation is a matter of loading a car, moving it to yards for placement on a train, removing it at another yard, and delivering it. The result is that a given car spends 90 percent of its time waiting and only 6 percent moving a load; the remaining time, it moves empty (Bailey, 1967).

These patterns are dictated by the requirements of the typical consumer but clearly make no sense for those who ship large volumes of material. Such users have no need to pool their loads with enough other users to make up a full train. Their requirements may be a full trainload. Modern electric power plants are in this position. A trainload of coal contains no more than 13,000 tons. Depending upon distances and speeds, total annual deliveries of one to three million tons a year could be made by a single train devoted to this service.

This is well within the requirements of a modern electric station. A rough tabulation of data on capacity and coal use suggests that plants consume an average of about 2.5 tons of coal per year for every kilowatt of capacity. (The exact relationship depends upon the thermal efficiency of the plant, the heat content of the coal, and the hours of operation, and so differs widely among plants.) Thus, it requires about 400 mw of capacity to justify purchase of a million tons of coal per year; a plant of this size is now considered relatively small. Plants of a million kilowatts are becoming common and would use at least 2.5 million tons of coal per year. (Alternatively, if the operating assumptions of chapter 7 are applied to a 1,000 mw plant using coal with 12,000 British thermal units (Btu) per pound, it would consume about 3 million tons of coal per year.)

Nevertheless, a combination of lethargy and the morass of encrusted regulatory tradition long precluded development of a trainload based concept despite the mutual advantage to customer and railroad. Consumers had to threaten withdrawing business to secure concessions. Three alternatives were presented—the coal pipeline (see below), EHV, and a shift to nuclear power. The response in the late fifties was the unit train. A train was "dedicated"—i.e., made up entirely of coal cars to move from a particular mine to a specific power plant. It then shuttled directly back and forth on the prearranged run. Arrangements were made for more rapid loading and unloading. An ingenious variety of devices were adopted. The usual method is to turn the car upside down; in some cases, special couplings are installed so that this turning can be accomplished without uncoupling. At one TVA plant, dumping is effected by electronically opening the car bottom as it passes (slowly) over a pit. However, coal freezing in more northern climates apparently precludes more widespread use of this method.

Finally, the railroads offered rate reductions if the user supplied the equipment. However, considerable variations seem to have prevailed in the attractiveness of the concession. Some users preferred to use railroad equipment. Others found the saving justified the purchase or lease of equipment. In some cases, the coal company was involved; in others, the utility. Rates in general were conditioned on shipment volumes and loading and unloading speeds.[2]

These changes proved quite profitable to all concerned. Clearly, a more intensive use of transportation equipment and manpower is produced by the arrangement. Thus, one study indicated that in 1965 unit trains yielded a higher than average net income per ton mile despite much lower charges. The rates were about 6.33 mills a ton mile compared to an average of 12.66, but the respective nets were 1.3 and 1.0 mills (Bailey, 1967, p. 5). Unfortunately, our field interviews indicated that electric utilities feel that

---

[2] See Glover, Hinkle, and Riley (1970) for a study of nine cases of unit train use.

the well-known erosion of this saving by rate rises was aggravated by the precarious position of the railroads. Innumerable comments were interjected about poor service, lack of reliability, and indifference.

Truck haulage is also restricted by the direct and public relations limitations on widespread movements. Truckage is more expensive for long hauls, and coal trucks are considered a traffic bottleneck and destructive of roadways. Thus, most movement is of a short-haul nature.

Coal movement by pipeline was originally proposed in 1890 but was first demonstrated in 1952 when Consolidation Coal started a 12 inch diameter pipeline pilot operation. This pipeline carried a slurry of approximately 50 percent finely ground coal and 50 percent water. The experience of Consolidation Coal gained in this pilot operation was tested in a full scale 10 inch pipeline from Cadiz, Ohio to Cleveland Electric's power plant at Eastlake on Lake Erie. This pipeline was 108 miles long and began operation in 1957. Although the economics of the operation are not known in detail, it could transport coal at a lower cost than *conventional* rail movements (Reichl, 1962, p. 7). This pipeline operated until 1963 when it terminated operation because the New York Central Railroad had offered lower rates by rail in unit train shipments (*Chemical Week,* March 16, 1968, p. 78).

In 1970 a 273 mile, 18 inch coal slurry pipeline began operation between Black Mesa, Arizona and the Mohave power plant in southern Nevada. The pipeline system is designed to pump 660 tons of coal per hour in a slurry of half coal and half water.[3] Coal slurry takes nearly three days to reach the Mohave plant and must cross rather remote and rugged terrain. At the power plant, the slurry is stored in the 6 million gallon active storage tanks. The slurry goes through a centrifuge to remove most of the water before being burned in the power plant (*Electrical World,* February 15, 1971, p. 44–46).

The cost of coal transportation by pipeline is dependent on such factors as the size of the pipeline, the type of terrain crossed, and right-of-way costs. Coal movement by pipeline is particularly attractive where a direct rail route does not exist such as in the Black Mesa–Mohave case. Only two pipelines for coal slurry have been constructed in this country, and the total tonnages moved have been an insignificant portion of total movements of coal. Most states have not passed legislation providing the right of eminent domain permitting the acquisition of right-of-ways. In the West, such pipelines would probably cross federal lands and require Environmental Impact Statements. Many utilities are having difficulty building power plants fast enough to meet the rapidly growing demands for electricity, and their ability to use coal is in doubt. Therefore, companies may be reluctant

---

[3] Includes 10 percent inherent moisture in the coal.

to tackle the right-of-way problems inherent in building a coal slurry pipeline. The future potential of coal slurry by pipeline is indeterminate at best.

The costs of transportation are not easily quantified, but a later section of this chapter presents rough data for particular cases. Hottel and Howard (1971, p. 45) attempt a review of general rate levels that may be consulted for further information.

A final consideration in coal logistics arises from trade-offs between transportation costs and investment in higher quality coal. A higher Btu per ton coal is cheaper per Btu to transport and burns better; however, this quality is most easily obtained by washing and other forms of preparation. Thus, a company with very cheap transportation costs finds that cleaning costs more than it can save and insists on coal delivered as mined. Companies in the Northeast generally face high coal transportation costs and find it desirable to pay the premium for higher coal quality.

PATTERNS IN COAL DISTRIBUTION

The tables in this chapter provide an elaborate reworking of USBM data on coal distribution. The separations are designed to lessen the complexity. Thus, table 4.1 shows shipments from the primary coal producing districts, table 4.2 shows shipments from secondary coal producing districts, and table 4.3 shows the roles of different methods of transportation.

Prevailing distribution patterns usually follow the dictates of locational economics. Coal use, as noted, is greatest near coal fields and the method of transportation employed is the cheapest available. Thus, in 1969, over two-thirds of the coal produced was consumed in ten states, and eight mining districts accounted for over 86 percent of total deliveries to electric utilities (see table 4.1). Moreover, the vast majority of the deliveries to the ten states were from districts which are nearby.

Indiana, Ohio, and Illinois mines make the majority of their utility coal sales within the state; in turn, the utilities in the states get their coal primarily from mines within the state. The variation is, however, considerable. Indiana coal, for example, has the highest proportion of sales intrastate, but the state's utilities have the highest dependence on nearby states.

While western Kentucky does provide the majority of that state's utility coal, that area and four other Appalachian districts (1, 3, 6, and 8) sell the majority of their coal outside the state in which it is produced. The remaining Appalachian districts (2, 7, and 13) also have markets quite heavily concentrated in nearby areas. Among the districts west of the Mississippi, the largest of them shipped only 5.2 million tons of coal to utilities. Again, the majority of the coal is sold within the state (see table 4.2).

Most of the coal was shipped primarily by railroad. About 30 percent was moved by water, 10 percent completely by truck, and about 6 percent by conveyor belts, private railroads, and other special methods (see table 4.3). Most of the water shipments were barge deliveries by river. However, lake and tidewater shipments were also made. Some 76 percent of 1969 domestic shipments to utilities by lake were to Michigan; 21 percent, to Wisconsin. The tidewater shipments were to East Coast destinations from Maryland northwards, and involved initial rail shipment.

Truck and other methods are inherently limited to short distances, and most shipments by these techniques are within a state. The exceptions to this rule are invariably shipments to contiguous states. These methods account for a larger proportion of deliveries in the West than in the East. However, the data somewhat understate the role of trucks since only the primary method of shipment is distinguished. Truck deliveries to railhead or barge terminals, for example, are not tabulated. Similarly, the initial rail hauls to tidewater are not distinguished.

A SUMMARY OF TRANSPORTATION PRICE PATTERNS

In dealing with coal shipping costs, at least three major transportation webs must be considered—those for each of the main supply areas—Appalachia, the Middle West, and the West. In the first two cases, the possibilities range from an ability to build mine mouth plants in the service area or be served by short barge hauls to long single-car-rate rail trips.

Western coal could either be delivered by rail to plants in the consuming area or used at a mine mouth plant that would use high voltage lines to transmit the power. As noted above, problems arise with both approaches. Several different cases arise with western coal. There are the local markets, but they are limited. To make matters worse, the most favorable markets are not necessarily located where cheaply available coal is mined. For example, Colorado is one of the larger markets, but local coals often have to be mined underground.

Several different distant markets may be considered. First, various markets exist on the West Coast. At least three subregions can be distinguished—the Northwest, Northern California, and Southern California. The second of these markets is somewhat less favorably situated in relation to coal deposits than the other two. California utilities would undoubtedly be forced by the state's prohibition of coal use to adopt the mine mouth plant alternative, but utilities in the Northwest believe that both mine mouth and local plants would be permissible.

As of 1973, the transportation cost for utilities buying coal east of the Mississippi seems to range from negligible amounts to perhaps as much as $0.25 per million Btu for a particularly unfavorable situation. The first

TABLE 4.1

Coal Flows from Principal Districts of Origin in the United States to Electric Power Plants in 1969

(thousand tons)

Destination	District 1	Districts 3 & 6	District 4	District 8	District 9	District 10	District 11	Other districts	Total shipments
				Principal Flows					
Pennsylvania	14,955	5,727	—	16	—	—	—	5,489	26,187
Ohio	99	4,150	21,838	3,755	2,041	—	—	786	32,669
Indiana	—	—	—	1,209	6,331	2,623	12,226	—	22,389
Illinois	—	4	—	—	3,063	26,622	656	48[a]	30,393
Michigan	99	1,144	13,829	4,661[b]	790	286	412	211[b]	21,432
West Virginia	1,622	6,928	1,066	4,231	—	—	—	—	13,847
North Carolina	—	—	—	15,823	—	—	—	248	16,071
Kentucky	—	—	—	2,768	10,443	2,447	38	—	15,696
Tennessee	—	—	—	6,994	5,084	1,188	20	352	13,638
Alabama-Mississippi	—	—	—	—	5,501	—	—	9,874	15,375
Total of Above	16,775	17,953	36,733	39,457	33,253	33,166	13,352	17,008	207,697
Undisclosed	157	2	99	37	98	915	85	60	1,453
Other States	13,790	13,577	579	20,871	7,846	14,965	281	24,356	96,265
Total U.S. Deliveries	30,722	31,532	37,411	60,365	41,197	49,046	13,718	41,424	305,415
Canada	—	4,137	—	20	—	—	—	2,420	6,577
Total Deliveries	30,722	35,669	37,411	60,385	41,197	49,046	13,718	43,844	311,992

Secondary Flows

State									
Massachusetts	833	51	—	924	—	—	—	53	1,861
Connecticut	1,895	62	—	50	—	—	—	25	2,032
Other New England	—	980	—	2	—	—	—	—	982
New York	5,270	5,291	244	1,792	—	—	—	294^c	12,891
New Jersey	688	3,480	335	221	—	—	—	194	4,583
Wisconsin	—	—	—	348	2,796	4,826	191	35	8,531
Minnesota	—	—	—	—	490	2,905	90	1,106^d	4,591
Iowa	—	—	—	—	312	2,204	—	1,160	3,676
Missouri	—	—	—	—	—	5,029	—	3,899	8,928
Dakotas	—	—	—	—	—	1	—	3,272	3,273
Delaware-Maryland	4,615	3,703	—	26	—	—	—	—	8,344
Virginia	16	—	—	7,610	—	—	—	614	8,240
South Carolina	—	—	—	3,660	—	—	—	—	3,660
District of Columbia	473	10	—	88	—	—	—	193	764
Georgia-Florida	—	—	—	6,150	4,248	—	—	841	11,239
Total of Above	13,790	13,577	579	20,871	7,846	14,965	281	11,686	83,595

Source: USBM Bituminous Coal Distribution.

Notes: For summary of district definitions, see note following table 4.3.

a This presumably represents the first shipments of Commonwealth Edison's purchase of low sulfur coal from Wyoming; the shipment was deduced from matching 48 thousand ton differences between total shipments to Illinois and the sum of reported components and total shipments from District 19 and the sum of its reported components.

b District 8 deliveries deduced by subtracting all other components from total district deliveries. This plus reported components allow inference of District 2 deliveries by subtraction from state total. Given District 2 deliveries to New York, per note c, deliveries of District 2 to Michigan can be checked by subtraction of components from district totals.

c Deliveries from District 7 deduced by subtracting other components from district total. Given this figure and the reported components, deliveries from District 2 may be inferred by subtraction from total deliveries to state.

d Deliveries from District 21 deduced by subtraction from the district's total shipments; this permits deducing deliveries from districts 22 and 23 combined by subtraction from state total.

TABLE 4.2

Coal Flows from Secondary Districts of Origin in the United States to Electric Power Plants in 1969

(thousand tons)

Destination	Secondary Eastern Districts of Origin				
	District 2	District 7	District 13	Other Districts	Total
Pennsylvania	5,489	—	—	—	5,489
Ohio	786	—	—	—	786
Michigan	197[a]	14	—	—	211
North Carolina	—	248	—	—	248
Tennessee	—	—	352	—	352
Alabama-Mississippi	—	—	9,874	—	9,874
Total of above	6,472	262	10,226	—	16,960
Massachusetts	—	53	—	—	53
Connecticut	—	25	—	—	25
New York	187[b]	107[b]	—	—	294
New Jersey	—	194	—	—	194
Wisconsin	34	—	—	1	35
Virginia	—	614	—	—	614
District of Columbia	—	193	—	—	193
Georgia-Florida	—	—	841	—	841
Total of above	221	1,186	841	1	2,249
Undisclosed	37	1	—	—	38
Canada	2,420	—	—	—	2,420
Total: this table	9,150	1,449	11,067	1	21,667

Destination	Secondary Western Districts of Origin							
	District							Total
	15	18	19	20	21	22 & 23	Others	
Illinois			48[c]					48[c]
Wisconsin	—	—	1	—	—	—	—	1
Minnesota	48	—	—	—	894	164	—	1,106
Iowa	229	—	155	—	—	—	776[d]	1,160
Missouri	3,885	—	14	—	—	—	—	3,899
Kansas-Nebraska	1,117	—	22	—	—	—	—	1,139
Dakotas	—	—	228	—	3,044	—	—	3,272
Colorado	—	—	323	—	—	—	2,663[e]	2,986
Utah	—	—	—	409[f]	—	—	—	409
Montana	—	—	—	—	—	599	—	599
Wyoming	—	—	3,077	—	—	—	—	3,077
New Mexico	—	3,249	—	—	—	—	—	3,249
Arizona-Nevada	—	438	—	634	—	—	—	1,072
Alaska	—	—	—	—	—	139	—	139
Undisclosed	19	—	—	3	—	—	—	22
Total	5,298	3,687	3,868	1,046	3,938	902	3,439	22,178

Notes to Table 4.2

Source: Same as table 4.1.

Note: For summary of district definitions, see note following table 4.3.

ᵃ See note b, table 4.1.

ᵇ See note c, table 4.1.

ᶜ See note a, table 4.1.

ᵈ Consists of deliveries from District 12; these are the district's only electric power shipments.

ᵉ 514,000 came from District 16; 2,149,000 from District 17; in both cases these are the only deliveries to electric power from the districts.

ᶠ Deduced by subtraction from total deliveries from District 20.

81

TABLE 4.3

Transportation Methods Employed for Shipment of Coal to Electric Utilities, 1969

(thousand tons)

Method	District 1	Districts 3 & 6	District 4	District 8	District 9	District 10	District 11	Other districts	Total
Road	17,851	14,635	19,984	46,637	12,582	25,429	8,701	17,747	163,566
River	—	9,816	3,909	6,104	22,050	18,621	1,838	7,838	70,176
Lakes	214	5,035	4,857	3,037	1,011	1,401	535	2,672	18,762
Tidewater	3,040	2,678	—	2,679	—	—	—	96	8,493
Truck	9,617	3,505	8,661	1,928	5,554	3,595	1,571	15,491	31,571
Other	n.a.	n.a.	n.a.	—	—	n.a.	1,073	n.a.	19,424
Total	30,722	35,669	37,411	60,385	41,197	49,046	13,718	43,844	311,992

Source: Same as table 4.1.

Note: Except for District 11 the bureau aggregates the figures on other methods with truck shipments in showing the shipments by district.

NOTES TO TABLES 4.1 to 4.3.

These figures were taken and in many cases deduced from the Bureau of Mines data. The bureau treats the data as confidential despite the fact that the consumers in the electric power industry regularly and freely report closely related data on coal consumption. For example, most of the detailed data on shipments by conveyors and private railroads are aggregated with those on truck shipments although the major uses of such special methods can easily be determined in the literature. In practice, some substantial discrepancies arise.

Moreover, some supposedly concealed figures may be inferred by subtraction. A single component of a given total, for example, may not be published but may be readily calculated.

Summary Definitions of Districts
(see USBM for details)

District   1: Maryland, the eastern half of the Pennsylvania coal fields and three counties in West Virginia
District   2: The rest of Pennsylvania's coal fields
District   3
    and 6: Northern West Virginia and the state's panhandle
District   4: Ohio
District   7: Eastern portion of Southern West Virginia and eastern half of Virginia coal fields
District   8: Rest of West Virginia and of Virginia, Eastern Kentucky, Northern Tennessee
District   9: Western Kentucky
District 10: Illinois
District 11: Indiana
District 13: Alabama, Georgia, and Southern Tennessee
District 15: Missouri, Kansas, and Oklahoma
District 16: Northern Colorado
District 17: Southern Colorado plus small area of New Mexico
District 18: Rest of New Mexico and Arizona
District 19: Wyoming
District 20: Utah
District 21: The Dakotas
District 22: Montana
District 23: Alaska, Washington, Oregon

situation prevails mainly for AEP and Allegheny; both can be served by short barge hauls and both can build mine mouth plants in their own service areas. However, AEP seems significantly better situated than Allegheny for use of such mine mouth facilities.

A cost of around $0.05 per million Btu would be applicable to some users of longer barge hauls such as TVA and companies near coal fields such as Union Electric and Duquesne. The costs seem to mount to around $0.10 for more distant locations within or near coal producing states; this figure might, for example, apply to Chicago, Detroit, Cleveland, or Toledo. Similar rates seem to prevail for more distant points on the barge delivery network—Minneapolis or the west coast of Florida. Somewhat higher rates would apply to rail shipments to southeastern utilities, and it appears that unit train rates to more distant markets such as in the Northeast or Wisconsin would reach $0.15.

The western situation cannot be characterized so neatly, since wide differences in distances prevail and only a few rates now exist. The coal is located quite far—1000 miles or more—from the major markets. The available evidence suggests that rail transportation costs for this coal would run *at least* $5.00 a ton outside the upper Midwest.[4] Since the heat content is often as low as 8,000 Btu/pound, this means about $0.30 a million Btu in transportation. Moreover, it is not clear that rail rates can actually be kept to this level. Some sources predict costs as high as $0.60 a million Btu for delivery in the Middle West. (In this study a $0.20 per million Btu transportation rate in 1973 dollars is assumed for the upper Midwest (e.g., Minnesota) and a rate of between $0.30 to $0.60 is used for transportation to Chicago.

Of course, mine mouth plants could be built and the electricity transmitted. It is not clear that this would prove to be a cheaper method of transportation, and it involves some serious disadvantages. Limitations on water supply are a chronic problem in the West so that sites might be difficult to find. Objections on environmental grounds have slowed progress in power line construction. One company in the West indicated to me that it feared a mine mouth plant and its transmission facilities would take about as long to build as a nuclear plant. There are possible offsetting advantages in that the power lines would not involve the rising costs after the plant starts operation that are likely with railroads. The impacts of regulation are more complex. The most probable situation is that regulations will lessen the overall attractiveness of western coal use, but the comparative impact on mine mouth plants versus those near load centers is unclear.

Many different situations also prevail with inland transportation of oil. It is generally agreed that pipelining is the most economical method for sustained deliveries to inland markets of low-sulfur residual oil. Estimates secured from industry sources suggest that a cost of around $0.05 a million Btu might arise for the most likely deliveries—from the nearest seaports to large midwestern markets such as the Chicago area and inland power plants in the Southeast. Such figures clearly are only applicable to situations in which the pipeline can operate over an extended period; requirements for more rapid amortization because the oil is only needed for the remaining life of an old power plant could greatly raise costs. A secondary problem arises from construction lead times. Unless the pipeline became

---

[4] This figure is based on a tabulation of prevailing rates provided by the traffic department of a major coal company. The $5.00 rate from Montana to Illinois was the lowest reported rate and involved use of customer owned cars. A 6 mill a ton mile cost was suggested by one observer interviewed as a reasonable estimate of the cost including that of the cars.

snarled in disputes over its environmental impacts, it could be built in about two years. This is much faster than the lead time of a new plant but slower than the time (about eighteen months) required to convert an old plant to oil.

For those located on the country's inland waterways, barge transportation constitutes the next most satisfactory approach. The public data suggest that barge shipments from New Orleans are costing Commonwealth Edison in Chicago about $0.10 per million Btu, and private sources confirm this figure. Such respondents also indicate that costs to more distant points such as Pittsburgh or Minneapolis would be about $0.13. A substantial number of coal consuming utilities could be reached by this method. Indeed, the possibility arises that the deliveries could mount to a level at which certain already crowded points on the inland waterway system would prove bottlenecks to adequate deliveries.

Another water shipping route is available to power plants on the Great Lakes—the Saint Lawrence Seaway. The main drawbacks are the limits it imposes on the size of ships that may be used and its winter closing. The need to use smaller ships and the necessity to store oil raise costs. Data on this situation are not readily available, but the oil prices paid by companies with plants on the Great Lakes suggest an extra cost of about $0.15 in upstate New York.

CONCLUSIONS ON PLANT LOCATION AND TRANSPORTATION COSTS

This chapter has reviewed the plant location and transportation problems of the electric utility industry. We have seen that trade-offs can be made between transmission of electricity and transportation of fuel. If favorable economics prevail, it may be preferable to locate plants nearer fuel sources and transmit the electricity over distances longer than those of transmission from plants located within the service area. However, many problems involving the ability to find acceptable sites and reduced fuel choice flexibility potentially limit the prospects for locating plants in close proximity to a fuel source.

Coal transportation employs railroads, water, and trucks; oil transportation inland in the United States is most easily accomplished by use of barges when plants are located on waterways. However, large sustained general deliveries of oil would probably lead to extensive use of pipelines. Not only would pipelines be necessary to reach plants not located on navigable waterways, but pipelining would be cheaper. The comparative advantage of pipelines, moreover, might be increased by the congestion costs resulting from massive increases in traffic produced by efforts to ship large quantities of oil. These considerations and the normal variation of transportation costs with the method used and the distance involved imply that transportation costs of fuel differ significantly among regions. Summary data on typical relationships in different parts of the country are presented in this chapter and are used in chapter 7 as a component of comparisons of the total cost of generating electricity from different fuels.

5

Prospective Fuel Prices
in the 1980s

INTRODUCTION

Fuel prices are clearly a major influence on electric utility fuel consumption patterns and, therefore, this chapter presents projections of possible fuel price levels for the early 1980s. For reasons outlined in chapter 1, 1980 represents a reasonable limit to the ability to provide forecasts. After the early eighties, it is conceivable that radical developments could arise to alter the situation. Breakthroughs in coal mining technology might drastically lower mining costs below the levels projected here, or new problems could emerge to raise costs drastically. It would be extremely unwise to attempt quantitative evaluations of these prospects since no data exist on which to base such numbers. Moreover, everything that such numbers would imply can more easily be fathomed qualitatively. The general effect of a better or worse relative cost position than considered here for a particular fuel, will obviously be a corresponding improvement or deterioration in its consumption. It is most honest, therefore, simply to say that such possibilities could arise but cannot be quantified.

The discussion begins with a brief review of conceptual problems in supply analysis stressing difficulties in evaluating coal reserve data. To this discussion are added summaries of the literature on oil, gas, and nuclear fuel prices. The chapter concludes by combining the data in chapter 4 on transportation costs with the material in the present chapter to provide projections of delivered fuel prices in selected markets. It should be noted that the development of the costs of oil and gas from conventional sources can have a dual effect on coal. A sufficient rise in oil or gas prices relative to those of coal would improve the prospects for direct burning of coal in electric power plants and elsewhere. If the relative price rise is great enough, it could also lead to synthesis of oil and gas from coal. However, the sections on oil and gas deal only with their ability to compete directly with coal. The prospects for coal synthesis are treated in a separate section.

Since the analysis of coal supply requires rather involved manipulation of a wide variety of data, the details are presented in three appendices dealing successively with basic data on the coal industry, the prospects for eastern coal, and the prospects for western coal. Similarly, the complexities of appraising low Btu gasification costs are presented in a separate appendix.

Throughout the chapter, unless it is otherwise noted, the predicted prices for the 1980s are in 1973 dollars. Since the data are subject to considerable uncertainty, the adjustments are often quite rough to avoid a spurious appearance of precision.

Finally, it should be noted that expositional convenience overrode consistency in determining how each fuel is treated. Coal and natural gas are handled in the most appropriate fashion of considering mine mouth and well head prices, but it is more convenient to talk about oil product prices delivered on the U.S. coasts and about the cost of reactor cores installed in nuclear plants. This last method of treatment is particularly problematic since reactor cores are more appropriately considered as short-term capital expenditures than current expenses. Nevertheless, it seemed preferable to discuss all the fuels together despite the problems of maintaining comparability.

PROBLEMS OF ANALYZING ENERGY SUPPLIES

To develop meaningful evaluations of prospective fuel use, it is necessary to provide some examination of market conditions. Such a review cannot be conclusive, as available information is incomplete, but we may begin by recalling that with natural resources, temporal considerations are critical. Thus, the analysis may start by examining the determinants of supply and demand in a given period and their interaction. Given the outcome of the initial analysis, and the impact of technology and other forces, the state of demand and supply in the next period can then be examined. The analysis can be repeated until the end of the relevant planning horizon is reached (see Gordon, 1973 for a fuller discussion).

The literature on natural resources stresses that the potential price rises due to increasing demands and depletion of the best of the known resources can be offset by new discoveries and improved technology. Apparently discoveries have had a limited impact on the coal market. The location of resources is supposedly well known. On the other hand, improved technology in mining and transportation has had a critical role in the quarter century since World War II.

Existing work tends to ignore both the concept of supply and of its interaction with demand. One tradition stresses mere physical availability; another widely used approach is to deal directly with the equilibrium price with limited attention being given to a full discussion of the determinants of price. Collectively, these two approaches can be used to give some rough idea of market trends if considerable caution is exercised.

The traditional starting place for analysis of coal supply has been the U.S. Geological Survey (USGS) data on coal reserves (Averitt, 1969). One standard argument takes the USGS figures and compares them to statistics on other fuels. It is argued that on any basis of evaluation the coal resources so dwarf the other available supplies that the country must inevitably rely on coal. It is easy to see the obvious flaws in such arguments, but the coal advocates counter with some justice that even after adjustment the advantage remains.

It is well known that the USGS figures may greatly overstate even the actual physical availabilities they attempt to measure. Schurr, Netschert, *et al.* (1960, p. 295–343) have reviewed the massive downward revisions of the initial USGS figures. Many of the reserves inferred by extrapolation of surface indicators proved not to exist. More adjustments may conceivably be required. Further adjustments may also be necessary for cases in which mining is precluded by whatever use the land is presently employed in. Very little information is available on this subject.

A 1971 Bureau of Mines report indicates that about 12 percent of the land in Appalachia is publicly owned—presumably for parks, forests, and government facilities (1971a, p. 36). The report also includes a survey of the availability for coal mining of a *portion* of the state owned land in West Virginia. It appears that only 30 percent of the state owned land could be used for coal mining (p. 37). Clearly, this tells us very little, and by any naive method of evaluation, it would be concluded that limited amounts of land are removed from mining in this fashion. However, it is conceivable that this land might contain a disproportionately large fraction of the coal reserves. More critically, other preemptions may exist on private land.

The typical comparisons, moreover, are between inflated coal estimates and proved reserves of other fuels—the part of physical availability actually commercially developed. The defenders of reserve figures contend that, even after adjusting the coal figures for overstatement and adding in prospective discoveries of other fuels, the disparity in availability remains. This may be true, but it is almost totally irrelevant. The contention only proves that several generations in the future coal may be the only remaining fossil fuel. By that time, the technology to utilize economically such virtually inexhaustible energy resources as nuclear fusion, solar energy, and the earth's heat may have been developed.

What really is critical is that this is entirely the wrong approach. By the time that one records all the potential sources of energy, the total exceeds the amount that can be used between now and the day the sun becomes a nova and destroys our earth. The relevant question is the order in which this energy is to be consumed. Moreover, the market acts to make developments after the next generation irrelevant. Discounting at the market rate of interest makes present values of more distant incomes negligibly small.

Some deplore this as shortsighted neglect of future generations. It is pointed out that our mortality causes us to ignore the needs of the next century. This is basically incorrect since the economic pure theory of exhaustion shows that high enough expected demand could be anticipated by the market (see Gordon, 1969 and 1974a). The essence of the theory is that the rising prices produced by shrinking supplies generate profits that encourage saving resources for future periods. The counterinterpretation is that the process frees future generations from the lack of foresight in the present. Consider, for example, the massive changes during the twenty-eight years prior to 1973. It is extremely doubtful that planners in 1945 could have foreseen the impact of computers, the jet plane, petrochemicals, or the copying machine—to name a few major developments.

In any case, the point at issue is the comparative cost of exploiting and processing the different fuels. This is an area in which publicly available data for all fuels are, deplorably, nearly nonexistent. Even the most relevant portions of the data—the figures relating to the portion of potential supply that has been proven for commercial use—remain company secrets. While the reasons for such secrecy are understandable, the lack of information makes it difficult to judge industry claims about what would constitute appropriate public policies. Finding a mechanism by which the information could be released and used without impacts on competition among firms would greatly help evaluation of public policy issues. It might be useful in some cases for the government to collect and evaluate information on the longer-run developments companies do not consider because of their low present worth.

It is indeed deplorable that while the U.S. government is quite willing to promote development of coal production and utilization technology, no meaningful effort has been made to secure the data needed for an adequate analysis of coal supply possibilities. Since reserves are better known and cost estimating techniques well established, the task would be far easier than for oil and gas.

PROSPECTIVE DEVELOPMENTS OF COAL MINING COSTS

Since this study deals with electric utility fuel use, the coal analysis is confined to steam coals—those used in boilers, and separate analyses are made of eastern and western coal producing regions.

Eastern coal refers here to the established coal mining regions east of the Mississippi River. These can be divided into two main areas. The first—Appalachia—stretches from Pennsylvania to Alabama and has long been the leading United States coal producing region. Most of the remaining production has occurred in the Eastern Interior or Middle Western region—Illinois, Indiana, and Western Kentucky (see Appendix A).

West of the Mississippi lie substantial coal reserves, many of which are low in sulfur content and can be cheaply strip mined. The largest and most promising reserves are in North Dakota, Montana, and Wyoming. As of 1973, production in the West was far smaller than in the East, but expectations were widespread that substantial expansion would occur. The coal was considered attractive both as a fuel for electric utilities east of the western fields and on the West Coast and as a basis for a synthetic fuel industry.

Eastern coal, in contrast, is beset by the problems of sulfur emission control regulations that restrict its use, and by sharply rising production costs. These cost increases involve rising material and equipment prices, the direct impact of labor problems on wages and productivity, and the effects of the 1969 revision of federal mine health and safety law. The drastic tightening of regulations under the new law can be considered an indirect response to labor discontent. Underground coal mining has long been notorious as a dirty, dangerous, and unhealthy occupation. The coal mine health and safety regulations are one way to correct the situation but so are payments of wages that compensate workers for enduring the working conditions. Sharp rises in the already high levels of miners' pay were negotiated in the three-year contract the United Mine Workers signed in 1971. (A similarly favorable contract was signed in 1974, but it is not treated here except to the extent that the projections implicitly anticipated such developments.)

However, these developments are only part of the labor problems of the industry. Expanding demand, the retirement of older workers, and declining productivity have necessitated the hiring of inexperienced workers. This, in turn, tends further to reduce productivity. The problems are compounded by labor unrest that has produced wildcat strikes, extensive use of seniority rights to change jobs, and similar actions that lower productivity by disrupting normal routines.

Rising costs have encouraged a shift to greater reliance on strip mining but, for reasons discussed in Appendix A, it is unlikely that strip mining can economically displace underground mining in the East. Therefore, the cost of underground mining serves as the best available index of future eastern steam coal prices. The evidence reviewed in Appendix B suggests that such prices were no more than $0.18 per million Btu in 1969, rose to $0.30–$0.35 by 1973, and will reach a price (in 1973 dollars) of $0.40 to $0.50 by 1980. New contract prices in 1974 rose well above this predicted 1980 level, as the producers were able to take advantage of the favorable climate produced by sharp oil price rises. We surmise, however, that the long-term pressure of nuclear competition will force prices down to the level projected here.

Data examined in Appendixes A and C suggest that the critical question about western coal is the extent to which cheap strippable coal can be produced. Known strippable coal supplies are much less ample than is often implied in discussions of western coal, and resistance to strip mining may limit exploitation, in any case. The evidence suggests that, to the extent strippable reserves are available, they can be exploited at $0.25 per million Btu or less in 1973 dollars—a modest absolute rise from the $0.15 levels many mines enjoy in 1973. A $0.20 to $0.25 range is used here. In short, eastern coal prices have risen sharply and may continue to do so. Western prices will increase less, but only if strippable resources are available.

THE PRICE OF OIL

Adelman's massive study of the world oil market has made it abundantly clear that the primary influence on world fuel prices will be the price of Middle Eastern oil. Since the debates over oil were outlined in chapter 1, these need not be repeated. We may simply note that Adelman's view is that the Middle East is clearly capable of supplying the world's demands for oil with costs of no more than $0.20 a barrel at least until 1985 and that it is highly likely that this situation can continue for a considerably longer period. Were this true, it would be quite clear that not only coal but also nuclear power can remain competitive only because oil prices are kept far above their true costs by the policies of the producing states. Even if we add transportation costs of, say, $0.50 a barrel, and desulfurization costs of $1.00 a barrel for a total of $1.70, oil selling at or slightly above its true economic cost would unquestionably be the cheapest fuel to use (see chapter 7).[1] Residual oil prices, as Adelman points out, are likely to be less than crude prices for various reasons, not the least of which is that otherwise crude would be burned directly, so that the hypothetical minimum crude oil price can be used directly as a measure of possible lower limits to residual oil prices (1972a, p. 176–7). Of course, it is not forecast that these limits will be attained; the figures serve to show the margin for price reduction that prevails.

The Adelman arguments about costs seem quite reasonable, but it is difficult to guess whether the right combination of public policies in consuming countries and weaknesses in cooperation among exporting countries will occur. Neither Adelman's thesis nor more pessimistic models of future energy supply are discussed in detail here; instead, a compromise position is adopted for the analysis in this study. Residual fuel oil price pro-

[1] Adelman (1972a, p. 76) sets Middle East costs in the middle eighties at no more than $0.20. He indicates that freight rates will be at Worldscale 40 (Worldscale is a system of base prices to which actual rates are related; Worldscale 40, for example, means prices 40 percent of the base figure, p. 77). The Worldscale rate from the Persian Gulf to the U.S. East Coast by the Cape of Good Hope was $9.29 a long ton (p. 334). At Worldscale 40, the rate was $3.72 a ton or about $0.50 a barrel.

jections are simply set at levels roughly comparable to those prevailing in mid-1972; i.e., well below currently inflated world oil prices. This provides an objective reference point from which the author and reader can readily modify the analysis. In mid-1972, high-sulfur oil was selling for a net price of about $2.50 a barrel (or about $0.40 a million Btu)—a rise from 1969 levels that can roughly be accounted for by rises in Venezuelan taxes of around $0.70 to a total of around $1.75. Oil with less than 0.3 percent sulfur was selling for a net price of about $4.00 per barrel (about $.67 a million Btu)—i.e., despite subsequent rises in Venezuelan taxes, the price was at about the same level paid in 1971 by the East Coast utilities using low-sulfur oil. Thus, the sulfur removal premium was in the $1.50 a barrel range. Given the standard, more optimistic estimate of $1.00 a barrel for desulfurization costs (see e.g., Robson, 1970, p. 83), this would indicate that a scarcity rent on sulfurization capability of as much as $0.50 a barrel was earned.

West Coast prices of low-sulfur residual oil were around $0.80 per million Btu in 1972. These higher prices were attributed by oil and electric power industry sources mainly to the lack of desulfurization facilities. Low-sulfur oil from Indonesia and Alaska was the main source of the low-sulfur residual oil.

The expedient adopted for projection, however, is that East Coast low-sulfur oil prices (in 1973 dollars) return to $0.67 per million Btu as the disappearance of the scarcity premium for desulfurization is offset by a slight price rise over 1972. This rise would bring high-sulfur oil prices to $0.50. West Coast prices are assumed to have reached parity with those on the East Coast. These are deliberately conservative estimates designed to insure that we make no erroneous assumption about oil's competitive relation to other fuels, and not forecasts of actual prices.

THE FUTURE OF NATURAL GAS AS AN ELECTRIC UTILITY FUEL

The basic issues about future use of gas as an electric utility fuel are the nature of prevailing regulations and their impact on supply and demand conditions. Regulatory issues extend beyond those relating to field price controls discussed in chapter 1. Since substantial amounts of gas have been purchased by electric utilities in the West South Central region under long-term contracts, the regulations affecting resale of the gas must also be considered. (Deregulation is the more interesting case because its absence implies additional gas supplies will be inadequate. Should this lead to rationing, the utilities are likely to have low priority.) California utilities, in contrast, expect their gas supplies to be lost in the 1970s.

It appears that even the most optimistic forecasts about the market clearing price for gas in the absence of field price regulation suggest that gas's viability in the electric power industry would be limited by the oil prices assumed here. Erickson and Spann (1972, p. 105), for example, project a 1980 field price (in 1972 dollars) of $0.69 per 1,000 cubic feet. Assuming a price rise of about 5 percent in 1973, this implies a $0.72 price in 1973 dollars. Since 1,000 cubic feet contains only slightly more than a million Btu, these figures can serve as estimates of the price per million Btu of gas. The oil prices assumed here imply delivered oil prices near the gas fields that would be lower than Erickson and Spann's gas prices.

Therefore, at least for expositional purposes, it may be assumed that gas would not be competitive as an electric utility fuel if deregulation were adopted. The oil price projections already represent a situation in which coal faces more intense competition from other fossil fuels than many observers predict. Rather than attempt to deal with a multiplicity of cases, the assumed oil prices can also serve as a proxy for low gas prices, especially since low oil prices, given the low cost of producing Middle Eastern oil, are much more probable than low gas prices.

A final question is the impact of deregulation on electric utilities with existing long-term gas supply contracts. In a competitive market, if gas could be sold to other gas users at a level sufficiently above the price of an alternative fuel to cover the costs of conversion, the rise in gas prices would provide an incentive for utilities to shift to the alternative. Utilities now buying gas in intrastate markets might, for example, sell to interstate pipelines. It is unfortunately easy to conceive of regulatory practices that would preclude this result. The Federal Power Commission might refuse to permit resale at the new higher price for gas, or local regulatory agencies might insist that all the savings be passed on to consumers.

SYNTHETIC FUELS FROM COAL AND OIL

Both fears of rising oil and gas prices and concern about cheaper ways to control sulfur oxide pollution have created interest in synthetic fuels from coal and oil. A main distinction among coal synthesis alternatives concerns the degree to which the coal is upgraded in transformation. One can easily gasify coal; coal gas was originally the fuel source for municipal gas companies. However, such gasification processes have in the past produced a gas with much lower Btu content per cubic foot than natural gas. Thus, the transportation cost per million Btu of such coal gas is much higher than for natural gas. Use of the gas would also require adjustment of equipment designed for burning natural gas. Two solutions to this problem are possible. First, the gas can be increased in Btu content by adding hydrogen. Second, systems can be devised in which it is feasible to utilize the low Btu gas.

Coal liquefaction is a different matter. Conversion of coal to a synthetic crude oil (again requiring some form of hydrogenization) has long been considered, and various technologically proven but overly expensive techniques have been developed. The idea of developing simpler processes to produce low-cost boiler fuels has been a relatively recent phenomenon. One possibility receiving particular attention is solvent refining.[2] The process involves heating a slurry of coal, solvent, and 30–40 pounds of hydrogen per ton of coal. The heated slurry then undergoes a series of processing steps that can include sulfur removal by well-established processes. The main end product then becomes a clean fuel usable in electric power plants; this can be supplied in a liquid or solid form. Products such as chemicals and light oils are also produced, and addition of an extra step of coking can increase the oil yield and produce coke. Even without coking, these other products produce a large fraction (47 percent) of the process revenues so that it is not strictly correct to say that the process is devoted only to clean fuel production (see Hottel and Howard, 1971, p. 162–70). Another source of boiler fuel would be the char residual from a process producing high quality synthetics.

Given the wide variety of basic approaches, not to mention all the variants to each, the various locations of coal, and the many potential uses, a number of possible cases could be conceived. However, solvent refining and low Btu gas are being stressed for the electric power industry while high Btu gas and synthetic crudes are being considered for markets in which premiums for their special properties can be earned. Because of its high transportation costs, low Btu gas might be made at the power plant in order to utilize the product while it is hot. The same consideration also makes it desirable for solvent refining to occur at the generating station. The mine mouth power plant alternative discussed above might be relevant. Presumably the cheapest source of coal would be used.

While the present discussion deliberately avoids examination of technical details, it may be noted briefly that the concepts for making low Btu gas involve first using the proven German Lurgi process and then developing superior alternatives by the 1980s. One problem is that highly caking coals such as are found in the eastern United States are difficult to use in the present design of the Lurgi process (see Hottel and Howard, p. 146). However, since sulfur removal technology for gas is well developed and indeed routinely used for natural gas, cleanup of the gas would be simple for all such processes.

The national "gas shortage," perhaps accentuated by the much discussed availability of oil shales as a crude oil substitute, has inspired priority of consideration for processes to synthesize high Btu gas over those to

---

[2] The process was developed by Spencer Chemical and Pittsburg and Midway Coal has carried out the testing; both are owned by Gulf Oil.

synthesize crude oil. Stress, moreover, seems placed upon taking advantage of the low mining costs of western coals and concentrating activity in that region. Use of eastern coals, however, has not been ignored. Hottel and Howard suggest that it may be that the potential of lower processing costs and the certainty of lower transportation costs *could* make synthetic crude oil a more attractive product than high Btu gas (p. 217-21). In addition, it should be noted that processes for the synthesis of gas from naphtha—a petroleum product—are well established and involve lower processing costs than coal gasification.

The various interrelationships involved here lead to a hierarchy of possible outcomes. These are best expressed by indicating the requirements necessary to permit liquefaction or gasification of coal to be competitive. The prospects for high-grade substitutes may be treated first. In the case of liquefaction, it is simply necessary for coal liquids to be cheaper than oil from all other sources—imported, domestic (including Alaska), and shale oil. Apparently, this will be a most difficult test to pass under any circumstances. Even if we leave aside the possibility that oil prices will not rise greatly, shale may suffice to preclude economic manufacture of synthetic crude oil from coal.

The 1972 National Petroleum Council (NPC) report (p. 206) indicates that at a 10 percent cost of capital oil from shale would cost (in 1970 dollars) $4.32 to $4.47 a barrel if the concentration of bitumen in rock ran 30 gallons per ton. The required price rises to $5.58 to $5.79 with a 15 percent cost of capital. Large quantities of shale are available in that concentration or better; the NPC estimates that at least 54.2 billion barrels of syncrude could be produced from such shales. As Appendix A implies, this is just about the contribution to supplies possible if known strippable western coal reserves were devoted entirely to liquefaction.

The NPC's estimates for coal liquefaction costs are much higher (p. 171). At a 10 percent cost of capital, the estimated costs (in 1970 dollars) with first generation commercial plants are $6.25 to $6.75 a barrel; this rises to $7.75 to $8.25 at 15 percent. Building later, larger plants is expected to reduce costs by $0.50. This cost is based on coal costing $2.75 to $4.00 a ton. The report interprets this as implying a $0.12 to $0.30 per million Btu coal cost but notes that the high cost, which implicitly assigns the highest mining cost to the lowest Btu coal, is unlikely to occur (p. 168). Under the more plausible assumption that the lowest costs per ton apply to lignites with 13.5 million Btu/ton, the appropriate low cost is $0.20. Similarly if only higher (17 million/ton) Btu coals are mined at a $4.00/ton cost, the highest cost would be $0.24 a million Btu. These are only slightly below the coal costs projected here. These data clearly add up to the conclusion that synthesis of oil from coal will occur, if ever, only after the best shale resources are exhausted.

The existence of oil competition for gas makes evaluation of high Btu gasification prospects quite complex. Oil can displace gas directly or serve as a feedstock for synthesis. Those users such as industrial consumers who can easily shift to oil will do so once gas becomes more expensive. While other customers may be willing to pay a premium for gas, oil synthesis as well as coal synthesis sets a ceiling on the possible gas price rise. Without going into details, the NPC figures on coal gasification costs provide one useful set of indicators. The cost in 1970 dollars using the coal prices assumed above would run $0.90 to $1.10 per million Btu if capital costs were "levelized" (see chapter 7) at an 18 percent a year capital charge. At a 15 percent cost of capital the costs rise to $1.20 to (apparently) $1.40 (NPC, 1972, p. 168).[3] The report indicates that gasification conversion efficiency is 67 percent so that 1.5 million Btu of coal are required for each million Btu of gas; therefore, a penny rise in the price per Btu of coal raises the price per Btu of gas 1.5 cents. Thus, the respective price ranges for gas using $0.40 to $0.50 eastern coal would be $1.32 to $1.40 with levelizing at 18 percent and $1.63 to $1.70 if the cost of capital is 15 percent. All these costs are clearly higher than the Erickson-Spann 1972 dollar price estimates for natural gas, so even without making adjustments to put the prices on a comparable basis, doubts can be expressed about the prospects for synthesis of high Btu gas from coal. Moreover, it should be recalled that these costs apply to liquefaction and gasification of the cheapest-to-mine available coal. Appendix A suggests that the ability to meet national demands for oil and gas from these cheapest fields is unproven at best. The costs of expanding output beyond the levels producible from known low cost coal reserves is subject to as much uncertainty as applies to the costs of other energy sources.

Turning to simpler processes to produce boiler fuels, evaluation is hindered by obsolescence of much of the available data. Solvent refining can be treated briefly here, but a more detailed evaluation of low Btu gas appears as Appendix D. A useful discussion of solvent refining economics appears in Hottel and Howard (1972, p. 162–6). They show that the process produces substantial amounts of coproducts and that the economics are quite sensitive to the income received on such coproducts. Their calculations indicate that with high coproduct incomes and the costs prevailing in the late sixties, solvent refining could produce a boiler fuel that would have a price per million Btu only $0.03 greater than the price per million Btu of coal. Less favorable by-product income would raise the required premium of solvent refined boiler fuel over coal prices to $0.19.

---

[3] The report only gives one figure called the lowest figure; the high is derived by assuming that the high of the range is, like the low, $0.30 above the high for the 18 percent levelizing factor case. Note also that the two capital charge rates cannot be directly compared. The 15 percent relates to after-tax return on investment; the 18 percent also includes capital recovery and taxes.

However, a more recent review of solvent refining by Catalytic Inc. indicates that costs would run around $0.35 to $0.40 a million Btu plus the price of the coal (Jimeson and Maddocks, 1973, p. 20). In handling solvent refining here, it is assumed that the noncoal costs in 1973 dollars will be at least $0.10 per million Btu. This figure represents a rough effort to adjust the Hottel and Howard low estimate for inflation and the questionable prospects of high by-product income. However, the Catalytic Inc. $0.40 figure is used as the high estimate.

The calculations in Appendix D indicate that the cost in 1973 dollars per million Btu of coal gas made by the Lurgi process would be 1.3 times the price per million Btu of coal plus $0.47. Improved gasification processes would lower costs to 1.15 times the coal cost plus $0.31. Oil gas would cost 1.1 times the oil cost plus $0.22. This would suggest that the comparative economics of low Btu gas and solvent refining remain to be proved.

Fuller evaluation of the prospects for synthesis of boiler fuels must await the consideration, in chapter 7, of total costs of electric power generation. However, the final section of this chapter presents the synthetic fuel prices implied by the various delivered prices of coal and oil considered in these projections.

REACTOR CORE COSTS

Nuclear reactors receive their fuel in single loadings of cores—the processed uranium—that are used for several years and then processed to recover usable fuel. At least in terms of the magnitudes involved, the economics are quite different from those of fossil fuel. A basic difference is that since several years' supply is obtained at once, interest costs for the fuel are involved. Another special feature is that the processing expenses are a far greater portion of final costs than is true for fossil fuels (although the relationships would be quite similar in oil should oil producing country taxes decline sharply).

The importance of processing is critical to understanding of future nuclear fuel costs. Table 5.1 presents Atomic Energy Commission (AEC) figures on the cost breakdown that may be used to illustrate the argument. Only the mining or milling costs are sensitive to any deterioration in ore quality. The deterioration would raise mining and ore concentration costs since more material would have to be handled. If the problem were only increased difficulty of mining, rises would only be in the mining stage.

At the very least, the small contribution of ore costs to reactor core costs greatly blunts the impact of ore price rises. Even a doubling raises costs to the utility by only 27 percent. More critically, the later stages are believed, at least on balance, to involve potential for cost reduction. Both the impact of greater experience and economies of scale are expected to contribute to

TABLE 5.1

Components of Reactor Fuel Costs for 1,000 Megawatt Nuclear Plant

	Million dollars	Percent of total
Uranium procurement	8.5	27.4
Milling	1.3	4.2
Enriching	10.6	34.2
Fabrication	7.6	24.5
Subtotal	28.0	90.3
Interest	3.0	9.7
Total	31.0	100.0

Source: AEC 1971, p. 91.

cost reductions. To be sure, enrichment of uranium ores may be a problem area. The U.S. government has owned the enrichment plants and provided the services at prices that may be below that required to justify commercial ventures. Efforts are under way to put enrichment on a commercial basis. The first stage would be adjustment of federal charges, and efforts have been made to encourage commercial ventures. Nevertheless, it is felt that gains elsewhere will suffice to offset any rises in this sector.

Moreover, many observers of the uranium supply situation (e.g., Schurr, et al., 1971, p. II–72–83) believe that stable uranium ore prices can be maintained. This combined with the possibilities for reduced processing costs suggests that reactor fuel costs will remain stable. Since these costs are essentially captial costs, provision of the actual figures is delayed until chapter 7.

CONCLUSIONS ON DELIVERED PRICES OF
FOSSIL FUELS IN THE 1980s

This chapter has developed assumptions about future electric utility fuel prices summarized in table 5.2. The table first lists the prior assumptions about each fossil fuel and then presents the delivered prices in Chicago suggested by the data in chapter 4. Then, the prices of coal and oil gas and solvent refined coal implied by the cost assumptions stated above and various fuel input prices are shown.

The choice of Chicago as a reference point primarily represents an expositional device. It is particularly convenient to start the analysis by examining conditions in Chicago and then to proceed to modify the conclusion for other locations. Chicago is a doubly important consumption center. Data about conditions there are particularly ample. Secondly and more critically, it is a strategically located market. Situations can arise in

TABLE 5.2

Projected Prices of Electric Fuel in the 1980s (1973 dollars)

(cents per million Btu)

	Low estimate	High estimate
Basic Prices		
Eastern coal price f.o.b. mine	40	50
Western coal price f.o.b. mine	20	25
High sulfur oil price c.i.f. coastal markets	50	50
Low sulfur oil price c.i.f. coastal markets	67	67
Transportation to Chicago		
Eastern coal	10	10
Western coal	30	60
Fuel oil	5	10
Delivered Prices in Chicago		
Eastern coal	50	60
Western coal	50	85
High sulfur oil	55	60
Low sulfur oil	72	77

Gas and Solvent Refined Coal Costs

Cost of fuel input	Price of gas			Price of solvent refined coal	
	Lurgi gas	Advanced coal gas	Oil gas	10 cent processing	40 cent processing
20	73	54	44	30	60
25	80	60	49	35	65
30	86	65	54	40	70
35	93	71	60	45	75
40	99	77	65	50	80
45	106	82	70	55	85
50	112	88	76	60	90
55	119	94	81	65	95
60	125	100	87	70	100
65	132	105	92	75	105
70	138	111	97	80	110
75	145	117	103	85	115
80	151	123	108	90	120
85	158	128	113	95	125
90	164	134	119	100	130
95	171	140	124	105	135
100	177	145	130	110	140

Source: see text.

which the Chicago outcome would directly indicate the national picture. Failure of western coal to compete in Chicago implies that western coal use would be confined to the relatively limited markets nearer the coal fields. The ability of oil to compete in Chicago, in contrast, indicates strength throughout the eastern United States since Chicago is one of the most distant oil markets, at least for pipeline delivery.

The comparative attractiveness of fuels depends on the total cost of their use rather than fuel prices alone. Thus, a full evaluation of competitive conditions appears in chapter 7, which discusses the additional costs such as extra capital facilities for handling the fuel or controlling the resulting pollution. Nevertheless, the data suggest great uncertainties about even the comparative prices per million Btu. Western coal might or might not be cheaper than eastern coal or low-sulfur oil. Eastern coal's position relative to high-sulfur oil is similarly unclear.

Section D suggests that even with assumptions about Chicago prices most favorable to coal of $0.50 coal price and $0.60 high-sulfur oil price, coal gas would be more costly than oil gas. Solvent refining's cost level relative to coal gas largely depends on attaining low processing costs. At least in a computational sense, however, very high coal prices favor solvent refining over gasification. The formulas provided by the sources penalize gasification but not solvent refining for conversion losses. This causes computed gas but not solvent refined coal prices to increase by more than the increase in coal prices. Since perfect conversion is impossible, it is likely that this advantage is largely illusory.

SUMMARY

The present chapter has shown that the price of eastern coal has risen sharply since 1969 and further rises are expected. The critical problems are difficulties in maintaining productivity advances rapid enough to offset sharply rising wages, the problems of labor unrest, and the expense of complying with the Coal Mine Health and Safety Act. Western coal costs will rise somewhat more modestly so long as strip mining is possible. World oil prices have also risen rapidly—not because of increased scarcity but because of effective cartelization by the producing nations. However, these rises can eventually be limited by extensive development of both conventional oil and gas and oil shale in the United States. Moreover, some observers feel the cartel could be undermined by proper policies in the consuming countries. Uranium price rises are likely to be far smaller than those for coal. This suggests serious problems both for the ability of coal to compete as the basis for synthesizing close substitutes for oil and gas, and as fuel for generating electricity. Chapter 7 reviews this latter issue in detail.

Appendix A

BACKGROUND ON COAL RESOURCES
AND PRODUCTION

To aid understanding of the prospects for the coal industry and the techniques used here to evaluate them, it is useful to examine some of the basic data about coal resources and production.[4]

The comments made above about the drawbacks of overinterpretation of coal "reserve" figures can be further illustrated by noting more about the nature of the data. In practice, the USGS reports several different reserve figures—each based on a different measurement concept—and others have attempted further refinements. One source of difference is the precision of measurement. The degree of knowledge can range from precise measurement of the seam to rough estimates undocumented by exploration. Other variations are produced by efforts to adopt very gross indexes of economic viability. Very rough criteria such as exclusion of coal at depths greater than 3,000 feet are adopted.

Most reporting systems use a mixture of information accuracy and reserve characteristics criteria in distinguishing concepts of reserves. For example, the USGS's most comprehensive figure indicates that 3.2 trillion tons of coal are estimated available at depths less than 6,000 feet. A second figure of 2.9 trillion limits inclusion to coal at depths less than 3,000 feet. The deletion is justified both because these reserves have never been accurately measured and because they are likely to be uncompetitive for many generations at best. When estimates for unexplored areas are removed, the figure falls to 1.6 trillion tons (Averitt, 1969, p. 12–13). This figure can be reduced further in several ways. A chart in the USGS report (p. 38) shows that only 8 percent of the 1.6 trillion tons has actually been measured, and the rest were estimated by less precise mapping techniques. The chart also provides the basis for subdividing the figure by depth and thickness. The National Petroleum Council (NPC) coal report (1973) employs similar concepts to produce two further concepts of reserves. NPC's initial figure includes only coals at depths of less than 1,000 feet and of sufficient thickness. This is defined as 28 inches or more for bituminous coal and 5 feet or more for subbituminous and lignite. These concepts lead to a reserve estimate of 394 billion tons. The NPC then uses a USBM report on strippable reserves to determine the strippable portion of the total. The underground reserves are deduced by subtraction.

The USBM (1971b, p. 11–13) has data that were compiled using a com-

---

[4] In addition to the primary sources cited, the annual compilation, *Bituminous Coal Data*, by the National Coal Association is quite helpful. It largely reports USBM figures but collects them in a more convenient form. While the *Minerals Yearbook* only provides full data for a single year, *Bituminous Coal Data* provides data for several years.

plex process for isolating the economically recoverable strippable coals. Three different figures were provided—the total strippable resource, the recoverable resource, and the reserves. The first figure showed all remaining reserves that met minimum criteria of strippability—both a large enough seam and a small enough overburden. It was postulated that the specific requirements would differ among and, in some cases, within states. Coal seams as thin as 12 inches were considered possible strippable resources in Missouri and Oklahoma, but Rocky Mountain coals were not considered unless the seams were thicker than 60 inches. Similarly, the maximum allowable overburden ranged from 40 feet in Oregon to 200 feet in some Wyoming fields. Wyoming was one of the states in which the ceiling on overburden depths differed among fields—from 60 to 200 feet. Recoverable resources were calculated by applying a recovery factor set at 80 percent everywhere except in western Kentucky for which 90 percent recovery was assumed.

Then an effort was made to determine which recoverable resources were actually economically minable. One requirement was a sufficiently low ratio of overburden to seam thickness. Again, different standards were applied to different areas. The allowable maximum ranged from 1.5 to 1 in some parts of Wyoming to 30 to 1 in Arkansas. A wide range of additional barriers to use were considered to eliminate the exploitation of other resources. Such barriers included land unavailability either because sale was unlikely or because the surface use was for purposes such as towns and railroads, poor quality of the coal, and poor mining conditions. The net effect of the analysis was to reduce an estimated 118 billion tons of strippable resources to 45 billion tons of strippable reserves (USBM, 1971b, p. 16). Using this USBM figure, the NPC inferred gross underground reserves of 349 billion tons. This it reduced further by eliminating all underground lignite, bituminous seams less than 42 inches thick, and subbituminous seams less than 10 feet thick, and applying the traditional 50 percent recovery factor. This left a total of 104.6 billion tons of underground and 150 billion tons of total reserves—this is but 5 percent of the largest USGS estimate of 3.2 trillion.

A few efforts have been made to determine how much coal was minable at some specified cost level. Thus, the Bureau of Mines (1971a) published the results of its survey of reserves and their mining cost in Appalachia. The survey was limited to the resources available to firms producing more than 100,000 tons of coal. Such firms had 31 billion tons of reserves. About 5.7 billion tons could be mined at 1967 prices, and total recoverable reserves amounted to 13 billion tons if prices were $2.00 above their 1967 level (and, implicitly, costs were unchanged). This contrasts radically with the 256 billion tons of measured and inferred reserves indicated by USGS data as adjusted by NPC for subsequent production, and the NPC's 140 billion ton estimate of reserves after the thinner and deeper seams were excluded (1973, p. 116–7).

It is, of course, quite difficult to interpret the USBM survey. In particular, nothing is available to determine the relative contributions of nonresponse, failure to contact nonmining coal landowners, preemption, and lack of economic viability. Certainly the level of economically viable reserves under mine company ownership appears at the sort of level required to meet needs over a generation or so. Thus, the figure may amount to the coal industry analogy to the proved reserve concept for other fuels.

Indeed, the critical point that can be made about all these reserve estimates is that they seem to confirm the argument presented above that the figures inadequately treat economic viability. Another problem is that the uncertainty attached to the estimates may be as great as that for ultimate resources of oil and gas. In fact, the very nature of the estimating process is antithetical to rational economic analysis. No method is provided to assess the economic implications of the different ad hoc criteria of viability.

Despite these drawbacks, it may be useful to present here a tabulation of reserve figures for selected states (table 5.3). The most striking feature of

TABLE 5.3

Alternative Estimates of Coal Reserves

(million tons)

State	Total estimated reserves[a]		Resources determined by mapping and exploration[b]	NPC reserve estimate[b]	Strippable reserves[c]
	0–6000 ft.	0–3000 ft.			
Wyoming	545,710	445,710	120,684	29,912	13,971
North Dakota	530,680	530,680	350,649	36,230	2,075
Montana	378,701	378,701	221,698	38,968	6,897
Colorado	371,715	226,715	80,679	13,280	500
Alaska	265,089	260,089	130,087	6,012	4,411
Illinois	239,756	239,756	139,372	60,007	3,247
Kentucky	117,952	117,952	65,332	31,925	1,758
Utah	115,250	80,250	32,070	9,305	150
New Mexico	109,479	88,479	61,455	2,120	2,474
West Virginia	102,034	102,034	101,186	68,023	2,118
Pennsylvania	79,650	79,650	69,686	36,603	752
Indiana	56,779	56,779	34,661	11,177	1,096
Washington	51,183	36,183	6,183	1,500	135
Ohio	43,864	43,864	41,568	17,242	1,033
Total of above	3,007,842	2,686,842	1,453,310	362,304	40,617
U.S. total	3,210,060	2,872,955	1,556,840	394,106	44,986

[a] From Averitt, 1969, p. 12–13.
[b] From NPC, 1973.
[c] From USBM, 1971b.

these data is the predominance of states west of the Mississippi in all categories of reserves. As table 5.4 shows, this predominance is particularly
pronounced for the Rocky Mountain states, but the coal is subbituminous
or lignite. The great advantage of western coal, however, is low-sulfur
content.

Until production patterns are discussed, the only appropriate comments
relate to the strippable coal reserve figures. Two different issues arise in the
East and in the West. As far as the eastern figures are concerned, the
critical question is whether the cutoff points adopted allowed inclusion of
more coal than is likely to be economic. Historical data show that stripping
has been forced to go deeper and deeper over time, and considerable
speculation prevails that it will be difficult, if not impossible, to continue to
develop the large strip mines that are so important in the Middle West. For
example, Gambs (1970a) talks of the difficulties of securing large blocks of
strippable coal in the Middle West. Both electric utilities and coal companies operating in the area indicated in field interviews that these difficulties were such that they expected few new large strip mines would be
developed. As is shown, such large strip mines are rare in Appalachia outside Ohio (where difficulties in opening large strip mines are also expected).

The crucial point about western strippable reserves is that close examination of the data suggests that the amounts are far too small to justify the
extravagant claims about reliance on western coal. This may be illustrated
by noting the implications of devoting all the western coal resources to
gasification. It is expected that a gas plant would operate for thirty years so
that the 26.6 billion tons of western strippable coal could be produced at an
annual rate of 890 million tons. With coal content as high as 17 million Btu
per ton, this is an annual input availability of 15.1 quadrillion Btu. With a
67 percent conversion efficiency, this permits output of 10 quadrillion Btu
of gas. At 1,000 Btu/cubic foot of gas, an annual output of 10 trillion cubic
feet of gas would be possible. This hardly suffices to satisfy a growing
market that amounted to 21.9 trillion cubic feet in 1971 and which the
NPC (1972, p. 62) projected would range from 15 to 32 trillion cubic feet in
1985. Comparable conclusions would be reached about the ability to serve
demands for liquids or to power the electric utility industry. In short,
known strippable coal reserves are by themselves grossly inadequate to supply the United States with its fuel. The case for heavy reliance on coal must
rest on the discovery of more strippable reserves or very sharp rises in the
costs of other fuels.

Turning to production patterns (table 5.5), it becomes clear that the distribution is quite different from that of reserves. The eastern states, being
more favorably located relative to markets, have long been the dominant
producing areas. The three largest states alone produced over half the 1971
output. Over the last fifty years, the major changes have been in the

TABLE 5.4
Western Coal Reserves
(million tons)

	Strippable resources	Strippable reserves			
		Low sulfur[a]	Medium sulfur[b]	High sulfur[c]	Total
Colorado (bituminous)	870	476	24	0	500
Utah (bituminous)	252	6	136	8	150
Arizona (subbituminous)	400	387	0	0	387
Montana (subbituminous)	7,813	3,176	224	0	3,400
Montana (lignite)	7,058	2,957	540	0	3,497
Montana (total)	14,871	6,133	764	0	6,897
New Mexico (subbituminous)	3,307	2,474	0	0	2,474
Wyoming (subbituminous)	22,028	13,377	65	529	13,971
North Dakota (lignite)	5,239	1,678	397	0	2,075
South Dakota (lignite)	399	160	0	0	160
Total bituminous	1,122	482	160	8	650
Total subbituminous	33,548	19,414	289	529	20,232
Total lignite	12,696	4,795	937	0	5,732
Western total (all ranks)	47,366	24,691	1,386	537	26,614
U.S. total	117,987	31,762	4,038	9,186	44,986
West as percent of U.S. total	40.1	77.7	34.3	5.8	59.2

Source: U.S. Bureau of Mines, 1971b.
[a] Less than 1 percent.
[b] 1–2 percent.
[c] Greater than 2 percent.

TABLE 5.5
Regional Distribution of Coal Output in the United States, 1971

State	Total output	Thousand tons of: Under-ground	Strip	Auger	Output as percent of U.S. total All methods	Under-ground	Strip	Auger	Percent strip mined
Kentucky	119,389	53,216	56,766	9,406	21.6	19.3	21.9	54.3	47.5
Eastern	71,569	37,353	24,981	9,236	13.0	13.5	9.6	53.3	34.9
Western	47,819	15,863	31,786	170	8.6	5.7	12.3	1.0	66.5
West Virginia	118,258	92,437	21,747	4,074	21.4	33.5	8.4	23.5	18.4
Pennsylvania	72,835	44,289	28,002	544	13.2	16.1	10.8	3.1	38.4
Illinois	58,402	29,446	28,956	—	10.6	10.7	11.2	—	49.6
Ohio	51,431	12,862	37,595	973	9.3	4.7	14.5	5.6	73.1
Virginia	30,628	21,631	7,168	1,829	5.5	7.8	2.8	10.6	23.4
Indiana	21,396	1,765	19,631	—	3.9	0.6	7.6	—	91.7
Alabama	17,945	6,751	11,121	73	3.2	2.4	4.3	0.4	62.0
Tennessee	9,271	3,543	5,412	316	1.7	1.3	2.1	1.8	58.4
New Mexico	8,175	977	7,198	—	1.5	0.4	2.8	—	88.0
Wyoming	8,052	141	7,899	12	1.5	0.1	3.1	0.1	98.1
Montana	7,064	20	7,044	—	1.3	0.0	2.7	—	99.7
North Dakota	6,075	—	6,075	—	1.1	—	2.3	—	100.0
Colorado	5,337	3,329	2,008	—	1.0	1.2	0.8	—	37.6
Utah	4,626	4,620	6	—	0.8	1.7	0.0	—	0.1
Missouri	4,036	—	4,036	—	0.7	—	1.6	—	100.0
Oklahoma	2,234	193	2,039	2	0.4	0.1	0.8	0.0	91.3
Maryland	1,644	176	1,365	102	0.3	0.1	0.5	0.6	83.0
Kansas	1,151	—	1,151	—	0.2	—	0.4	—	100.0
Arizona	1,146	—	1,146	—	0.2	—	0.4	—	100.0
Washington	1,134	32	1,102	—	0.2	—	0.4	—	97.2
Iowa	989	418	571	—	0.2	0.0	0.2	—	57.7
Alaska	698	—	698	—	0.1	—	0.3	—	100.0
Arkansas	276	41	236	—	0.0	0.0	0.1	—	85.1
Total	552,192	275,888	258,972	17,332	100.0	100.0	100.0	100.0	46.9

Source: USBM Minerals Yearbook.

relative position of the states. The many fluctuations in coal output preclude a simple description of these developments. The most persistent trend
has been a growing output in Kentucky that caused it to become the largest
coal producing state in 1971. Ohio and Virginia are the only other leading
producing states with similar tendencies to growth. In contrast, Pennsylvania output has been heading downward since the twenties, and West Virginia output in 1971 remained well below the 176 million ton level attained
in 1947.

Table 5.6 examines another feature of mining patterns—the ability to
operate large mines. Chapter 4 pointed out that the unit train is most economically served by such large mines, and it is often argued that at least up
to a point mining costs are lower with larger mines. However, these scale
effects are not substantial enough to create natural monopolies. It is not
possible to supply total demands from a few large mines. Reserve limitation and other sources of diminishing returns limit the optimal mine size

TABLE 5.6
Role of Mines Producing 500,000 Tons or More in 1971

State	Output of mines (thousands of tons)			Output as percent of area total		
	Total	Under-ground	Strip	All methods	Under-ground	Strip
Kentucky	53,437	24,496	28,941	44.8	46.0	51.0
West Virginia	48,695	45,787	2,909	41.2	49.5	13.4
Pennsylvania	33,196	28,957	4,239	45.6	65.4	15.1
Illinois	55,497	28,311	27,186	95.0	96.1	93.9
Ohio	30,535	10,615	19,920	59.4	82.5	53.0
Virginia	5,848	5,848	—	19.1	27.0	—
Indiana	20,243	1,620	18,624	94.6	91.8	94.9
Alabama	6,455	4,392	2,063	36.0	65.1	18.6
Tennessee	1,050	1,050	—	11.3	29.6	—
New Mexico	8,175	977	7,198	100.0	100.0	100.0
Wyoming	6,953	—	6,953	86.4	—	88.0
Montana	6,657	—	6,657	94.2	—	94.5
North Dakota	5,351	—	5,351	88.1	—	88.1
Colorado	2,248	510	1,738	42.1	15.3	86.6
Utah	1,462	1,462	—	31.6	31.6	—
Missouri	3,185	—	3,185	78.9	—	78.9
Oklahoma	1,528	—	1,528	68.4	—	74.9
Kansas	765	—	765	66.5	—	66.5
Washington	1,093	—	1,093	96.4	—	99.2
Total U.S.[a]	294,169	154,025	140,146	53.3	55.8	54.1

Source: USBM *Minerals Yearbook.*

[a] Includes 1,146,000 tons from Arizona and 650,000 tons from Alaska in the single strip
mine that produced all of each state's output. Other states not shown—Maryland, Iowa,
and Arkansas have no mines of 500,000 tons or more.

to one far smaller than total coal demands. The data in the table use the only available disaggregative statistics on large mines—that of USBM. A drawback of these figures is that they relate to mines producing 500,000 tons a year or more. This output level is far less than the needs of a modern power plant, and it would have been preferable to have data on the role of mines large enough to meet a power plant's needs. In any case, large mines as defined by USBM tend to dominate output in the West and Middle West but are less important in Appalachia. These differences in the regional importance of large mines, moreover, are more pronounced for strip mining. Nationally, the trend towards dominance of large mines has prevailed for many years.

Appendix B

EASTERN STEAM COAL COSTS

The present section is an effort to piece together from the available literature and from discussions with the coal industry, a projection of the market price of eastern steam coal. Economic analysis of coal supply has long been virtually nonexistent. At least until the late 1960s, such analysis appeared simple and, therefore, unnecessary. Coal market conditions seemed extremely stable, and the industry made its regular modest but useful contribution to energy supplies. Everyone assumed that coal would continue this role, and some even believed the industry was destined to resume its earlier importance in the energy markets. Subsequent events have destroyed the apparent stability of the coal markets. Cost conditions have radically changed. This has made it much more important to know more about prospective coal economics. Unfortunately, the new turmoil has also made it much more difficult to predict probable developments.

Available data are inadequate to permit analysis of the long-term competitive supply function of coal, so instead an effort is made to determine the location of a critical point on the long-term supply curve for the 1980s, that is, the cost of producing a level of steam coal output at least as great as that prevailing in the early seventies. This output level appears both the most interesting and the easiest to treat. The industry appears to be effectively competitive, so it seems valid to adopt the purely competitive model as the basis of the analysis.

Appraisal of the relationship between the price consumers are willing to pay and the price producers require for such output levels is basic to the present analysis. If, as the evidence suggests, the supply price is greater than the price consumers are willing to pay for this quantity of output, we can presume that actual output must contract to bring supply and demand in balance. Conversely, if the price consumers would pay were above the supply price, we would expect higher output. Thus this approach can at least establish the probable direction of output change, and help policy makers appraise the basic situation. (Should they desire more detailed information they can undertake the detailed studies proposed in the main text.)

The critical consideration in the argument about the greater ease of projecting the supply price for maintaining current output is the basic role assumed by large underground mines. Prior discussions (chapter 4 and Appendix A) suggested that such mines are likely to be necessary if output is to be maintained. Throughout the eastern United States, it has never been possible to secure all the needed coal without reliance on some large underground mines. Moreover, large strip mines have been extensively developed only in the Middle West and Ohio. Appendix A suggested that depletion problems might hinder the opening of additional large strip mines in these areas. An earlier discussion of coal distribution indicated that the replacement of large underground mines with many small strip mines imposes serious transportation cost penalties. All this implies that, at least unless underground costs mount alarmingly, it is unlikely that output can be maintained without reliance at the margin on large underground mines. Thus, the market price required to maintain output must be at least as great as the projected costs of large underground mines. While the possibility of such alarming cost rises cannot be completely ruled out in practice, here it is theoretically disregarded. Only relatively modest cost rises unlikely to force a shift to total reliance on strip mining are considered.

It is recognized here that the Mine Health and Safety Act clearly provided a major impetus for strip mining, since compliance was much more expensive underground. It is unlikely that strip mine reclamation laws will become severe enough to offset this, at least in the Midwest. The difficulties in the hills of Appalachia, however, will be considerable, and some danger exists that a ban of mining of steep slopes will produce significant cost increases because of shifts to more expensive-to-mine seams (see U.S. Council on Environmental Quality, 1973). Even so, the role of strip mining may exceed that which would have arisen without the new health and safety regulations. It still seems unlikely, however, that this incentive will suffice to cause strip mining to displace large underground mines entirely. With this in mind, we can note that the advantage of concentration on large underground mines is that their cost trends seem much less sensitive to depletion effects than do those of strip mines.

The argument also involves a second assumption, which is more difficult to evaluate—that a movement to production of low-sulfur coals will not basically upset the conclusions. In long-run equilibrium, the price of low-sulfur coal would exceed the price of high-sulfur coal (adjusted for any transportation cost differentials) by the cost of sulfur stack gas scrubbing. Several possible cases can arise. There might be enough low-sulfur coal to cover total demands without need for use of any high-sulfur coal. Alternatively, the market left to low-sulfur coal might be limited to strip mined coal, or, finally, the large underground mine might remain viable.

Here the last outcome is assumed to occur. This conclusion is based upon contentions in interviews with coal and electric power industry sources that low-sulfur coal resources will be expensive to develop. As usual, those notoriously inadequate "reserve" figures are the only published data on the alternative of eastern low-sulfur coal. They indicate that some 36 billion tons of coal with less than 0.7 percent sulfur exist in the East—mainly in eastern Kentucky and West Virginia.

The availability of this coal is unclear. Certainly, electric utilities have not had widespread success in securing such coals. Discussions with coal industry sources suggest that substantial expansion of the industry in the relevant areas would be necessary to make this coal available. The expansion, moreover, would apparently be quite expensive. The coal probably would be in deep, fairly thin seams, and extra problems would arise in concentrating demand on a small area. The cost impact of attracting both construction and mining labor could be accentuated by those of developing adequate transportation facilities.

Difficulties are aggravated by the long-term competition with coking coal demands. Indeed, steel industry ownership and contracts for exports have already apparently tied up the best reserves. This is not as critical by itself as many observers suggest. With sufficiently high demands, the coal could be bid away. What these existing commitments do indicate is that it will be difficult for others to offer high enough prices.

Readers familiar with attacks on the coal industry for failure to develop such low-sulfur coal mines may feel that the present argument relies too heavily on the assertions of interested parties. It is often said that the pessimistic statements about low-sulfur coal are merely public relations devices designed to pressure agencies that regulate air pollution into adopting looser sulfur oxide emission standards. Such arguments, however, seem to presume a far greater degree of collusion than seems likely to prevail under the competitive conditions discussed in chapter 3. It seems implausible that, given the fairly extensive searches for low-sulfur coal that have occurred and the high degree of competition among coal companies, the failure of such supplies to materialize is due to conspiracy. It is more probable that the underlying economics were unattractive.

Having argued for the importance and relative ease of analyzing large underground mines, it is now appropriate to point out that severe problems still remain after the scope of the inquiry is narrowed. The basic problems have already been outlined. The industry is in a severe disequilibrium for the reasons indicated above, and the underlying data base is grossly inadequate. The objective here is to appraise the prevailing disequilibrium state and then project subsequent developments as the industry moves to a new equilibrium. Such an evaluation must be pieced together by analysis of available price and cost data.

Moreover, by judicious selection of data, it is possible to isolate those developments that probably reflect long-term trends rather than transitory developments. One can achieve a clearer idea of costs, for instance, if one looks at impacts on firms shielded from short-term pressures by contracts. The discussion of productivity trends that follows does not try to separate productivity and depletion effects. The implicit assumption is that, while severe depletion of strippable resources may occur in underground mining, depletion of the cheapest-to-exploit reserves would have a smaller impact on costs than the other forces considered here. Costs are, as before, set as nearly as possible in 1973 dollars.

Before examining the cost side of the picture, we may first look at the price data. Much of it is unsatisfactory. The Bureau of Mines county averages reflect the effects of such factors as quality differences and whether the coal is sold to spot purchasers or on contracts. The data reported by electric power companies also average spot and contract purchases and include transportation costs. A number of expedients can be used to make the data more useful. Contract prices are more informative than spot prices, since the latter have in recent years reflected transitory supply-demand imbalances. The material on use of contracts reported in chapter 3, however, makes it possible to identify cases in which published data are minimally affected by spot market developments—that is, the companies buying mainly on contract can be identified. The prices then reflect underlying cost trends rather than temporary market imbalances.

Another indicator is provided by the data on mine mouth plants; such plants are generally supplied on long-term contracts and have relatively small transportation charges. Thus, their experience should closely reflect mining cost and price trends. Even so, it is unclear to what extent the price movements are satisfactory indicators of long-term trends. Rising capital costs are not incorporated in the prices under old contracts, but the extra expenses of adapting old mines for new health and safety measures are included. Thus, a new mine would have higher capital cost but probably could meet the new regulations more cheaply than an older mine. Which impact will dominate in the long run is not clear, but the approach used here should encompass the most reasonable possibilities. Again, the wide range of cases considered should implicitly include the net outcome.

A survey of steam coal prices over the past two decades may be used to supplement these data. A study made for the *1964 National Power Survey,* indicated that the average price of steam coal was *about* $0.15 a million Btu in 1961. The range extended from 12.5 to 16.5 cents (Vol. II, p. 351).

To trace subsequent and prospective developments, we may turn to the examination of price and cost developments since the FPC report. The price trend since 1961 has been towards at least some rise, and synthesis of available data suggests that prices were at least $0.18 by 1969. Since that time, prices appear to have risen sharply through 1972. The data show that sharp price rises have been reported by most consumers of Appalachian coal. The rise from 1969 to 1972 ranges from $0.10–$0.20, and the midpoint of the range seems roughly representative of typical increases for firms buying underground-mined coal on long-term contracts. It would appear, therefore, that coal costs in 1972 had hit at least $0.33 a million Btu in Appalachia.

The midwestern situation is much less clear since so many consumers rely on strip mined coals supplied on existing contracts. Thus, the lower price rises reported in this region may not be indicative of underground cost trends. Since the best available indicator of cost trends, the data on output per man day (OMD), suggests OMD declines in the Middle West have been only slightly less severe than in Appalachia, it seems reasonable to presume that underground mining costs there have risen similarly to those in Appalachia (see below). These conjectures were checked in discussions with a number of coal companies and electric utilities. They tended to quote figures in the range of $0.30–$0.35 per million Btu for prices prevailing in early 1973. It was suggested that the top of the range would be a more appropriate figure for coal from new mines.

As both a rough check on the plausibility of these estimates and as a means to forecast prices in subsequent years, it would be desirable to break down these prices into their component parts. Unfortunately, data on which to base such analyses are not readily available. Crude estimates can be made of labor costs per ton, however. Labor costs per ton equal average daily labor costs per worker divided by OMD. Therefore, we can analyze labor cost levels and possible trends by examining the behavior and prospects of daily wages and OMD.

At least until 1966, the coal industry displayed impressive rates of increase of OMD. The 1950–1966 annual average growth was 6.5 percent for the industry as a whole and 6 percent for underground mines. However, the average increase underground from 1966 to 1969 was only 2.2 percent. A 12 percent decline in average OMD underground occurred in 1970 and a 13 percent decline in 1971. OMD underground in 1971, therefore, was 23 percent below 1969 levels. Ratios of 1971 OMD to 1969 levels in individual states ranged from 65 percent in Ohio to 104 percent in Maryland (table 5.7). Discussions with industry sources indicate that this decline continued in 1972 and had not clearly disappeared by early 1973.

Further confirmation of coal industry assertions about OMD drops is provided by John W. Straton's surveys of coal mine experience (1972a and 1972b). Straton's fullest survey covered sixty-four mines and presented nu-

TABLE 5.7
Trends in Underground Output Per Man Day, 1969–1971

State	1969 OMD (tons)	1971 OMD (tons)	1971 as percent of 1969
Illinois	22.94	18.85	82.2
Indiana	17.73	16.02	90.3
Eastern Kentucky	15.58	12.42	79.7
Western Kentucky	25.64	18.47	72.0
Maryland	11.33	11.77	103.9
Ohio	17.34	11.29	65.1
Pennsylvania	13.92	10.56	75.9
Tennessee	15.79	14.94	94.6
Utah	16.55	14.01	84.7
Virginia	14.97	11.46	76.6
West Virginia	14.81	10.96	74.0
U.S.	15.61	12.03	77.1

Source: U.S. Bureau of Mines press releases.

merous tabulations of the data (often so detailed that only one or two mines were in a given category so that only the grosser disaggregations seem safe to use). Nationally, output per worker declined 26 percent. However, steam coal mines experienced a larger (30 percent) drop than metallurgical coal pits (23 percent). Among steam coal mines, the rates were 30 percent in Appalachia, 33 percent in the Midwest, and 21 percent for the two western mines sampled. The rate for steam coal mines using continuous methods (27 percent) was less than for those using conventional methods (33 percent). The difference between methods was greater in the Midwest (22 vs. 34) than in Appalachia (28 vs. 32).

The average absolute levels cannot be used directly for appraising present or prospective levels of OMD in large underground steam coal mines. The average is lowered by inclusion of metallurgical coal. It can command a higher price and so is mined under less favorable conditions than steam coal. Moreover, the average includes small mines and those designed under older techniques, and thus the typical large mine should exceed this average. Thus, it seems appropriate to assume an average somewhat above the 15–17 tons a man day level prevailing in Appalachia in 1969. The Illinois-western Kentucky range of 23–26 tons may more accurately measure the appropriate figures for large mines since they dominate in these areas. However, I will conservatively use a range of 20–25 tons for 1969 and assume a 25 percent decline occurred by 1972. This would imply a range of 15–18.75 tons OMD in 1972 and 1973.

Turning to future OMD prospects, the expectations are that OMD growth will be modest, but it is difficult to guess how to define this concept properly. Does it relate to present or old levels? We have little to go on other than estimates of what seems reasonable. It was expected that productivity advance in the seventies would be slower than in the sixties even without new regulations and that these would aggravate the problem.

It is probable but not certain that problems of resource depletion and slower technical progress have arisen. Thus, we hear many statements about the inability to secure large blocks of coal and particularly fears that large strip mine reserves are depleted in some areas (see Appendix A).

Similarly, it is agreed by the managers interviewed that little further technical advance is likely through improvement in current types of mining machinery. Some expect gains through some improved system of hauling coal to the surface, but the industry sources consulted disagree on the prospects for success in this area by 1980. Many fear considerable difficulties in reducing the labor unrest prevailing in the mines. Coal industry sources are, in short, extremely pessimistic about future trends and fear 1980 OMD will remain below 1969 levels. Thus, it seems desirable to explore a wide range of possibilities for OMD growth.

Roughly, if OMD were at 75 percent of its 1969 level in 1973, growth of 4.2 percent a year is required to restore OMD to 1969 levels (since to offset a 25 percent decline, a 33 percent rise is needed, and $1.33^{1/7} = 1.042$). This sort of performance would not be difficult to secure if the impediments to OMD growth could be resolved, but would be quite a difficult and impressive performance while the climate in the industry remains so unsettled. To be sure, the National Petroleum Council Coal Task Force did project a return of 1980 OMD to the 1969 level, but its figure was derived before the full decline in OMD was known. The NPC expected an OMD drop of only 19 percent and recovery starting in 1973. Thus, with the later data available, a lower 1980 figure might appropriately be assumed. In the absence of a sound basis for selecting that figure, it may conservatively be assumed that OMD does return to its 1969 level.

To represent a more favorable OMD climate, it could arbitrarily be assumed that somehow the industry manages by 1980 to raise OMD by 24 percent above 1969. This is the increase that would have occurred if OMD had grown steadily at a 2 percent per year rate from 1969 to 1980. However, since 1973 OMD may be only 75 percent of 1969, 1980 OMD would be 66 percent above 1973 (since $1.24/.75 = 1.66$). This implies a required average annual growth of 7.5 percent from 1973 to 1980. In any case, the implied 1980 OMD range is 25 to 31 tons. These assumptions, of course, essentially rule out the possibilities that, perhaps as a result of massive government research support, radically cheaper methods of coal mining emerge. This position simply reflects the basic approach of this study, which is to quantify only those developments that can be related to proven experience.

To complete the analysis of labor costs per ton, we should examine the labor cost per man shift. Some indication of the impact of these labor problems can be gleaned from the terms of the November 1971 contract between the United Mine Workers (UMW) and the coal industry. All labor contracts are difficult to interpret because of problems of averaging the gains of different labor categories and of valuing the fringe benefit changes. Estimates of the gains in the first year were set at around 16–17 percent, and estimated average gains over the three year period were said to be around 13 percent a year (apparently including the change in the welfare payments). For present purposes, a slightly different breakdown of the benefits is desirable. The main changes were large wage increases—the top daily earnings went from $37 in 1970 to $50 in 1973—and staggered increases in Welfare Fund contributions by the industry. These went from $0.40 to $0.60 when the contract took effect and ultimately rose to $0.80 in May 1974.

This cannot be directly related to costs without adjustments for the distribution of the work force among salary categories, average overtime, and fringe benefits. One coal industry source suggested that in 1972 the weighted average cost per man day was about $53—a figure that accounts for complications such as fringe benefits and the mix between wage and salary workers. Assuming that these costs rose roughly in proportion to wages, the 1969 figure would have been about $42 a day.

Looking forward, we may begin by noting that by the fall of 1973 wages under the UMW contract rose still further so that the weighted average labor cost was about $65.60 a day. The rise in wages in the UMW contract amounted to about 56 percent in the four years from 1969 to 1973—an average increase of 11.8 percent a year. However, consumer prices—the best indicator of the impact of inflation on wages—rose about 25 percent over the period covered, making an annual average of about 5.7 percent. Thus, the rise in real wages totaled about 25 percent for the full period or 5.8 percent per year. Extrapolation of this rate to 1980 implies a wage rate of $97 per day in 1973 prices, which may be rounded to $100. This rate may be too conservative since the growing difficulties in securing workers may cause acceleration in wage increases. It is therefore assumed for illustrative purposes that daily wages might be as high as $150, which happens to be slightly above the $143 wage implied by continuation of the monetary wage rate increases from 1969 to 1973.

Table 5.8 summarizes the combined implications of the assumptions on OMD and daily labor costs. The figures indicate that at a 25 ton per man day level, 1969 labor costs per ton would have been about $1.68, and this would have risen to $2.83—$1.15 above the 1969 level by 1972. For 10,500 Btu/pound midwestern coal this implies a 5.5 cent per million Btu cost rise. For 12,000 Btu/pound Appalachian coal, the price rise per million Btu is

TABLE 5.8
Estimated Labor Costs Per Ton in Coal Mining (1973 dollars)
(dollars per ton)

	Actual costs		Estimated costs for 1980			
			OMD at 1969 level		OMD 24% above 1969 level	
	1969 costs wages $42 a day	1972 costs wages $53 a day	wages $100 a day	wages $150 a day	wages $100 a day	wages $150 a day
Mine with 20 ton OMD in 1969	2.10	3.53	5.00	7.50	4.02	6.03
Mine with 25 ton OMD in 1969	1.68	2.83	4.00	6.00	3.22	4.83
	Cost increase 1969–1972		Cost increase 1972–1980			
Mine with 20 ton OMD in 1969	1.43		1.47	3.97	.49	2.50
Mine with 25 ton OMD in 1969	1.15		1.17	3.17	.39	2.00

Source: see text.

about 4.8 cents. When the same assumptions about wages and productivity trends are applied to a 20 ton 1969 level, we get 1969 labor costs of $2.10 a ton; $3.53 a ton in 1972. The rise then is $1.43—6.8 cents per million Btu for midwestern coal; 6.0 cents for Appalachian.

Before turning to future developments, it is useful to review other cost elements to see how adequately the rest of the $0.15 per million Btu cost rise from 1969 to 1972 can be explained. A further known cost is the increase in the payments to the United Mine Workers Welfare and Retirement Fund. By late 1972, $0.25 of the staggered rise of $0.40 a ton had occurred. Another apparent cost increase reported in unpublished U.S. Bureau of Mines studies of coal mining costs is a $0.50 a ton rise in supply costs. Thus, we have a cost rise total of $1.90 per ton for mines with 1969 OMD of 25 tons—$1.15 in labor, $0.25 in welfare payments, and $0.50 in supplies. The last two figures, plus the $1.43 rise in labor costs, imply a $2.18 a ton rise in costs for mines with 20 tons OMD in 1969. Thus, the explained cost increases range from $1.90 to $2.18. For 12,000 Btu/pound coal, this amounts to $0.08-$0.09 per million Btu; for 10,500 Btu/pound coal the corresponding range is $0.09 to $0.10. Thus, only a half to two-thirds of the apparent cost rise is explained by the present method—i.e., it is a conservative measure of cost effects.

In contrast, an alternative method of relating cost increases to estimates of new health and safety provisions may overexplain the cost rise. Here we take the estimate of the cost rises due to the Health and Safety Act. These figures include both the equipment cost and efforts to measure the productivity decline produced as a result of the regulations.

Straton reported the 1968-1971 cost increases the companies attributed to health and safety regulations. Those for steam coal were $1.53 for Appalachian continuous mines; $1.67, Appalachian conventional mines; $1.00, Midwest continuous; $1.27, Midwest conventional, and $1.37 for the two conventional western mines. In contrast, the sources interviewed argued that health and safety rules raised costs from $1.50 to $3.00. It appears part of these estimates reflect an effort to charge the Health and Safety Act for its contribution to lower coal mine productivity. However, the decline is the combined product of general labor unrest, the need to use new workers, and the law. These interact since the law requires more work and increases the need to hire. Differences in the estimates presumably reflect different allocations of the productivity decline among the three causes. Thus, what we have is a combined figure on health and safety equipment costs and a sizable part of the productivity decline effect.

How the wage increase over the period was handled in the cost estimating process is unclear, but presumably an extra charge of say the $0.40 of additional labor costs per ton if productivity were constant should be added to the health and safety cost. Another $0.25 must be added for the increased welfare payments. So given the $1.50–$3.00 estimate, the total cost increase ranges from $2.15 to $3.65. Since the higher end of the range presumably includes more of the productivity decline effect (i.e., omits fewer cost influences), it should be considered more relevant. Thus, there seems good reason to infer a cost increase of the previously estimated magnitude from these data.

Admittedly, these figures are highly imperfect and useful mainly because they are reasonably consistent with other data. However, any projection of prices cannot be justified unless we look at underlying costs. Turning to projections for 1980, the combination of assumptions stated above implies a wide range of cost increases—from $0.39 to almost $4.00. However, only the most optimistic combination of assumptions leads to cost rises of less than $1.00. For present purposes, therefore, $1.00 to $4.00 a ton cost rise may be presumed. To this we should add at least the $0.15 further rise in welfare payments. This translates into total cost rises of $0.05 to $0.17 per million Btu for 12,000 Btu/pound coal and $0.05 to $0.20, for 10,500 Btu coal. Assuming a $0.33 1972 cost price, the implied 1980 costs are $0.38 to $0.50 for 12,000 Btu/pound coal; $0.38 to $0.53 for 10,500 Btu coal. An alternative approach is to combine the absolute levels of labor cost estimates with the absolute level of welfare payments ($0.80), the $1.50 supply cost, a $0.50 estimate for other costs, and an estimate of capital costs.

The U.S. Bureau of Mines in its 1972 survey of strip-mining costs has developed a useful method for levelizing capital costs. The bureau carefully reports all capital expenditures and calculates their present worth at the time of initial operation. Then standard interest tables are used to determine the constant annual income that will exactly recover these investment outlays and the required interest on them. Efforts are made to adjust the figures to reflect the impact of tax accounting conventions. The amount available to repay investments appears on the books as depreciation plus profits after taxes. The bureau, therefore, first calculates book depreciation and subtracts this from total income requirements to determine the contribution that must come from after tax accounting profits. Then the income before taxes that will generate the required after-tax "profits" is determined under the assumption that 50 percent of gross profits are excluded from taxation because of the depletion allowance and that a 50 percent tax rate prevails. The first assumption implies that profits in coal mining are so low that the statutory limitation of depletion allowances to 50 percent of gross profits rather than 10 percent of the market price prevails. The two assumptions indicate that 75 percent of profits before tax are retained as profits after tax (the 50 percent not taxable plus half—25 percent—of the taxable half). Thus, profits before taxes are four-thirds of profits after taxes, and the required profits after tax must be multiplied by this ratio to determine necessary before-tax profits.

Discussions of capital costs suggest they range around $10 a ton. Under this assumption, at 12 percent interest and a ten-year life, annual repayments must equal 18 percent of initial outlays or $1.80 per ton, and $1.00 of this cost is depreciation. Another $0.80 must be earned as profits after tax. Four-thirds of $0.80 is $1.07 so that $2.07 of income is required to recover capital costs.

Table 5.9 summarizes the implications of these assumptions. These suggest that only in the most favorable circumstance would costs in 1973 prices be below $0.40 per million Btu. Therefore, while the two methods of cost projection literally imply costs of $0.37 to $0.59 per million Btu, the $0.40 to $0.50 range cited in the main text seems an appropriate choice. It

TABLE 5.9

Estimates of 1980 Total Costs of Coal Mining[a] (1973 dollars)

	Mine with 20 ton OMD in 1969	Mine with 25 ton OMD in 1969
a. Cents Per Ton		
Capital costs	2.07	2.07
Welfare payments	.80	.80
Supply and other costs	2.00	2.00
Total of above	4.87	4.87
Labor cost cases		
a. OMD at 1969 level; wages $100 a day	5.00	4.00
b. OMD at 1969 level; wages $150 a day	7.50	6.00
c. OMD 24 percent above 1969; wages $100 a day	4.02	3.22
d. OMD 24 percent above 1969; wages $150 a day	6.03	4.83
Total cost cases		
a. OMD at 1969 level; wages $100 a day	9.87	8.87
b. OMD at 1969 level; wages $150 a day	12.37	10.87
c. OMD 24 percent above 1969; wages $100 a day	8.89	8.09
d. OMD 24 percent above 1969; wages $150 a day	10.90	9.70
b. Cents Per Million Btu for 12,000 Btu/pound Coal		
Total cost cases		
a. OMD at 1969 level; wages $100 a day	.41	.37
b. OMD at 1969 level; wages $150 a day	.52	.45
c. OMD 24 percent above 1969; wages $100 a day	.37	.34
d. OMD 24 percent above 1969; wages $150 a day	.45	.40
c. Cents Per Million Btu for 10,500 Btu/pound Coal		
Total cost cases		
a. OMD at 1969 level; wages $100 a day	.47	.42
b. OMD at 1969 level; wages $150 a day	.59	.52
c. OMD 24 percent above 1969; wages $100 a day	.42	.39
d. OMD 24 percent above 1969; wages $150 a day	.52	.46

[a] This table represents in concise form material presented on pp. 111–121.

appears unlikely that conditions sufficiently favorable to secure costs lower than $0.40 will prevail. Conservatism dictates choice of $0.50 as an upper limit.

These figures may be roughly checked by simply computing forecasts based on the assumption that costs will grow at some constant rate. A range of between 4 and 10 percent a year seems appropriate to consider. Industry sources expect every component of costs to rise at least 4 percent, and at least one observer thought a 10 percent overall rise might prevail. Should 1972 costs have been as low as $0.25 a million Btu, 4 percent growth leads to 1980 costs of $0.34; this jumps to $0.40 with a 6 percent annual increase and to $0.54 with 10 percent. With $0.30 1972 costs, the corresponding 1980 figures are $0.41, $0.48 and $0.64. Thus, the present forecasts seem in line with the results of simple trend extrapolations.

Still another check can be provided by other discussions of coal price trends. One of the more widely quoted is by Hauser and Potter of Westinghouse. By simple trend projections, they developed an estimate that the national average cost of coal would reach $9.55 a ton which is about $0.40 per million Btu by 1980. Their method was simply to break down the costs of mining into their major elements. Cost indicators were selected for various components and the 1958–1968 trend for each indicator was calculated. For example, the Bureau of Labor Statistics (BLS) figure on hourly wages for production workers in mining was used to measure coal mine wage employee costs. Similarly, the BLS wholesale price index for construction machinery was the indicator of material cost. The trends were extrapolated to 1980, and the resulting values were summed to provide cost figures. A $1.50 cost was added to cover the expected impacts of the Mine Health and Safety Act. Productivity advance was essentially ignored. Moreover, a minor correction is needed to cover the difference between utility and metallurgical coal. The former might cost $0.02 or $0.03 less than the national average.

My former graduate assistant, Charles J. Johnson, deliberately tried a similarly naive method and managed to get about the same results. He computed an extremely short-term trend—1964–1969—for the cost of coal at mine mouth plants. The price for each year was an average for all mine mouth plants east of the Mississippi that operated in that year. Thus, the year to year change reflected both cost movements for existing plants and differences in costs between old and new plants. His extrapolation to 1980 produces a 33.4 cent per million Btu price. If it may be assumed that a Health and Safety Act effect of about $0.05 per million Btu reflects an independent development, the forecast rises to $0.38 or the same amount as the adjusted Hauser and Potter figure.

Gerard Gambs (1972) of Ford, Davis, and Bacon presented a quite different and even more pessimistic approach to price forecasting. He contends that by 1971 prices had already risen to $0.38, and he anticipates a further $0.16 rise by 1974. He argued that the 1971 coal wage contract would raise costs by $0.06. An equal increase would be produced by additional costs of the Health and Safety Act. The remaining $0.04 of the increase would be due to the necessity to compensate workers for the effects of black lung disease.

Appendix C

WESTERN STEAM COAL COSTS

Published data on prevailing costs of western coal indicate that mining costs of $0.15 per million Btu prevail. However, coal and electric utility sources expect f.o.b. mine costs in the West will rise to at least $0.20 and perhaps $0.25 a million Btu mainly because of the industry's expansion. The main factors will be that a somewhat more concentrated and, therefore, more expensive process of mine development will be required (i.e., the existing mines built up to their peak output levels more gradually than will be possible with many new mines), and labor shortages will push up wages. It is also conjectured that some of the present sales were made at bargain rates to interest potential new customers. The forecasts apparently abstract from inflation, and so may be considered to be in 1973 dollars.

A rough confirmation of these forecasts is provided by the *North Central Power Study* (1971, p. 10). It estimates that coal in the Dakotas, Wyoming, Montana, and Colorado could have been exploited in 1970 at costs ranging from 11 to 20 cents a million Btu, and that the cost range would rise to 14 to 25.5 cents by 1975. Extrapolating these increases to 1980 yields a range of 18 to 32.8 cents. The great bulk of the reserves, however, have projected 1980 costs less than $0.25 (see table 5.10).

However, it is not clear just how much coal would be available at these costs. Appendix A discussed the possible physical limits to supply. Another problem lies in opposition to land disturbance by strip mining. Here reclamation requirements would have a negligible effect. The available estimates on reclamation costs range quite widely. A major source of such differences is the variation in conditions among sites. In addition, the degree of restoration assumed can differ considerably. Nevertheless, it appears unlikely that even the most severe reclamation requirements would markedly increase costs. The determinants of reclamation costs differ markedly from case to case, and we can best see the maximum impact by combining assumptions that lead to the highest impact on costs. Thus, we may start by assuming that costs per acre are at the $6,500 figure that Peabody Coal reported would be the highest conceivable cost in Montana (see USGS,

TABLE 5.10

Hypothetical Supply Conditions for Western Coals, 1970–1980

(costs in cents per million Btu; volumes in million tons)

	Wyoming	Montana	Wyoming and Montana	North Dakota	North and South Dakota	Wyoming	Colorado	Total
1. 1970 costs	11–12	11–13	12–14	12.5–14	13–15	15–18	15–20	—
2. 1975 costs	14–15.3	14–16.6	15.3–17.9	16–17.9	16.6–19.1	19.1–23.0	19.1–25.5	—
3. 1980 costs	18–19.5	18–21.2	19.5–22.9	20.5–22.9	21.2–24.6	24.3–29.5	24.3–32.5	—
4. Reserves actual tons	19,000	14,459	5,625	3,049	553	2,699	600	45,985
5. 8,000 Btu pound equivalent of reserves	19,831	14,836	5,255	2,431	447	3,066	413	46,279
6. Recoverable reserves	15,865	11,869	4,204	1,945	358	2,453	330	37,024

Lines 1, 2 and 4 are from *North Central Power Study*.
Line 3 is line 2 × ratio of line 2 to line 1.
Line 5 is normalized using Btu contents listed in report; where a range is shown, average used.
Line 6 is line 5 × 0.8.

1974, p. 12–56). This estimate far exceeds any secured in either the prior published literature or my interviews with informed industry sources. Such sources suggest that 1.4 acres may be disturbed for every acre mined, and to be conservative we may assume that the $6,500 relates to acres disturbed so that a cost of $9,100 (i.e., 1.4 times $6,500) is incurred per acre mined. Coal contents per acre mined can range from 15,000 to 66,100 tons per acre, but at the low figure the cost would be $0.61 per ton. Similarly, the Btu contents also differ considerably, and if we assume a 7,000 Btu/pound lignite is involved, the cost per million Btu is only $0.04.

However, resistance to enduring massive amounts of ongoing stripping might lead to severe restrictions on how much production is allowed. These questions about supply suggest that western coal may not be as cheap as is often contended.

Appendix D

THE COST OF LOW BTU GAS

A comprehensive review of low Btu gas processes and their economics appears in a study by United Aircraft Research Laboratories (Robson, 1970). Unfortunately, these data are obsolete and so presented that the cost relationship can only be inferred by rough calculations. In particular, gas prices are presented based on specific fuel input prices, and the total nonfuel costs can best be inferred indirectly. Elsewhere in the report (p. 403–8) the conversion efficiencies are shown. These efficiencies and the assumed fuel prices can be used to infer the contribution of fuel expenses to total costs. Then the data do suffice to suggest the proportional contribution of capital recovery to the costs. Similarly the report explicitly indicates how much of the required income is supposedly recovered by sale of by-product sulfur. The present study adjusts these data to develop equations to show the cost of gas as a function of fuel prices.

Briefly, $P_g = EP_f + C$ where P_g is the price per million Btu of gas; E is the reciprocal of the conversion efficiency, P_f is the price per million Btu of the input fuel, and C is nonfuel costs of gasification. Only the first term on the right needs explanation. If efficiency is 0.67, for example, a million Btu of coal produces 666,667 Btu of gas, so $\frac{1}{.67}$ or 1.5 million Btu of coal are required to produce a million Btu of gas.

Actually, the United Aircraft report shows $P_g - P_s = P_r$ where P_s is the sulfur credit, but since P_s is given, P_g is easily calculated. However, the formulas developed here assume that massive gasification would produce so much sulfur that its price would decline so precipitously, and thus essentially no income would be secured from sulfur recovery. It is also assumed that inflation has doubled capital costs in 1973 dollars. Since every element but C in the equation is known, we can solve for C:

$$C = P_g - EP_f$$

Given C and the proportion of the costs represented by capital charges, the capital cost in 1970 prices can be isolated and adjusted as noted above. Thus, the adjusted nonfuel cost C' is $C + \alpha C$ where α is the proportion of nonfuel costs in 1970 prices represented by capital charges. [Proof $C - \alpha C$ are the old noncapital charges, αC the old capital charge, $2\alpha C$ the new capital charge so the adjusted costs are $C - \alpha C + 2\alpha C = C + \alpha C$.]

Three cases are considered by United Aircraft—coal gasification using the Lurgi process, an advanced coal gasification process, and an oil gasification process. With the Lurgi process, the net price of gas is $0.55 when gas is made from $0.20 per million Btu coal (p. 87).[5] The sulfur credit is worth $0.03 per million Btu of gas so its loss raises the required price to $0.58 (p. 87). The conversion efficiency is 77 percent (p. 403) so E is about 1.3. The fuel cost component then is about $0.26 implying a $0.32 nonfuel cost. At least $0.15 of this is capital recovery, so the adjusted nonfuel cost is $0.47. Thus:

$$P_g = 1.3\,P_f + 47$$

In the advanced coal gasification process, the net price needed using $0.20 coal and a $0.03 sulfur credit falls to about $0.40 or $0.43 if sulfur sales are not realized. The conversion efficiency rises to 87 percent (p. 405) so $E = 1.14$. This implies $0.22 fuel and $0.21 nonfuel costs. The capital cost component is about $0.10 so the adjusted nonfuel cost is $0.31 (p. 101). Thus here:

$$P_g = 1.14\,P_f + 31$$

Finally, oil gasification with $0.20 oil and a sulfur credit of about $0.02 involves a net gas price of about $0.45 a million Btu or $0.47 without the credit (p. 107). Conversion efficiency is set at 93 percent (p. 408) so E is about 1.1. Thus fuel costs are about $0.32 and nonfuel costs are about $0.15. About $0.07 of this is capital, so adjusted nonfuel costs would be $0.22 (p. 107). Thus:

$$P_g = 1.1\,P_f + 22.$$

---

[5] The report presents costs per kilowatt hour generated, and these were converted to costs per million Btu by use of the plant thermal efficiencies (reported in Robson, p. 278). Figures are also provided on "costs per million Btu" but, as Hottel and Howard (p. 149–50) point out, these are costs per million Btu of fuel processed. This was confirmed by dividing the figures in Robson by the conversion efficiencies. The figure used for advanced coal gas is roughly an average for the two cheapest processes discussed by Robson (p. 104).

6

Power Generation and the Environment

INTRODUCTION

The rapidly evolving efforts to improve the quality of the environment have become a major influence upon the electric power industry. Since the middle sixties, pressures have mounted generally to eliminate the undesirable side effects of economic activities.

A growing and more centralized governmental apparatus has been established for this purpose. A Council on Environmental Quality (CEQ) is attached to the Executive Office of the President; the council formulates basic policy. The formerly scattered enforcement efforts are consolidated in an Environmental Protection Agency (EPA). However, its activities are supplemented by those of state, local, and regional bodies. This formal apparatus has been directed at controlling pollution in a broadly defined sense that includes issues beyond the air, water, and radiation problems stressed here. Even so, another critical controversy—that of optimal power plant siting—is often handled by separate agencies.

Air pollution may be used as an illustration of how these institutions attempt to operate. A rapidly changing, fairly complex system of pollution control regulations operates in the United States. The federal government, presently through EPA, establishes basic standards. The states are required to translate these into specific compliance programs for their areas. These, in turn, must receive EPA approval, and EPA may impose its own plan if the local actions are deemed inadequate.

The basic EPA rules provide for two levels of air quality: a primary standard sufficient to protect health "with an adequate margin of safety" and a secondary standard to eliminate other damages. For each pollutant, a maximum annual average level of concentration and one or more standards for shorter periods are provided. Each pollutant is subject to its own quite specific standards. Their nature is best suggested by examining a particular case. For example, the primary standard for sulfur oxides is an annual average concentration of less than 0.03 parts per million (ppm); the maximum allowed in any twenty-four-hour period is 0.14 ppm but this must not be exceeded more than once a year. The corresponding secondary standards are 0.02 and 0.1 ppm, and it is also required that in any three-hour period concentrations not rise above 0.5 ppm—again a standard that may be exceeded only once a year. The federal standards only set an *upper* limit to the amount of pollution the states may allow.

The complexity of these rules and their rapid change precludes an adequate survey here. As noted in chapter 1, the President's April 1973 energy message, for example, proposed relaxation in the secondary standard for sulfur oxides. It may be noted that the basic approach involves not only overall quality goals already noted—ambient air standards—but also specific rules for emission sources designed to insure attainment of ambient air criteria. The specific source rules may not be directly related to the ambient air rules. Indeed, the EPA's own rules for emission standards applied to new sources (see below) are based on what EPA believes to be practically realizable abatement levels. These could be more than needed in some regions. It may also be noted that technical problems arise in converting the emission standards to a standard basis, since several different measuring rods can be used.

Adding support to government regulation, a profusion of private groups is seeking to promote a better environment. They have mounted massive publicity campaigns. Each of them can sue private organizations or even the government to stop some objectionable actions. The electric power industry has been the center of many of these controversies. Power plants create many undesirable impacts on the environment. At least 60 percent of the heat consumed is wasted and must be disposed of. In addition, nuclear plants involve radiation problems while fossil-fuel burning releases air pollutants.

Many different contaminants are discharged into the air from electric power plants and other sources. Both the amounts and effects of these pollutants differ considerably. A limited number have received primary attention—carbon monoxide, particulate, sulfur oxides, hydrocarbons, and nitrogen oxides. However, carbon monoxide is largely (66 percent) generated from transportation equipment. Electric utility combustion of fuel adds about 0.1 percent of the total (U.S. EPA, 1973b, p. 44). Roughly similar conditions prevail for hydrocarbons. Electric power is most important in generation of sulfur oxide, particulate, and nitrogen oxide pollution. The respective contributions of the industry to the 1970 total were 57.2, 14.5, and 20.7 percent of total emissions and 70.6, 49.3, and 21.7 percent of fuel use related discharge (U.S. EPA, 1973b, p. 44).[1]

Were this not enough, the industry is enmeshed in what can most simply

---

[1] Those interested in the details of the effects and control of these pollutants may consult the series of reports prepared by advisory committees to the National Air Pollution Control Administration (NAPCA) and its successor in EPA. Each major pollutant was the subject of both an *Air Quality Criteria* report on effects and one or more *Control Techniques* studies. These reports were used as a major background source for subsequent sections.

be called land use controversies. For a wide variety of reasons, objections are raised to the use of particular lands for power plants and transmission lines.

The present chapter treats successively the environmental issues that are presently most critical for the electric power industry—particulates, sulfur oxides, nitrogen oxides, radiation, waste heat, and siting.

PARTICULATE MATTER

Historically, particulate matter has been the central issue of air pollution. Whether particles create the greatest total damage, they certainly cause the most obvious effects—soot and smoke. By the same token, the long concern evolved a similarly long history of control and produced the development of an extensive effective control technology.

The most obvious impacts of particles are that they soil the surroundings and darken the air. However, even more serious damage may be caused by breathing the particles. Substantial evidence exists of respiratory damages from exposure. Difficulties arise, however, in establishing the exact causation, since other pollutants—notably sulfur oxides—are present. Some evidence suggests that it is the combined effect that is critical.

Coal is clearly a far greater source of particulate matter than other fuels. The others contain small amounts of contaminants but coal contains substantial—about 10 percent—amounts of waste. EPA figures indicate that an average of 80 percent of the ash would be discharged if no treatment were provided (U.S. EPA, 1973a, p. 1–1.3). Therefore, a 10 percent ash, 12,000 Btu/pound coal would release 6.7 pounds of particulate per million Btu burned. In contrast, a million Btu of residual fuel oil releases 0.05 pounds of particulates; a million Btu of gas, 0.02 (U.S. EPA, 1973a, p. 1.3–2 and 1.4–2).

Particulate control standards of various degrees of severity have prevailed for many years and have inspired a wide range of control devices. In the electric power industry the most widely used of these is the electrostatic precipitator. It operates by electrically charging the particles so that they collect on a surface grounded to produce an opposite polarity. Under ideal conditions, these precipitators can remove 99 percent or more of the particles. Thus, presumably these precipitators would enable most of the electric industry to meet government air quality standards.

It should be noted, however, that the sulfur in the coal contributes to the ionization of the particles, and thus precipitator performance deteriorates when sulfur contents are lowered. Efforts have been made, with varying degrees of success, to overcome the problem. A larger precipitator may be installed; the precipitator may be located to treat hot gases rather than at the end of the cycle (See Henke, 1970); scrubbers may be used instead of precipitators. All these methods are in use. In each case, examples of both success and difficulties with the process can be provided. A further problem is that very large plants, particularly in dry climates such as in the Southwest, could still produce serious effects on visibility even with stringent particle control.

The 1971 EPA criteria applying to emissions per million Btu from new electric power plants limit particulate emissions to 0.1 pounds per million Btu. Given the 6.7 pound uncontrolled emission level and 99 percent precipitator efficiency, 0.067 pounds or less than the allowable amount would be discharged.

The large amount of particulate pollution coming from the power plants of the sixties clearly reflects prevalence of standards weak enough to allow use of less efficient pollution control devices. Compliance with the EPA standards means adding the best available precipitators. The literature indeed is replete with reports of such purchases.

SULFUR OXIDES

The recognition of the sulfur oxide emission problem is much more recent than that of particulates, and abatement technology, at least for coal-fired plants, is not yet perfected. By 1973 concern was mounting rapidly that the difficulties could not be economically surmounted. Sulfur oxides form through reaction during combustion of sulfur present in the fuel with atmospheric oxygen. All fossil fuels contain varying amounts of sulfur, but its removal causes considerably different problems for each type.

As with most pollutants, the exact effects of sulfur oxides are imperfectly known. The best established impact is that under rare special weather conditions sulfur oxides can accumulate and can contribute to numerous deaths such as occurred in Donora, Pennsylvania, in 1948 and London in 1952.[2] Clearly, this by itself would only justify methods to reduce or disperse the emissions under such circumstances. However, evidence exists that at least in conjunction with particulate matter, continued high exposure to sulfur emission creates damage to health. The oxides are corrosive enough to damage plants and materials.

In 1971, EPA established emission standards for all new fossil-fired steam generating plants using more than 250 million Btu per hour. At a 9,000 Btu heat rate, this implies about 28 megawatt electric (MWe) of plant capacity. The standard for sulfur oxides is a maximum of 1.2 pounds of sulfur oxides per million Btu in a coal-burning plant and 0.8 pounds in an oil-fired plant. EPA data indicate that each pound of sulfur in fuel

---

[2] The Donora episode did not involve pollutants from electric power plants in the area (U.S. Public Health Service, 1949). The London "killer smog" appears to have resulted from the widespread use of coal probably including that in power plants.

produces 1.9 pounds of sulfur oxides, so the restriction amounts to a *sulfur* limit of about 0.6 pounds per million Btu of coal and 0.4 pounds per million Btu of oil (U.S. EPA, 1973a, p. 1.1–3 and 1.3–2). The implied sulfur content per pound of fuel (the usual way sulfur contents are measured) naturally depends on the Btu content per pound. A 12,000 Btu/pound coal could contain 0.76 percent sulfur by weight, but this falls to 0.51 percent with 8,000 Btu/pound coal (each 1,000 Btu drop in heat content lowers permissible sulfur levels by about 0.06 percent).

The conversion for oil is more complex since it is measured in volumetric rather than weight terms. The standard implies that oil containing 6 million Btu per barrel could contain about 2.4 pounds of sulfur per barrel; this rises to 2.5 pounds if the barrel contains 6.3 million Btu. This also implies a percent weight of sulfur of about 0.7 percent. The difference between oil and coal standards proves largely to reflect the higher Btu content of oil.

Sulfur emission control, particularly when coal is burned, has proved difficult to achieve in practice although many remedies are possible in principle. The possibilities for reducing the impact of sulfur oxide emissions are to use a naturally lower sulfur fuel, somehow reduce the sulfur content before combustion, remove the sulfur from the stack gases, or simply to spread the emissions over a wider area. At the very least, however, actual use is limited by construction lead times for the special facilities when the method adopted takes advantage of existing techniques. These delays are necessarily longer when new technology is to be used.

Very tall smokestacks are the usual means of effecting the dispersion approach. Certain electric utility officials vigorously advocated this technique, and indeed numerous very tall stacks were installed (see Sporn and Frankenberg, 1967). This may have proven at best a temporarily acceptable solution. EPA regulations such as those of 1971 no longer can be met through mere dispersion.

Natural gas has become quite attractive as a boiler fuel because it is delivered with virtually no sulfur. This is not necessarily because the natural sulfur content is low. Sulfur compounds are easily and routinely removed from gas before pipeline transmission because they can corrode pipelines and are undesirable from a health standpoint. However, natural gas is unlikely to be competitive as an electric utility fuel. Should price controls remain, increased gas supplies will be unattainable; deregulation probably would raise prices to levels at which natural gas will no longer be competitive in the electric utility market.

A more complicated situation arises with oil. As with natural gas, the natural sulfur content differs among crudes. Moreover, residual oil—the principal electric utility petroleum fuel—is higher in sulfur content than the crude from which it is refined. Residual oil is a mixture of lighter oils and a residuum in which the sulfur concentrates during refining. In the past, this sulfur was not removed. The situation is aggravated by the United States' past reliance on residual oil from the high-sulfur crudes of Venezuela. Relatively cheap (perhaps as little as $0.50 a barrel) and simple techniques can reduce the sulfur levels to around 1 percent. The main short-term barrier was the need for installations of the necessary capacity, and projects for such installations are well underway.

Unfortunately, considerably greater difficulties arise with prevailing standards of 0.5 percent or less sulfur. At lower levels of sulfur removal, treatment can be provided by the simpler processes required to treat the middle distillates that are blended with the residuum to produce residual oils. Severe sulfur removal requirements can only be met by treating the residuum itself—a more complex process. Estimates of the total costs of reducing sulfur levels below 0.5 percent differ widely, but most estimates in the published literature indicate costs of around $1.00 per barrel (see, e.g., Robson, 1970, p. 83).

It can then become economically attractive to resort to blending high-sulfur residuals with distillate oil made from low-sulfur crudes from Nigeria or Libya. Direct burning of low-sulfur crude oil also becomes a possible alternative. The greater volatility of the crude creates safety problems, but technology for safe burning is well established. Japanese experiments provided the initial evidence; their work has been duplicated in the United States, and some utilities have undertaken crude oil burning.

Coal involves more sulfur removal problems, and more ways to effect control have been considered. The use of naturally occurring, low-sulfur coal is limited. As chapter 5 shows, the most ample sources of such coals are in western coal fields quite distant from major coal burning plants, but the eastern situation is *apparently* much less promising.

Full removal of sulfur from coal is possible only by transforming it into some synthetic fuel. Sulfur in coal comes in two main forms—pyritic and organic. Much of the former is separable from the coal by washing and gravity separation, but the organic sulfur is chemically bound and can only be released by a chemical transformation of the coal. An FPC report indicates the proportions of pyritic sulfur typically ranges from 20 to 60 percent of the total (1968, p. 92). Results of cleaning experiments suggest that in most cases because of the high proportion of organic sulfur and the inability completely to remove pyrites, generally less than half the sulfur is removed by cleaning (U.S. NAPCA, 1969d, p. 38). Cost estimates for the different processes range from $0.50 to $1.00 per ton.

Moreover, technical problems arise in using low-sulfur coals. As noted, the sulfur apparently greatly assists the ionization of particles in electrostatic precipitators, and so lower sulfur content means greater difficulty in particle emission controls. The problem of boiler flexibility also affects substitution possibilities. Many low-sulfur fuels differ substantially in other characteristics, such as higher ash content, ash composition, and combustion characteristics. Thus, boiler clogging problems can arise.

Another method for control would be through utilization of the various synthesis processes discussed in chapter 5. It is apparently fairly easy to remove the sulfur during the synthesis process. The problem, as noted, relates to lead times. The quickest approach would be to adopt the Lurgi process despite its drawbacks; otherwise new technologies must be developed.

Finally, it has been proposed that the stack gases be scrubbed. This process can be used for any fossil fuel, but it was thought particularly applicable to coal (largely because no other alternative seemed readily available). A bewildering profusion of different techniques producing sulfur products ranging from sludges that create serious waste disposal problems to marketable sulfur were considered (many reviews of these are available to the determined reader but see especially M. W. Kellogg, 1971 and Hottel and Howard, 1971). Confidence in stack scrubbing, particularly among the electric utilities, has rapidly declined in the early seventies. In the late sixties, it was often argued that fairly cheap processes would emerge by the middle seventies (see, e.g., National Coal Association, *Bituminous Coal Facts*, 1970). Subsequently, as research proceeded, cost estimates (discussed in chapter 7) have been raised sharply, and expectations that the processes would be quickly available have nearly vanished (see Garvey, 1972; Garvey is a vice-president of the National Coal Association). The most optimistic views arise abroad. A U.S. government team was sent to Japan in 1972 to examine sulfur oxide control technology. Most of the work reported involved oil, but one scrubber for a coal powered unit was examined. This scrubber, using American technology, had operated successfully for four months by the time of the visit. While many features of the plant such as size and design were similar to those prevailing in the United States, the study group noted that higher SO_2 inlet concentrations, wider variance in boiler loads, and higher inlet ash concentrations in U.S. plants might create problems in employing the process in the United States (Elder, 1972, p. 18–36). Actually, what the report described as a boiler comparable in size to those in the United States was only rated at 156 MWe. Similar questions can be raised about other more recent claims about the availability of scrubbers (e.g., those in U.S. EPA, 1974).

Clearly unless these problems are resolved, severe difficulties are in store for the coal and electric power industries. In time, the electric utilities can find alternatives; either better ways to use coal will be developed or a shift away from the fuel will occur. Society, in any event, should be prepared for a *possible* failure to develop alternatives that involve coal.

NITROGEN OXIDES

This third major coal-associated pollutant also forms in combustion. The oxides can form simply as the heat reacts on the oxygen and nitrogen in the atmosphere, but nitrogen chemically bound in the fuel reacts more readily. Coal produces larger emissions than other fossil fuels in part because it has a high proportion of such chemically bound nitrogen. The higher temperatures typical for coal furnaces are also a factor. The EPA criteria statement on nitrogen oxides suggests that their effects, other than in lowering visibility, are particularly unclear. It appears that some harm to health, materials, and vegetation arises, at least at high concentration levels.

Controls in this area are in their infancy. For example, the EPA's 1971 standard of 0.7 pounds of nitrogen oxides per million Btu appears but slightly below the 0.75 pounds of the uncontrolled emissions that the EPA estimates would be produced by burning of 12,000 Btu/pound coal (U.S. EPA, 1973a, p. 1.1–3).

Since nitrogen oxide formation is mainly influenced by the combustion process, modification of this process has been stressed as a control technique. Several factors influence the release of nitrogen oxides. The formation is increased at higher temperatures and at higher concentrations of air. Both a longer residence of the hot gas in the boiler and a more rapid cooling of the gas exiting from the boiler increase emissions. The abatement techniques most widely used include two-stage combustion and flue gas recirculation. The two-stage combustion approach involves introduction of air in stages; as a result, the partially burned fuel and combustion products cool before the completion of combustion. Recirculation of flue gases similarly dilutes the fuel and air and, therefore, lowers flame temperatures and emissions. Similar results can be produced by injection of steam or water into the boiler or by lowering the preheating of air (James, 1971, and National Academy of Engineering–National Research Council, 1972).

These methods are quite effective for gas-fired plants, can produce significant reductions in nitrogen oxide emissions from oil-fired plants, but are not yet usable for coal-fired plants. Among the problems with coal are increased dangers of flameouts or of unburned carbon in the ash and greater boiler corrosion. Stack gas scrubbers for sulfur emission control could also reduce nitrogen oxide emissions. However, this technology has not been perfected and is expected to be expensive (National Academy of Engineering–National Research Council, 1972, p. 4–7). Alternative combustion systems such as the combined cycle and the fluidized bed are expected to produce much lower levels of nitrogen oxides.

Clearly, then, the problems of nitrogen oxides ultimately may cause further difficulties for the coal industry. However, it is not presently possible to appraise the impact. It is argued below that sulfur pollution control difficulties alone may produce severe setbacks for coal, and thus the nitrogen problem may have limited supplemental impacts.

RADIATION

Moving from fossil fuels to nuclear power clearly eliminates the three problems discussed above, but leads to questions of radiation effects. The Atomic Energy Commission has long contended that the dangers were trivial, but vigorous criticism of that claim has appeared.[3]

The main admitted difficulties are with discharges of radiation from the plant and with storage of the still-radioactive spent fuel. Some concern is expressed about hazards faced by uranium miners and workers in processing plants. However, critics suggest that greater attention should be given to a serious plant failure that might cause massive release of nuclear material.

The danger of a serious accident is difficult for a lay observer to evaluate. Certain facts are fairly clear. Numerous safeguards are provided, and thus far the safety record has been excellent. No radiation-related fatalities or serious accidents have occurred in civilian reactors. Those concerned about the situation argue that as the industry becomes larger more accidents will occur, and inevitably one will cause severe loss of life. At the time of writing, critics were concerned over experiments that suggested that the safety devices intended to handle the unlikely situation of a sudden loss of coolant might not work. The defenders contend that the present record suggests that disaster is highly improbable and that improvements will arise from advances in safety technology and the benefits of greater experience with plant operation. It remains true, however, that there are difficult subjective questions about a tolerable level of risk.

The waste problem cannot be dismissed confidently. The potential for a rather substantial volume of wastes appears considerable. The Atomic Energy Commission presents arguments supported by the evaluations of outside observers that adequate techniques for storage have been devised, but, as is typical in nuclear debates, others dispute the argument.

The attack on radioactive emission standards, however, is easier to resolve. The main critics are Gofman and Tamplin, two scientists at the Lawrence Radiation Laboratory. They argue that, if the entire population

[3] The literature here is enormous, but a convenient summary appears in a 1973 report by the Atomic Energy Commission (WASH 1250). This report contains extensive references. The bibliography to this study also lists relevant reports published by the Joint Committee on Atomic Energy (e.g., 1969, and 1970b).

of the United States were exposed to the maximum permissible dose of radiation from a nuclear plant, an unacceptable number of cancer fatalities would be generated. Some controversy exists over the assumptions they make about the relationship between dosage and cancer deaths per unit of exposure. In particular, some of the researchers cited allege Gofman and Tamplin have misinterpreted the earlier results. However, this question is made far less critical by other considerations. First, the siting of nuclear plants insures that the actual exposure will be far below their hypothetical levels. Second, the actual emissions per plant will be well below the AEC standards Gofman and Tamplin used. The standards have been tightened; in fact, plants apparently are designed to emit significantly less than the allowed amounts. Gofman and Tamplin, moreover, only advocated stricter standards.

In short, there are various hazards from the existence of nuclear plants. Yet such plants eliminate all the air pollutants associated with fossil fuel plants. Thus, two poles of opinion have developed. One group contends that the allegations of damage are grossly overstated and the benefits quite clear, while the other contends the dangers justify considerable delays for increased use of nuclear power.

WASTE HEAT[4]

Power plants generate substantial amounts of waste heat. Traditionally, most of this heat was discharged into a nearby body of water. Power plants account for about 80 percent of the heat discharged into waterways (U.S. Council on Environmental Quality, 1970, p. 34). Concern is widespread about the impacts of these heat discharges. The problem is somewhat different from those with conventional pollutants. The impact of heat is not as unambiguously harmful.

Fears about waste heat emphasize, but are not confined to, the impact on the waterways. The waste heat from all combustion processes is eventually discharged to the atmosphere, and some questions have been raised about the climatic impacts of this heat. Apparently, for at least the next fifty years or so, these direct impacts would be quite small on a global basis but might produce noticeable local problems. The main concerns about effects on the heating or cooling of the earth incidentally relate to fossil-fuel emissions of carbon dioxide, which could raise temperatures, and particulates, which could lower them. In any case, these questions have not yet greatly influenced policy; so the water effects that have been critical to policy are stressed here (see MIT, 1970, for a review of these issues).

Analysis is complicated by the numerous variables involved. Heat

[4] See the *1970 National Power Survey,* National Academy of Engineering (1972), and MIT (1970) for material on these issues.

produces changes in the complex ecological system of the waterways. The variation as well as the level of heat affects the outcome as do the impacts of any pollutants in the waste water. Thus, we must deal with the differences of the effect on each element in the system at a given location. Vast differences, moreover, exist in the prior nature of the ecology at different locations. Moreover, the desirability of some changes is difficult to assess.

Effects on fish and other larger aquatic animals are frequently emphasized in discussions of the waste heat problem. Generally, the heat makes the climate unfavorable to some species and stimulates growth of others. In an inland location, fishes desirable for commercial or sport fishing may be displaced, but a coastal plant's discharges could permit creation of shellfish beds. Thus, we have the double problem of determining whether the change is unfavorable and, if it is, whether the damage costs more than control.

Of course, other potentially more critical thermal effects can arise. For example, the taste of drinking water may be harmed by stimulation of growth of organisms, or the heat alone may raise tap water temperatures. However, it will suffice here to examine the implications of efforts to restrict discharges into natural waterways.

Obviously, the prohibition of discharges into water requires that the heat go elsewhere. It would be preferable ideally to reduce the initial waste or find an economic way to utilize it. This at least saves control costs and lessens any atmospheric effects. Unfortunately, the waste heat is usually difficult to employ, particularly when discharged from a fairly remote power plant. Indeed, some existing waste heat sale operations of utilities are being abandoned because other environmental regulations preclude continued operation of plants in large cities.

Nevertheless, it is often suggested that efforts be made to develop industrial complexes centering about a nuclear plant. Its waste heat would then provide process steam for the other facilities in the complex. Others advocate a total energy concept in which a neighborhood is served by a plant providing central heating and cooling and electricity. Presumably small fossil-fuel fired units would be used.

The ideas appear attractive in principle but do not seem to be promising practical solutions, at least in the 1970s. The already slow process of completing a nuclear plant would undoubtedly be even more retarded by efforts to build nuclear industrial complexes. Extra time would be required to line up participants. The already difficult site selection process would be complicated by the need to provide for the associated ventures. The proposals might easily involve greater regulatory problems, particularly because of greater intervention by outside groups. It is similarly not clear that usable waste heat can be generated economically.

Thus far only one felicitous combination of conditions seems to have arisen. In Midland, Michigan, the Dow Chemical Company presently produces its own steam from coal-fired power plants that create unacceptable amounts of pollution. It proved possible for Consumers Power to build a nuclear plant near enough to Dow for the latter to use the waste heat. Unfortunately a bitter controversy has arisen over this plant's alleged dangerous proximity to populated areas.

Some of the problems with total energy complexes are that they are difficult to install except in new communities and that the small plants involved may be uneconomical. Since the reuse option is not yet widely applicable, requirements to eliminate heat discharges into waterways must be met by using alternative discharge methods. Two main basic approaches exist—cooling towers and cooling ponds. The latter is simply a large artificial body of water in which the waste heat is discharged so the heat may dissipate into the atmosphere. The towers are a variety of devices for effecting a similar transfer.

Several approaches to towers may be taken with the basic distinctions being between natural and mechanical drafts and wet and dry cooling. The natural draft tower is a very tall hyperbolic structure that exposes the heated water to air; fans are used in the mechanical draft method. In both cases, the heat is released by the evaporation of the water. "Dry" methods operate on the same principle as an automobile radiator and involve separation of the heat by conduction or convection, and no water is lost by evaporation. However, they are much more expensive than wet methods and so are not yet used in large power plants (U.S. FPC, 1971, p. I–10-6–7).

The choice of methods is affected by numerous factors—most notably local land, water, and climatic conditions. Ponds clearly are impossible if the proper terrain does not exist and would be prohibitively expensive in urban and other high land cost areas. Ponds and wet towers need makeup water and thus the annual amount of water available and the regularity of its flow affect choice. Conflicting statements appear in the literature about the comparative total water requirements of the two methods; apparently, these differ with local conditions affecting the natural conditions of rainfall, evaporation, and seepages. Clearly, however, the towers require a steady flow of water while ponds can build up reserves in wet seasons to carry the plant through drought periods. Thus, the choice may be influenced either by the difference, whatever it may be, in total makeup water requirements or by severe seasonal fluctuations in water availability that mean only a pond can remain steadily operational. Alternatively, a utility may use both a pond and a tower.

Another influence is the marked difference among methods in the climatic impacts of their release of the heat to the atmosphere. Wet methods can create fogging or icing in the area of the plant and all methods release heat that can warm the area. The fogging and icing apparently are most serious with the wet mechanical draft methods. The much greater heights of a natural draft tower lessen ground effects. Ponds, if feasible, are better still since they spread out the discharge over a wider area.

While questions remain about the best methods to use, the techniques, nevertheless, are operational. Moreover, the costs of the controls apparently will not significantly alter the competitive position of different fuels. The main source of such differences would be the greater amount— 50 percent or more—of waste heat produced by a nuclear plant compared to a fossil-fuel-fired plant of equal size.

However, the literature suggests that unless dry cooling is adopted, differential cooling costs are too small to affect greatly the comparative economics of nuclear versus fossil fuel. Although reports sometimes provide "typical" cost figures for the different methods, the variation in local conditions makes actual cooling pond costs highly variable among sites. Tower costs are likely to vary less among sites, and so provide a more general basis of comparison. In any event, L. G. Hauser (1970, p. 14–17) of Westinghouse estimated that costs would run 0.09 mills per kilowatt hour for ponds, 0.21 mills for wet mechanical draft towers, 0.20 mills for wet natural draft towers, and 0.82 mills for dry cooling of nuclear plants. However, he used a somewhat lower capital charge than is now employed, and the respective figures rise to 0.10, 0.24, 0.24 and 1.06 mills per kilowatt hour if an 18 percent charge is used. (See chapter 7 for a discussion of these costing methods.) The respective costs per million Btu displaced, then, are 1.20, 2.67, 2.69, and 10.97 cents. These figures may be outmoded by subsequent inflation. For example, the lowest estimates provided in nuclear plant environmental impact statements issued in 1972 and 1973 indicate costs double those Hauser presented. Some environmental impact statements indicate much higher costs, which may include the extra costs of adding the equipment to existing plants. Therefore, a doubling may be a more appropriate adjustment of the Hauser figures for new plants.

Only differential capital cost figures are readily available to indicate the difference between nuclear and fossil cooling costs. The *1970 National Power Survey* (U.S. FPC, 1971, p. I–10–8) indicates capital costs of $5–8 a kilowatt for mechanical draft cooling towers in fossil plants; $8–11 in nuclear plants. The respective ranges are $6–9 and $9–13 for natural draft towers. This suggests a 40 to 60 percent excess of nuclear costs over fossil costs.

If we double Hauser's costs and round upward, nuclear cooling tower costs run about $0.06 a million Btu. If it is further assumed that this is 1.6 times fossil costs (i.e., using the highest nuclear/fossil capital cost ratio reported), fossil costs are 3.75 cents/million Btu. This 2.25 cent saving cannot significantly affect the subsequent analysis. The figures used are so rough that a $0.02 adjustment does not affect them materially. Therefore, differences in cooling costs are ignored in later discussions.

LOCATIONAL PROBLEMS

The final difficulty the industry faces is opposition to locating its facilities in certain areas.[5] In some cases, this is simply an extension of the pollution problems. One solution is to move the plant elsewhere. Certain moves, moreover, obviously can be beneficial. This would be true when the meteorological or geological conditions were better at the alternative site. Situations arise when it is the mere existence of the facility that is the issue. An absolute dislike of the installation may be involved, or the critics may believe that a better land use exists. Power plants and power lines appear excessively ugly to many people who oppose the construction.

Naturally, these arguments are difficult to settle. The social values of alternative uses or the costs of ugliness are extremely difficult to measure. In general, the evaluation involves unmarketed and unmarketable commodities. Of course, since much of the protest relates to recreational uses, some of the benefits can be valued but perhaps not to the extent that the appraisals can be conclusive.

In one sense the aesthetic objections may be easier to resolve than the preferences for another use. The latter normally cannot be altered by changes in the designs. Scenic vistas or little parks attached to the facilities are rarely going to be considered adequate compensation for whatever was lost. However, the appearance of facilities can be improved. It is possible to enclose a power plant in a building that could be attractively designed. Techniques for lessening the amount of land cleared for power lines have been developed, and more graceful pole designs have been employed.

Such gains cannot eliminate all objections. Certain facilities cannot be easily enclosed. Thus, a natural draft cooling tower is a vast structure that must be open. Some might consider it a great eyesore; others might consider the towers rather attractive.

There are further problems with the limitations of technology. Many propose using underground burial of power lines, but this is presently impossible for high voltage lines except over short distances. Techniques to permit burial have been proposed, but it is not clear when or at what cost they will be available.

[5] See, for example, U.S. Office of Science and Technology (1968 and 1970), Edison Electric Institute (1970), Electric Utility Industry Task Force on Environment (1968), and Working Group on Utilities (1968), for discussions of these problems.

SUMMARY

The chapter indicates that electric power generation involves air pollution, radiation, waste heat, and siting problems. However, the critical influences for interfuel competition appear to be sulfur oxide pollution controls for fossil plants and nuclear radiation. Sulfur oxide pollution controls are being vigorously enforced, and difficulties in compliance arise particularly for coal. Uncertainties about the safety of nuclear plants could eventually lead to restrictions on the use of atomic energy to generate electricity.

7

Costs of Power Generation
in the 1980s

INTRODUCTION

As has been previously suggested, fuel cost is but one element in the total economics of electricity generation. In the present chapter, enough is discussed about the nature of the electric power industry to indicate some of the other influences on fuel demands. Then a method of cost analysis called "levelizing" is outlined and applied to a variety of cases.

Four basic situations are discussed. First, the fuel choices possible in existing plants are considered. Second, the situation for new fossil-fuel-fired plants is examined. The third case relates to the slightly longer time horizon in which nuclear plants are alternatives to fossil-fired plants. The final analysis introduces a major improvement in fossil-fuel generating efficiency. A particular example—the advanced combined cycle (defined below)—is used here as the archetype of such innovations because it appears fairly promising and has been the subject of detailed quantitative evaluation. The analysis explores four alternative strategies towards sulfur oxides—no controls, the enforcement of the EPA new plant standards (see chapter 6) in all plants, the same rules supplemented by the requirement of scrubbers at least for plants using western coal in the West, and the use of a sulfur tax. (Once again many of the details of the discussion are presented in appendixes. They deal successively with the assumptions used here in levelizing and the algebra of the analysis, nuclear and fossil capital costs, the costs of sulfur emission control, the sulfur tax, and the advanced combined cycle.)

The analysis attempts to convey the wide range of outcomes possible given that the costs of using existing technologies, the ability to develop new technologies, and the nature of prevailing regulations, particularly in the environmental realm, are so difficult to predict. This returns us to a basic theme of this study—the inherent inability to describe more than reasonable possibilities. This chapter attempts to characterize the extent of the uncertainties involved.

The cost possibilities considered are limited largely to those that can be related to published estimates. However, the treatment of new fossil-fuel technologies involves some rough adjustments of the supporting data. Obviously things could be much better or worse than these guesses. Consideration of other possibilities, however, is an overly cumbersome way of stating the obvious—that the "best" estimates available could be badly inaccurate. The figures used are presented in 1973 dollars but try to project charges in relative real prices up to 1980. Despite possible further subsequent relative cost changes, no effort is made to project post-1980 cost changes and "1980" costs in 1973 dollars are used as a point of departure.

The limitations on the analysis noted in chapter 1 should also be recalled. In particular, it is *assumed* throughout that both stack gas scrubbing and nuclear power will be feasible alternatives by 1980. However, the data are sufficiently comprehensive so that the reader can determine the effects of contrary assumptions. Therefore, rather than lengthen the discussion by constant reminders of these two critical assumptions and the consequences of their invalidity, no further discussion is provided below of these issues, despite widespread concerns about both alternatives.

One severe problem—finding an acceptable plant site—has not been explicitly considered here. It is implicitly assumed that this problem either will be resolved or develop so that it hinders equally building of all types of plants.

INFLUENCES ON FUEL CHOICE[1]

At least in discussions of fuel choice, it is normally assumed that the electric utility industry is seeking the cheapest possible way to meet the demands it faces.[2] Thus, some idea of the nature of the demands and the ways that demands can be satisfied must be provided. For present purposes, it suffices to recognize that electric power fluctuates considerably from one time period to another. Thus, the industry distinguishes a base load maintained all the time and various other levels up to the peak load which may exist for only a few hours a year.

Like all rational firms, the electric utilities will, at each moment of time, utilize the cheapest-to-operate combination of available power sources. The industry talks of its load curve, in which the available sources are ranked in

[1] See the *1970 National Power Survey* (U.S. FPC, 1971) for a discussion of most of these issues.

[2] An extensive literature has arisen arguing that the regulatory process may encourage overinvestment in capital equipment. This contention is ignored here mainly because of the convincing criticism of the overinvestment argument by Baumol and Klevorick (1970) and the widespread use of cost minimizing analyses by electric utilities. In addition, from a social point of view, it is desirable to know which is the cheapest method, and the analysis shows which is the most capital-intensive method. This should allow the reader to infer what a tendency to overinvestment might imply. Similarly, no effort is made to deal with the possibility of altering consumption patterns by varying prices with demand intensity—the so-called peak load pricing concept, which has been widely discussed in the literature on public utility economics.

ascending order of cost; that is what economists would call the short-run marginal cost function. Those plants that have the lowest costs will be used to meet the base loads; those with the highest costs are used, if at all, only for peaks.

The optimization process is complicated by such factors as regulation, the unpredictability of demands, the limits to plant availability, and the ability to cooperate with other utilities. Regulation imposes severe restraints on the ability to react to unexpectedly high demands by cutting off power. At most, some utilities have arrangements to interrupt supplies to specific industrial consumers. Otherwise removing or reducing supplies causes regulatory agency disapproval. This need to meet demands combined with the imperfect ability to predict them requires that capacity be adequate to meet more than expected demands. In addition, no power plant can operate all the time. Under the most favorable circumstances, it is still desirable to perform regular preventive maintenance, and, even so, unexpected breakdowns (forced outages) can occur.

Cooperation among utilities can take many forms. First, two utilities with peaks at different times might exchange power with each delivering electricity during the other's peak period. In addition, larger plants may involve economies of scale in construction and operating costs but be too large to fit comfortably into a single company's system. The loss of the plant's availability might leave inadequate remaining capacity. This difficulty can be avoided by sharing the plant with one or more companies. Many devices exist for such sharing ranging from agreements to sell power on a sustained basis to joint ownership of the plant. Agreements to enter a joint venture may be made only for a single plant or be part of a broader cooperative program. The discussion of western mine mouth plants noted the development of a plan for construction of a series of plants. Elsewhere, joint operation may be part of a comprehensive program of integrated intercompany planning.

The main considerations involved are a need to maintain spare capacity to meet demand surges and offset unavailability of plants, a necessity to consider plant reliability as well as capital and operating costs, and an ability to use cooperation among utilities to reduce costs.

Further complications arise when we consider the historical evolution of the industry. In general, the higher the lifetime production of a plant, the more profitable it becomes to invest in reducing operating costs. Thus, were demands and technology stationary, the industry would design different types of plants to meet different loads. A base load plant would have much higher capital and lower operating costs than a plant for peak loads.

When growing demands and technical improvements are involved, it becomes possible to add cheaper new plants because of the ability to take advantage of economies of scale and because of the ability to introduce new technologies. As a result, each new plant addition would cause the position of all older plants on the load curve to deteriorate. Over the life of an individual plant, its rate of utilization would decline.

Conceivably, plant additions could proceed at such a rate that electric utilities would only build plants for initial use as base load units and serve all intermediate and peak loads with older plants. In practice, the industry has long found it efficient also to build units specially designed for peaking use. Such plants had the expected characteristics of lower capital costs but required use of fuels such as middle distillate fuel oils or natural gas that often were more expensive than the fuels used in base load units.

Whether this trend will continue is a matter of considerable discussion. As Appendix A points out, numerous statements have appeared that fossil plant efficiency cannot be significantly improved without the development of new technology. Moreover, many modern fossil plants were designed so that they are most efficiently operated as base load units (U.S. FPC, 1971, p. I-5-7). Similarly, it is likely that the operating costs of all nuclear plants built in the seventies will be quite similar. It is, therefore, possible that all plants might be built for a specific level of operations—base, intermediate, or peak load—and maintain constant outputs over their lives.

Another influence on the basic choice of plants is the large difference among construction lead times of different plant types. It is now feared that because of the elaborate regulatory process involved it may take as long as ten years to build a nuclear plant.[3] A conventional fossil-fuel plant may require up to five years. However, a gas turbine (a stationary adaptation of an aircraft jet engine) can be installed in less than two years. Delays in completion of planned plants and expectedly large demands have put a strain on capacity. As a result, gas turbines that were previously used mainly as peaking units were heavily ordered for more intensive use—as intermediate load units.

Finally, some attention must be given the degree of interfuel sub-

[3] As a check on these estimates, the completion dates for the plants ordered in the six month period ending April 1, 1971, were tabulated from Edison Electric Institute's semiannual survey of plant orders. Of twenty-five fossil plants, eleven were to be completed in 1975 and eight in 1974. Five were to start after 1975. Seven nuclear plants were ordered. One was expected in 1975, one in 1976, three in 1977 and the other two in later years. Another view is provided by the AEC's regular tabulation of nuclear plant data (Wash 1208). Its issue for March 1973 indicates that twenty-three nuclear units of at least 175 megawatts were operating. Of these one was in commercial operation four years after announcement; eight, five years after; nine, six years; four, seven years; one, eight years. Of the thirty-three units announced and ordered in 1972, two were to begin operation in 1978, seven in 1979, twelve in 1980, nine in 1981, and three in 1982. It may be noted, however, that buyer needs rather than lead times affected many of the choices of completion times. Many 1972 announcements involved two or more units for a single plant with deliveries staggered over time. Thus, one company ordered a unit for 1979 and a second unit in 1981. Six other units scheduled for 1981 operation were ordered simultaneously with units set for 1980. On the other hand, the various estimates of lead times may include the preannouncement planning period.

stitutability in both conventional fossil-fired plants (steam turbines) and gas turbines. With steam turbines, a distinction can be made between the absolute physical limits on flexibility in fuel use imposed by boiler design and the economic limits imposed by the costs of equipment to handle a particular fuel.

Basically, oil boilers must be larger than gas boilers; coal boilers, larger than oil. Thus, coal to oil or gas and oil to gas shifts are always physically possible but changes in the reverse direction can only occur when the boiler was designed to permit this. In addition, a boiler designed for use of specific types of coal may have limited flexibility in adapting to coals of radically different characteristics. For example, considerable concern has been expressed about the ability of plants designed for use of eastern coals to shift to western coals (see, e.g., Frankel, 1969, p. 22). Discussions with informed sources suggest that actual experience is mixed. While some reports of severe problems have been made, others indicate modest difficulties in conversion.

Moreover, special handling equipment is needed for each fuel. For oil and gas, the primary requirement is pipe to deliver the fuel to the boilers. In the case of oil, it is also necessary to have receiving and storage facilities. Their installation is the most time-consuming part of an oil conversion; the limited amount of required adjustment of the boiler can be completed when the plant is undergoing its annual period of preventive maintenance so no extra service time is lost. Since coal is a solid, it is much more difficult to move, and the facilities for receiving, unloading, and moving the coal are significantly more expensive than those for oil and gas. Moreover, large amounts of land for coal handling and storage are required, and its acquisition might prove extremely expensive, particularly in urban areas.

The gas turbine, however, has been limited to use of gas or middle distillate oils such as kerosene. Some discussions have appeared (e.g., U.S. FPC, 1971, p. I–8–4) indicating that it will become possible also to use heavier oils, and one informant indicates that at least one company has already been able to burn a low-sulfur residual fuel oil (which tends to be somewhat lighter than more widely used grades of residual oil) in a gas turbine. A 1973 report (Arizona Public Service, 1973, p. 9–4) indicates that the techniques for using heavier oils are not perfected and may involve reduction of plant efficiency.

With these facts in mind, some basic points about the economics of fuel choice may be considered. First, it may be noted why four different fuel choice cases were proposed earlier in this chapter. Each reflects the possibilities available over different time horizons. At any point in time, the only way to alter fuel use for the next two years is to make whatever possible conversions of existing plant fuel use capabilities and to add gas turbines.

New fossil-fuel plants can be added within five years and nuclear plants within a decade. New technologies can be added only after they are perfected. Thus, lead times and plant flexibility are predominant influences in determining what choices are available.

Possible plant operating patterns and cooperation among utilities are key influences on the comparative economics of different options. The role of cooperation is simply that development of such coordination seems to make it possible for most electric utilities in the United States to build or participate in building the largest available units. Thus, the cost penalties of being forced to build smaller plants can essentially be ignored.

The basic issue about operating patterns of specific plants is how best to estimate their probable future behavior. An upper limit clearly is set by the probable level of forced and scheduled outages. Considerable controversy has arisen about whether it will be physically possible to maintain operating rates for complex modern nuclear and fossil plants as high as the 80 percent rate generally used by the Atomic Energy Commission (AEC). Similarly, questions arise about the ability to reduce the large amount of planned maintenance now required with gas turbines.

It is conceivable that for many years physical availability may be the only limit to nuclear power uses. It may have the lowest operating costs of any nonhydroelectric plant type (see below). Thus, until enough nuclear capacity exists to cover base loads completely, nuclear plants may be used whenever available. One effect of this may be to prevent similarly high utilization of fossil plants. Moreover, the lower the total cumulative utilization, the less attractive extra investment will be. This will be influenced by the utilization rates prevailing in each year of remaining operations. Older plants naturally have the disadvantage of lower current operating rates and shorter remaining lives than newer plants. A final complication is that it is generally more expensive to retrofit, i.e., add equipment to existing plants, than to install the same equipment in a new plant. The old plant is unlikely to have the space and configuration to permit an optimal installation.

In what follows, therefore, these distinctions prove fundamental to the analysis. The assumptions about available options, the costs they involve, and the operating rate must reflect all these propositions.

METHODS OF ELECTRIC INDUSTRY INVESTMENT ANALYSIS

Electric utilities, following the well-established economic theory of present value cost minimization, make their investment decisions by choosing the optimal combination of plants to meet expected needs. Such analyses are enormously complicated and may be heavily influenced by the peculiarities of a specific company. Thus, the widespread approach in published comparisons of different types of power generation is to measure the costs under simplified assumptions. The convenience of this approach is a major justification for its employment here. Moreover, it appears that the underlying data are subject to so much uncertainty that the apparent precision added by a more sophisticated evaluation method would be spu-. rious.

The starting point for the simplification is the well-known principle in financial analysis that the case of constant annual net cash flows (the difference between cash receipts and expenditures) is the simplest to analyze. Evaluation can proceed by use of the widely tabulated annuity tables showing the constant annual payment per dollar of investment that will recover with interest the initial investment. A convenient further assumption is that the constant annual flows result from constant output per year and constant net cash flow per unit of output.

In this particular case, each unit of output makes an equal contribution to repaying the investment. The annuity formula factor multiplied by the actual investment shows the required annual income. Dividing the annual total by the expected output yields the required income per unit of output. To an economist, this amount is not a cost but rather a measure of one of the infinite number of income streams that could recover the relevant costs—the investment and interest on it. However, the industry shorthand term—"levelized cost"—is so convenient and widely used that it will be employed here.

Appendix A reviews the specific assumptions used in levelizing costs. It may be noted here that an annual charge rate of 18 percent is employed. This represents a figure that had come into use by 1973 as a result of rising interest rates and seems a reasonable figure given prevailing interest rates and the capital structure of the electric power industry. A range of operating rates from 50 to 75 percent is considered. Steam turbine fossil plants are assumed to require 9,000 Btu to generate 1 kilowatt-hour (kwh).[4] Other assumptions specific to individual cases may be found in the appendixes.

THE FUTURE FUEL CHOICE SCENARIOS

As noted, the material in the prior chapters can be combined with that in the appendixes to this chapter to provide scenarios of possible fuel uses. A vast number of cases can be considered. However, four basic types of variations may be distinguished—in the location of fuel use, in the options open to the electric utility, in the costs at that location, and the public policies applying. It was argued earlier that Chicago represents a convenient point of

[4] This also means a million Btu produces 111 kwh in a conventional fossil-fuel plant and so the equivalent concepts of a cost per million Btu used in a conventional fossil plant, and a cost per 111 kwh are used here (see Appendix A).

reference since it is a particularly distant market for oil and the nearest major market east of the Mississippi for western coal. Therefore, Chicago is used here as a reference point. Conclusions for Chicago are modified to cover other areas when appropriate.

The four types of available options have already been outlined earlier in this chapter—existing plants could be modified, new conventional fossil plants could be built, capacity to build nuclear plants could be developed, and choices could be made among new conventional fossil plants, the advanced combined cycle, and nuclear plants. The specific cost assumptions used come from chapters 4 and 5 and the appendixes to this chapter; the relevant figures appear in table 7.1.

As previously noted, the only policy variations considered relate to sulfur emission controls. Two basic approaches are considered—regulation and a sulfur tax. To achieve a basis for comparison and to handle special exceptions that might be granted, calculations are also made of the comparative economics in the absence of sulfur regulations. For present purposes, stress is placed on the assumption that sulfur regulations can be met at least in the East by use of scrubbers, low-sulfur coal, or low-sulfur oil. The possibility that scrubbers might be required for low-sulfur fuel is also discussed. Sulfur taxes are represented by the 1972 Nixon Administration rate proposals (see Appendix D).

Before turning to the specific cases, it is desirable to make a few basic points about the sulfur tax. When such a tax is in effect, the user of a particular fuel will adopt an emission control technique only if the resulting tax reduction is at least as great as the cost of controls. Otherwise it would be cheaper to pay the tax. Therefore, table 7.2 lists the tax savings possible from different shifts in fuel use strategy. The basic comparisons are those relating to methods of burning the same fuel more cleanly.

The clearest situation arises with the consequences of a sulfur tax on oil users. Table 7.1 indicates that an oil-using firm would pay a premium of $0.17 a million Btu to secure low sulfur oil, but table 7.2 suggests that the tax saving will just equal this cost if the tax rate is $0.15 per pound of sulfur. Thus, it would appear that the sulfur tax would not raise the cost of oil by more than would a requirement to use low-sulfur oil. Thus, the tax discourages the use of low-sulfur oil as a control strategy, but it remains to be seen whether the higher oil cost might encourage a shift to another fuel. For present purposes, it is presumed that the imposition of the sulfur tax implies that those who remain oil users would buy high-sulfur oil and pay the tax.

The wide variation in estimates of sulfur oxide stack gas cleaning costs produces a similar variation in the possible responses. Generally speaking the taxes are large enough to produce scrubber use only if costs are at the low-estimate level. A quick comparison between tables 7.1 and 7.2 makes

TABLE 7.1

Assumptions about Electric Power Costs in Chicago in the 1980s
(cents per million Btu displaced)

	Low	High
Delivered prices of fuel		
1. Eastern coal = cost of fuel use in existing plant not subject to sulfur regulations	50	60
2. Western coal = cost of fuel use in existing plants not subject to sulfur regulations or under EPA standards	50	85
3. High-sulfur fuel oil = cost of oil use in new plants not subject to sulfur regulations	55	60
4. Low-sulfur fuel oil = cost of oil use in new plants subject to EPA standards	72	77
Capital costs for special facilities		
5. Cost of adding oil capability to existing plants	5	10
6. Extra cost of building new coal rather than oil-fired plant	10	25
7. Cost of adding stack gas scrubber to existing plant	30	85
8. Cost of adding stack gas scrubber to new plant	15	57
Costs of fuel use in existing plants not subject to sulfur regulations		
9. Eastern coal use cost (same as line 1 above)[a]	50	60
10. Western coal use cost (same as line 2)	50	85
11. Oil (high-sulfur) use cost (lines 3 plus 5)	60	70
Costs of fuel use in existing plants subject to EPA sulfur limits		
12. Eastern coal use cost (lines 1 plus 7)	80	145
13. Western coal use cost (same as line 2)	50	85
14. Oil (low-sulfur) use cost (lines 4 plus 5)	77	87
Cost of fuel use if all existing plants use sulfur oxide stack gas scrubbers		
15. Eastern coal use cost (same as line 12)	80	145
16. Western coal use cost (lines 2 plus 7)	80	170
17. Oil (low-sulfur) use cost (lines 14 plus 7)	107	172

this clear. For use of a scrubber to be beneficial, its costs, as noted, must be less than the sulfur tax *reduction*; otherwise it would be cheaper to pay the tax. In no case are the savings shown in table 7.2 greater than the *high* estimates of scrubbing costs for new or existing plants shown in table 7.1. However, except in the case of scrubbers for existing plants using Appalachian coal, the savings are greater than the *low* estimates of scrubber costs.

As a result, rather complex calculations are required to indicate the impacts of the sulfur tax. In those cases in which the scrubber will be used, it is necessary to calculate the net cost of emission control—the cost of the scrubber plus the tax remaining because the scrubber is not perfectly efficient. Table 7.3 provides such figures for eastern coals. When scrubbers are not used, of course, the total tax must be included in the cost of coal use. In table 7.4, the data from the prior tables are combined to provide figures on

TABLE 7.1. *Continued*

	Low	High
Costs of fuel use in new plants not subject to sulfur regulations		
18. Eastern coal use cost (lines 1 plus 6)	60	85
19. Western coal use cost (lines 2 plus 6)	60	110
20. Oil (high-sulfur) use cost (same as line 3)	55	60
Costs of fuel use in new plants subject to EPA sulfur plants		
21. Eastern coal use cost (sum of lines 1, 6, & 8)	75	142
22. Western coal use cost (lines 2 plus 6)	60	110
23. Oil (low-sulfur) use cost (same as line 4)	72	77
Cost of fuel use if all new plants use sulfur oxide stack gas scrubbers		
24. Eastern coal use cost (same as line 21)	75	142
25. Western coal use cost (lines 22 plus 8)	75	167
26. Oil (low-sulfur) use cost (lines 23 plus 8)	87	134
Coal breakeven price with nuclear when coal not subject to sulfur regulations		
27. Both plants at 75 percent utilization	51	32
28. Both plants at 50 percent utilization	66	38
29. Nuclear plant at 75 percent utilization and coal plant at 64 percent utilization	32	14
Coal breakeven price with nuclear when coal subject to EPA sulfur limits		
30. Both plants at 75 percent utilization (lines 27 minus 8)	36	−25
31. Both plants at 50 percent utilization (lines 28 minus 8)	51	−19
32. Nuclear plant at 75 percent utilization and coal plant at 64 percent utilization (lines 29 minus 8)	17	−43
Oil breakeven price with nuclear		
33. Both plants at 75 percent utilization	69	41
34. Both plants at 50 percent utilization	93	52
35. Nuclear plant at 75 percent utilization and oil plant at 64 percent utilization	50	32

Source: see text.
[a] References in parentheses are to lines in this table from which figures are drawn.

the cost of fuel use when a sulfur tax is imposed and the optimal ajustment to the tax is made.

Comparison of the situation in Chicago then can be made entirely by use of tables 7.1 and 7.4. From table 7.1 comes summary data on the relative cost position when no sulfur regulations, imposition of the EPA standards, or scrubber requirements on all fuels is the prevaling policy; Table 7.4 handles cases in which a sulfur tax of either of the levels suggested by the Nixon Administration is imposed.

For the all fossil fuel cases, the data in tables 7.1 and 7.4 are arranged so that direct comparisons may be made between the total costs of using each fuel. The cheapest-to-use fuel will be chosen. In the nuclear cases, the

TABLE 7.2

Sulfur Tax Saving Produced by Alternative Control Strategies
(cents per million Btu)

		Benefit of emission control strategy		
Fuel previously used	Precontrol tax	Use western coal	Use low-sulfur oil	Use 90 percent efficient scrubber
a. Savings when tax is 10 cents per pound of sulfur				
Appalachian coal	25	19	23	23
Midwestern coal	38	32	36	34
High-sulfur residual fuel oil	13	7	11	12
Western coal	6	0	4	5
b. Savings when tax is 15 cents per pound of sulfur				
Appalachian coal	38	29	35	34
Midwestern coal	57	48	55	51
High-sulfur residual fuel oil	20	11	17	18
Western coal	9	0	6	8

Source: Computed using assumption in text.

critical requirement is that the predicted price of a given fossil fuel be less than the breakeven price. The relevant breakeven prices are also in table 7.1, and their use is explained below.

Clear dominance of a given method of generation prevails only when the least favorable assumptions about its cost position indicate lower costs than do the most favorable assumptions about the cost position of rival fuels. This condition proves far too stringent, and looser criteria must be adopted based on rough appraisals of the reasonability of the numbers.

Fuel Choice for Existing Fossil-Fuel Plants. In the absence of sulfur regulations, oil use in existing plants would be unlikely in Chicago since the assumed minimum possible cost of oil use (line 11 of table 7.1) just equals the highest expected cost of eastern coal use (line 9). However, the relative competitive position of eastern and western coal is quite unclear. To be sure, the highest costs considered for western coal exceed the highest figure for eastern coal, but western coal costs could be sufficiently below those of eastern coal to pose a severe competitive threat.

It is reasonable to infer that in markets west of Chicago western coal would be in a strong position because it would cost less and eastern coal would cost more than in Chicago. However, the prospects for penetration of markets east of Chicago by western coal do not appear promising in this case. Similarly, on the east coast where coal use costs might range from $0.55–$0.65 and oil costs might be around $0.55 per million Btu, oil would remain quite competitive under the price assumptions stated here.

The imposition of EPA sulfur emission rules would be expected to cause marked deterioration of the competitive position of eastern coal, and the data in section d of table 7.1 support this expectation. The highest estimated values for western coal and low-sulfur oil use are only slightly above the low figure for eastern coal use costs. It is quite doubtful that so favorable a situation for eastern coal will develop since the low cost estimate probably greatly understates scrubber costs (see Appendix C). Western coal has good, but not guaranteed, prospects of being preferable to oil. It is true that high oil prices and environmental pressures have led some eastern utilities to purchase western coal.

Moreover, it appears quite probable that this Chicago situation is representative of the national prospects for use of eastern coal in conventional power plants. There are likely to be few places in which eastern coal has a locational advantage over the other fuels sufficient to outweigh the high cost of scrubbers. Thus, we can expect that the market for fuel for

TABLE 7.3

Net Sulfur Emission Cost for Stack Gas Scrubber Users
(cents/million Btu)

	1 Tax in absence of scrubber use	2 Tax saving due to scrubber use	3 Net tax[a]	4 Scrubber cost	5 Net emission cost[b]
10 cent/pound of sulfur tax					
Old plant					
Appalachian coal	25	23	2	30	32
Midwestern coal	38	34	4	30	34
New plant					
Appalachian coal	25	23	2	15	17
Midwestern coal	38	34	4	15	19
15 cent/pound sulfur tax					
Old plant					
Appalachian coal	38	34	4	30	34
Midwestern coal	57	51	6	30	36
New plant					
Appalachian coal	38	34	4	15	19
Midwestern coal	57	51	6	15	21

[a] These figures are the remainders of columns 1 minus 2.
[b] These figures are the sums of columns 3 and 4.

TABLE 7.4

Cost of Fuel Use in Chicago Under Sulfur Tax
(cents per million Btu displaced)

	10 cent/pound of sulfur tax		15 cent/pound of sulfur tax	
	Low	High	Low	High
1. Eastern coal price	50	60	50	60
2. Stack gas scrubbing cost for old plant	30	85	30	85
3. Tax	38	38	57	57
4. Tax saving if scrubber used	34	34	51	51
5. Residual tax if scrubber used or total tax if scrubber not used	4	38	6	57
6. Eastern coal use cost in existing plant [low (1 + 2 + 5)[a]; high (1 + 5)]	84	98	86	117
7. Western coal price	50	85	50	85
8. Sulfur tax on western coal	6	6	9	9
9. Western coal use cost in existing plants (7 + 8)	56	91	59	94
10. Extra cost of building new coal instead of oil plant	10	25	10	25
11. Cost of western coal use in new plant	66	116	69	119
12. High-sulfur oil price	55	60	55	60
13. Sulfur tax	13	13	20	20
14. Oil use cost in new plant (12 + 13)	68	73	75	80
15. Cost of adding oil use capability	5	10	5	10
16. Oil use cost in existing plant (14 + 15)	73	83	80	90
17. Eastern coal price	50	60	50	60
18. Extra cost of building new coal instead of oil plant	10	25	10	25
19. Stack gas scrubbing cost for new plant	15	57	15	57
20. Tax saving if scrubber used	34	34	51	51
21. Residual tax if scrubber used or total tax if scrubber not used	4	38	6	57
22. Eastern coal use cost in new plant [low (17 + 18 + 19 + 21); high (17 + 18 + 21)]	79	123	81	142
Summary for existing plants				
23. Eastern coal use cost (6)[a]	84	98	86	117
24. Western coal use cost (9)	56	91	59	94
25. Oil use cost (16)	73	83	80	90
Summary for new plants				
26. Eastern coal use cost (22)	79	123	81	142
27. Western coal use cost (11)	66	116	69	119
28. Oil use cost (14)	68	73	75	80
Summary for competition with nuclear power				
29. Eastern coal effective price (22 minus 18)	69	98	71	117
30. Western coal effective price(9)	56	91	59	94
31. Oil effective price (14)	68	73	75	80

Source: Presents in tabular form material discussed on pp. 147–157.

[a] Figures in parentheses refer to line numbers within this table.

existing plants would be split between oil and western coal. Since we cannot be sure which of the last two fuels will serve Chicago, it is not possible to determine the dividing line between oil and western coal markets. It is surely unlikely, however, that western coal could be transported economically all the way to the east coast.

In practice, the universal requirement of scrubber use only makes sense when fuels of equal sulfur content are used. Otherwise, a low-sulfur fuel is subject to arbitrarily higher standards than a high-sulfur fuel. Thus, the sensible concept of universal scrubber requirements is that sulfur limits are set so low that only the combined use of low-sulfur fuel and a scrubber meets the regulations. Nevertheless, for the sake of completeness, data are shown on the cost of fuel use with scrubbers for eastern coal as well as oil and western coal. Again the results are rather inconclusive. However, to the extent that oil is more likely to incur costs at or above the high end of the cost range, western coal may have a slight advantage but not enough to cause deep penetration into the eastern market. If we translate this into the implications for the locations near the western coal fields at which scrubber requirements are most likely, they suggest that a shift to oil is unlikely to result. Coal would be much cheaper than oil in such locations.

The data on lines 23–25 of table 7.4 indicate that the sulfur tax also implies that only low scrubber costs and high prices for rival fuels would permit viability of eastern coal in Chicago. Generalization to other regions of sulfur tax conclusion for this and other sulfur tax cases is complicated by the fact that lower taxes are applicable to Appalachian coal than those for midwestern coal. If midwestern coal can compete in Chicago given the sulfur tax, the lower tax on Appalachian coal implies that it can compete in any market to which transportation costs are not significantly greater than the $0.10 per million Btu cost of delivering midwestern coal to Chicago. In cases in which midwestern coal is not competitive in Chicago, however, it is possible that the lower tax on Appalachian coal might suffice to permit its continued viability. The relevant cases are those in which scrubber costs are so high that it is preferable to pay the full tax rather than undertake abatement measures. In these cases, with coal prices at $0.40/million Btu f.o.b. mine, a coal burning plant would pay a $0.25 a million Btu tax given a $0.10 per pound of sulfur rate; therefore, the cost of coal for a mine mouth plant would be around $0.65. If the tax were $0.38 because a $0.15 per pound of sulfur tax were imposed, the cost to a mine mouth plant rises to $0.78. The corresponding Chicago costs for western coal are such that the cost of transportation further east would make it unlikely that western coal could compete. Similarly, the oil price estimates are such that most utilities fairly close to Appalachian coal fields probably would find coal cheaper than oil. However, utilities on the east coast would find oil cheaper.

Fuel Choice in New Plants—Fossil Fuel Only. The main cost differences between an existing coal-fired-plant fuel choice and those in new plants is that oil use in the former involves a retrofitting penalty and in the latter leads to saving the cost of coal handling facilities. This implies oil is a more attractive alternative in new plants than in old ones. The critical question, therefore, is whether this improvement suffices, in each of the five policy cases considered, to alter fuel choice. Such a development does occur in Chicago when no sulfur regulations prevail; the highest assumed oil use cost equals the low estimates for the cost of using eastern or western coal.

However, in all cases where some form of policy to control sulfur oxides is imposed, the qualitative ranking of oil as a new plant fuel remains about where it does in the corresponding cases for existing plants. At the assumed prices, oil use remains quite likely to be cheaper than eastern coal use even when the lower tax on Appalachian coal is considered, but its position relative to western coal is less certain. However, once again, this suggests that east of Chicago oil would be more likely to be used than western coal, should oil prices return to relative 1972 levels.

Fuel Choice in New Plants—Conventional Fossil Fuel and Nuclear. The main problem with fossil fuel–nuclear comparisons is keeping track of all the possible comparisons without extending the analysis to unmanageable lengths. One basic simplification made here is that only the high allowable breakeven prices are explicitly considered. The low estimates of breakeven prices almost invariably imply that nuclear power is the cheapest way to produce electricity. The basic conclusions we may make from this information are fairly straightforward. At best, fossil fuel is likely to be competitive in Chicago only when nuclear capacity reaches a high enough level that the rate of utilization falls well below 75 percent. This suggests that only oil on the east coast or western coal plants serving areas near the mines could possibly be competitive with nuclear power.

This may be seen by tracing through some of the critical cases. The initial benchmark for comparison is the $0.51 per million Btu maximum breakeven point for a coal plant not employing scrubbers when it and the nuclear alternative are utilized at a 75 percent rate. By the construction of tables 7.1 and 7.4, this price is relevant for all cases involving western coal except forced scrubber use and all cases for eastern coal but the imposition of EPA sulfur limits or forced scrubber use. In particular, it was noted above that level sulfur taxes have uncertain effects on scrubber use and abatement measures reduce rather than eliminate the tax. A convenient way to handle comparisons is to consider an "effective price" of using a fuel when it is subject to a sulfur tax that is comparable with the breakeven price excluding scrubber costs. Obviously this effective price includes the actual delivered price before sulfur tax of the fuel and the sulfur tax paid. In addition, when scrubbers are used, their cost is added to the effective price rather than sub-tracted from the breakeven price. Such effective prices appear on lines 29–31 of table 7.4.

Turning to the actual cases, it may be noted that even in the absence of any form of sulfur emission control policy, the low estimate of delivered prices ($0.50 per million Btu for eastern and western coal) is so close to the $0.51 maximum breakeven price considered that the viability of coal is questionable. This also means that the ability to comply with EPA sulfur limits by western coal use may not suffice to make it a viable alternative when such limits are imposed. Table 7.4 makes clear, moreover, that the sulfur tax raises the effective cost of coal use well above $0.51/million Btu.

The cases involving either forced scrubber use with coal or imposition of EPA sulfur limits on eastern coal are handled by comparing the delivered price of the coal to the $0.36 per million Btu breakeven price relevant to the relative economics of a coal-fired plant with scrubbers and a nuclear plant when both are utilized at a 75 percent rate. This breakeven price is so far below the expected delivered prices of eastern and western coal in Chicago that forced scrubber installation would rule out use of eastern or western coal, and the EPA rules that implicitly necessitate scrubber use also preclude employment of eastern coal.

The oil comparisons all are made with the $0.69 per million Btu breakeven price applicable between oil and nuclear plants when both operate at a 75 percent rate. This breakeven price assumption implies that the absence of sulfur regulations would make oil use preferable to nuclear plants since the assumed delivered price of high-sulfur oil is estimated at only $0.55 to $0.60. However, the $0.72 to $0.77 price per million Btu of low-sulfur oil is so high that the EPA sulfur regulations prevent oil from competing against nuclear power in Chicago. Similar conclusions apply for forced scrubber use since a minimum $0.15 per million Btu scrubber cost plus $0.72 low-sulfur oil prices means effective costs of $0.87/million Btu or more than the allowable price of $0.69. Similarly, only when $0.55 per million Btu oil bears a $0.10 per pound of sulfur tax is the effective price below the breakeven price.

In sum, the estimates for Chicago suggest that the absence of sulfur con-trol policies makes it possible but by no means certain that fossil fuels can remain competitive with nuclear power. However, oil at its relative 1972 price may be the cheapest fuel in Chicago and therefore in much of the East except for companies located near coal fields. Western coal would be competitive near where it is mined and possibly as far east as Minnesota.

The imposition of the EPA sulfur limits or forced scrubber use appears to rule out *eastern* coal use in competition with nuclear power anywhere in the United States; the allowable breakeven price when scrubbers are used is below the low estimate ($0.40/million Btu) of mine mouth coal costs. The

EPA rules leave the cost of western coal use unchanged but, by necessitating employment of low-sulfur oil, raise the cost of oil use. Thus, use of these emission rules makes the position of western coal relative to oil better than it would be in the absence of regulation. In the presence of regulation, western coal could be competitive in Chicago but by so narrow a margin that its use further east is unlikely. Oil would not be competitive with nuclear power in Chicago but might be so on the east coast. Forced use of scrubbers rules out oil and western coal use in Chicago, but utilities near western coal fields might find it possible economically to use this coal instead of nuclear energy.

Finally, only a small possibility of oil use rather than nuclear fuel use in Chicago arises if sulfur taxes are used. When a $0.10 per pound tax prevails, oil might be barely competitive at the prices assumed here. This suggests that the $0.10 per pound tax might allow oil use throughout the eastern United States. The $0.15 a pound tax makes oil use uneconomical throughout the east since east coast effective costs would be at least $0.70/million Btu. Coal use in Chicago would be uneconomical, and even mine mouth plants with effective eastern coal costs of $0.59 (the effective Chicago cost at a $0.10 per pound of sulfur tax less transportation) would be above the breakeven price with nuclear plants. However, western coal could remain competitive at plants serving areas near the coal fields.

The effects of different operating rate assumptions may be treated more tersely. The case of 75 percent utilization of nuclear plants and only 64 percent employment of fossil plants sharply lowers the breakeven price. The resulting $0.32 per million Btu breakeven price when coal plants without scrubbers are possible totally rules out eastern coal use anywhere whatever public policy may be. The mine mouth price of eastern coal is expected to exceed $0.40 a million Btu. However, western coal with a $0.20–$0.25 mine mouth cost per million Btu could be competitive near the coal fields. A sulfur tax of $0.15 a pound, however, amounts to a cost of $0.09 per million Btu and could raise western coal use costs above the breakeven price as would the requirement to use scrubbers. The $0.17 breakeven price associated with coal plants using scrubbers implies no coal use when scrubbers are required, and the $0.53 oil breakeven price can only be met on the east coast by high-sulfur oil with low prices.

Lower operating rates not only favor fossil plants over nuclear but also oil over coal. At the prices assumed here, the combined impact could make oil the preferred fuel throughout the eastern United States for plants operating at a 50 percent rate. The allowable high breakeven price for oil of $0.93 is above even the high estimate of delivered prices under a $0.15 per pound of sulfur tax. Thus, for every policy situation but imposed use of expensive scrubbers, oil would be viable in the eastern United States. The position of coal relative to nuclear power is much weaker, and the distinct possibility exists that even in locations east of the Mississippi in which coal is cheaper than nuclear power, oil could be cheaper still.

Fuel Choice in New Plants—Conventional Fossil, the Combined Cycle, and Nuclear. As noted, the position of coal could be improved by introduction of new technology to generate electricity from fossil fuels. To examine possible prospects, the economics of the combined cycle may be reviewed. Table 7.5, the derivation of which is explained in Appendix E, presents possible breakeven prices for the combined cycle relative to the other alternatives and estimates of synthetic gas prices. The data show that the combined cycle would be much cheaper than using scrubbers with eastern coal. The lowest breakeven price in this case, $0.92 per 111 kwh, is well above the $0.70 per 111 kwh high estimate for gas from eastern coal or oil. This $0.70 price also makes gasified eastern coal in the combined cycle cheaper than use of western coal in a conventional plant in Chicago. Similarly, the $0.84 lowest breakeven price with low-sulfur oil is below the high estimates for gas from oil or eastern coal. Without discussing the details, it should be apparent that this cost advantage over conventional fossil plants should prevail throughout the United States. Thus, success with the combined cycle would clearly make it the preferred fossil-fuel generating technique.

However, this does not answer the questions of which would be the cheapest combined cycle fuel and whether the combined cycle would permit fossil fuels once again to be competitive with nuclear power. The fuel choice is simply a matter of selecting the lowest-cost, usable fuel. The price assumptions used here imply that oil gas would be cheaper than any form of coal gas. Thus, the present assumptions imply that oil would be the fuel used. However, its use might not necessarily be as an input for gasification. It is not yet clear whether gasification would be a cheaper way to make oil usable in a combined cycle than treatment of low-sulfur residual oil.

The estimated high breakeven prices with nuclear power would allow the combined cycle to become competitive, but the low breakeven prices would leave the situation more precarious. For example, if the breakeven price per 111 kwh were as low as $0.47, no form of gas could compete. Thus, the most prudent conclusion is that the combined cycle or other improved generating techniques are promising but not guaranteed routes towards restoring the ability of fossil fuel to compete with nuclear power.

Conclusions on Fuel Choice. The present analysis suggests that even the fairly limited range of cost variation considered is not sufficient to indicate the exact fuel use choice that electric utilities will make. However, the

TABLE 7.5

Costs of Advanced Combined Cycle and Competitive Generating Techniques in Chicago in the 1980s

(cents per 111 kwh except as indicated)

	Low estimate	High estimate
Net cost advantage[a] of combined cycle over conventional coal plant		
1. at 75 percent utilization	27	58
2. at 64 percent utilization	33	68
3. at 50 percent utilization	43	88
4. Delivered price of western coal	50	85
Breakeven price per 111 kwh of combined cycle fuel compared to western coal in conventional plant		
5. at 75 percent utilization $(1 + 4)$[b]	77	143
6. at 64 percent utilization $(2 + 4)$	83	153
7. at 50 percent utilization $(3 + 4)$	93	173
8. Delivered price of eastern coal	50	60
9. Scrubber cost	15	57
10. Delivered price plus scrubber cost $(8 + 9)$	65	117
Breakeven price per 111 kwh of combined cycle fuel compared to eastern coal in conventional plant		
11. at 75 percent utilization $(1 + 10)$	92	175
12. at 64 percent utilization $(2 + 10)$	98	185
13. at 50 percent utilization $(3 + 10)$	108	205
Net cost advantage[a] of combined cycle over conventional oil plant		
14. at 75 percent utilization	12	43
15. at 64 percent utilization	15	51
16. at 50 percent utilization	20	65
17. Cost of low sulfur oil	72	77
Breakeven price per 111 kwh of combined cycle fuel compared to conventional oil plant		
18. at 75 percent utilization $(14 + 17)$	84	120
19. at 64 percent utilization $(15 + 17)$	87	128
20. at 50 percent utilization $(16 + 17)$	92	142

assumptions used indicate that oil and western coal represent a severe threat to eastern coal in existing plants and new fossil plants. An even more severe threat is posed in the long run by nuclear power.

It is appropriate at this point to reflect upon what these calculations do (and do not) mean. Obviously, they involve the self-imposed limitation of not considering extreme variations outside the ranges treated here. As noted, there are those prepared to argue that costs will indeed be such that coal will prove to be the best short- and long-run choice. The argument to date has been that such a development has no stronger support than the obvious statement that the best cost estimates are none too good. Success for coal will be neither easy nor automatic. The risks of high costs of using other fuels are great enough to justify efforts to improve coal's competitive

TABLE 7.5 *Continued*

	Low estimate	High estimate
Breakeven price of combined cycle fuel per 111 kwh compared to nuclear plant		
21. Both at 75 percent utilization	60	108
22. Both at 64 percent utilization	67	124
23. Both at 50 percent utilization	81	154
24. Nuclear at 75 percent utilization and combined cycle at 64 percent utilization	47	100
Cost of gas for combined cycle[c]		
25. Gas from eastern coal		
Cost per million Btu of gas	88	100
Cost per 111 kwh for plant with 54.5 percent thermal efficiency	61	70
Cost per 111 kwh for plant with 57.7 percent thermal efficiency	58	66
26. Gas from western coal		
Cost per million Btu of gas	88	128
Cost per 111 kwh for plant with 54.5 percent thermal efficiency	61	89
Cost per 111 kwh for plant with 57.7 percent thermal efficiency	58	84
27. Gas from oil		
Cost per million Btu of gas	81	87
Cost per 111 kwh for plant with 54.5 percent thermal efficiency	56	61
Cost per 111 kwh for plant with 57.7 percent thermal efficiency	53	57

[a] See text for basis of calculation, p. 182.

[b] Figures in parentheses refer to line numbers within this table.

[c] Gas costs as indicated by table 5.2 for fuel prices assumed in table 7.1. Coal based on advanced gasification process; oil assumes use of high sulfur oil. Adjustment for higher thermal efficiencies based on method explained in Appendix A.

position. This requires developing both better use technology and cheaper methods of safe, environmentally acceptable mining. Given all the barriers that must be overcome, success is not guaranteed, and society ought also to be working on other alternatives.

This leads to consideration of the various policy trade-offs available. It can be argued that the best of all possible worlds would be produced by insuring that low-cost oil is readily available. It is clear from chapter 5 that imported oil prices close to marginal costs abroad would be so low that much of the United States would most cheaply secure its electricity from oil. This, of course, would require that the massive rises in oil prices since 1971 be reversed and oil prices move nearer the true economic cost of production. This approach would avoid both the expensive alternatives associated with coal and the risks of nuclear power.

This is not to say that this is truly an attainable or preferable state. As chapter 1 noted, many doubt whether oil prices could indeed be lowered. For that matter, the whole question of what constitutes a preferable environmental condition remains in doubt. In particular, some would be prepared to argue that the remaining sulfur emissions inevitable from oil use are less desirable than the risks of using nuclear power. Others more timidly argue that even the higher levels of sulfur emissions resulting from uncontrolled coal burning are preferable on balance to the alternatives at least in the short run.

Moreover, declines in foreign oil prices may not be essential to insure that oil becomes the principal fossil fuel used by electric utilities. The data in this chapter suggest that one possible development is that oil could compete at prices well above those assumed here. Chapter 5 pointed out that some observers believe that a fairly modest rise in prices combined with removal of public policies that hinder oil and gas supply expansion could produce a substantial increase in domestic oil and gas output. Therefore, domestic oil and gas could prove to be cheaper than coal, so the decline of coal use is far from completely dependent upon the collapse of OPEC.

Even if oil prices are well above those assumed in the scenarios, oil competition may still prove formidable for coal. It may be noted that the $1.42 per million Btu estimate of the high cost of using coal in a new fossil plant employing sulfur oxide scrubbers is constructed so that it represents the maximum allowable price of oil. The $1.42 estimate implies that low-sulfur oil prices could be as high as $8.50 a barrel. As chapter 5 suggests, this estimate is not directly comparable with forecasts of crude oil prices, but some indicators of the relationship can be provided. The critical considerations are that high-sulfur residual oil will sell for less than the price of crude, and that low-sulfur oil prices will ultimately exceed the price of high-sulfur oil by an amount equal to the cost of desulfurization. With a $1.00 a barrel desulfurization cost, an $8.50 low-sulfur oil price implies a $7.50 price for high-sulfur oil, and thus crude oil prices could exceed $7.50 per barrel and still be the preferred fuel for electric power generation. The more optimistic forecasts of U.S. liquid fuel supply potentials indicate that crude oil prices could be below this critical figure.

Whatever public policy may become, the implicit trends through 1972 towards strict sulfur emission controls made it most probable that up to 1980 a substantial amount of oil conversion and switching to western coal would be necessary because stack scrubbing would either be unavailable or too expensive. Import policy has tacitly tended to make oil available to meet these needs.

Moreover, the very sorts of estimates presented here have, as chapter 8 shows, inspired the electric utilities to move heavily into nuclear power.

This decision implies that at least for a considerable part of the early eighties much of the *new* fuel demand for electricity generation will be met by nuclear fuels. It will take a considerable amount of time to reverse the attitudes upon which these decisions were based—lack of confidence in the ability to burn oil or coal economically in an environmentally acceptable fashion. Thus, we have numerous forces making for a short-term decline in use of at least eastern coal and difficulties in insuring that coal will ever recover from the setback. Public policy must be designed to recognize these considerations. It must be decided whether these trends can and should be reversed.

Appendix A

GENERAL ASSUMPTIONS FOR LEVELIZING

As noted in the text, the essence of levelizing is converting capital costs into a charge per unit of output. Noncapital costs for conventional plants are generally divided into fuel and other components. However, for present purposes, a slightly different breakdown is preferable. Capital and nonfuel operating costs are measured net of sulfur oxide emission control costs. The control costs are then treated as a separate item. This allows consideration of control cost estimates that are different from those used in the sources of data on the other costs. Nuclear cost presentations usually differ from the normal treatment of conventional plants by the inclusion of a specific item for the special nuclear risk insurance that such plants are required to purchase. Other insurance costs for nuclear and fossil plants apparently are part of nonfuel operating expenses. Nuclear insurance is included here as part of nuclear fuel costs.

A critical problem in the analysis is conversion between the price of a fuel and the fuel cost per kwh. Part of the normalization involves putting the price per unit volume on a cost per million Btu basis as done in chapter 5. The basis of the conversion was left largely implicit and, here, except in the case of evaluating sulfur taxes, no further discussion of such conversion techniques is necessary.

The next step is to indicate the relationship between the cost per million Btu and the cost per kwh. This requires an assumption about the electric power produced by a million Btu. The requisite information is generally stated in the form of a heat rate—the number of Btu required to produce 1 kwh—or a plant thermal efficiency—the ratio of 3,413 Btu, the heat equivalent of 1 kwh, to the heat rate. For example, the "standard" assumption, used here, is that a modern conventional fossil-fueled plant has a heat rate of 9,000 Btu per kwh. This implies a thermal efficiency of about 38 percent. It can be directly calculated that a million Btu produce about 111 (1,000,000/9,000) kwh.

The 9,000 Btu heat rate assumption essentially indicates a belief that new base load fossil stations will match but not exceed the performance of the best plants built in the late 1960s. To understand the forces influencing the choice, it should be noted that utilization of the basic thermodynamic principles that higher initial operating temperatures and increased steam pressures raise thermal efficiency have been the main techniques for reducing heat rates. The *1970 National Power Survey* indicates that temperatures rose from about 800 degrees (Fahrenheit) in the best plants of the early forties to 1,000 degrees in new plants ordered for the middle sixties. Over the same period, steam pressures rose from 1,200 to 3,500 pounds per square inch (U.S. FPC, 1971, p. I–5–6).

These developments were produced by the introduction of new techniques and involved employment of stronger materials. As is usual in such situations, economic considerations limit the adoption of techniques to those with costs that can be recovered by the fuel savings produced. As a result, a wide difference prevails among the heat rates realized in various plants. It has been suggested that these differences are closely related to the type of fuel used. For example, the National Petroleum Council (1972, p. 232) indicates that the respective heat rates for modern coal, gas, and oil-fired plants are 9,000, 10,000, and 11,000 Btu. However, a survey of actual experience reported by individual companies suggests that use of these averages grossly oversimplifies the situation.

First, heat rates of 9,000 Btu or less are fairly rare. Second, such low rates have been realized in oil- and gas-fired plants, and conversely many modern coal-fired plants have significantly higher heat rates. The best oil-fired unit in 1970, New England Electric's unit three of the Brayton Point station, had an 8,725 Btu heat rate; only the coal-fired unit three of Duke Power's Marshall plant has a lower rate—8,636. The best gas-fired unit was Pacific Gas and Electric's Moss Landing unit number six with an 8,848 Btu rate—the eighth best unit reported (U.S. FPC, 1972, xxxiv–vi).

In looking at coal plant experience, it is similarly easier to identify those companies—notably American Electric Power, TVA, Duke, Consumers Power, and Detroit Edison—that have attained heat rates below 9,000 than to list "exceptions" to the standard rule of thumb. It may be noted, however, that coal-burning plants in the West are particularly likely to maintain higher heat rates. The Four Corners plant jointly owned by a group of western utilities in New Mexico, for example, had a 1972 rate of 11,186 Btu for units one through four and 9,662 for unit five; the Mohave plant, another joint venture, in Nevada, 10,989 Btu (company reports).

The failure of other plants to match the best attainable performance must reflect expectations that fuel savings would not justify investing in higher thermal efficiencies. Rising oil prices, however, should be expected to stimulate more widespread adoption of techniques to reduce oil heat rates at least to the level experienced by the best coal-fired units. Moreover, the general rise in fuel prices might cause all plant types to be built using technologies that further reduce heat rates. However, the literature on electric power economics contains many statements that the prospects of reducing thermal efficiencies of steam turbine plants were limited (see, e.g., U.S. FPC, 1971, p. I-5-6). A United Aircraft Laboratories study (Robson, 1970, p. 155–57) indicated that calculations of the underlying economics showed that the cost of the more expensive materials needed to lower heat rates exceeded the value of the fuel savings produced. As recent a study as the 1972 National Petroleum Council Report (p. 232) contended that new plant heat rates would only fall from 9,800 Btu, the level it considered the appropriate weighted average for all fuels, to 9,600 Btu by 1980. Given an apparent failure to incorporate the effect of rising fuel prices, this may understate the possibilities for lowering the heat rates.

In the present study, it is assumed, however, that all new fossil plants will maintain a 9,000 Btu heat rate. Oil plants are thus expected to utilize the techniques employed for coal burning, but no radical improvements in conventional coal plants are anticipated. Thus, it is assumed that synthetic fuels from coal and an advanced combined cycle will not be available until well into the 1980s. However, the implications of lower heat rates can be adequately suggested through the consideration provided here of new technologies involving higher thermal efficiencies.

The only situations in which heat rate assumptions for old plants are critical are those in which new capital investment is required to use a particular fuel. The higher the heat rate, the more fuel is required, and thus the more profitable is an investment that permits use of a cheaper fuel. Understatement of the heat rate understates the profitability of the investment. Nevertheless, a 9,000 Btu heat rate is used here for all old plants. This is an expositional simplification justifiable by the nature of the relevant cases, that is, conversion of old plants to oil and installation of stack gas scrubbers. In the first case, it may be preferable to bias the argument slightly against oil. In the second case, the cost ranges considered are so broad that they swamp the impact of any heat rate adjustment.

The only effect of environmental regulations on heat rates or net output considered here is the adjustments built into some of the estimates of stack gas scrubbing costs. Environmental regulations are often met by using some of the plant's power to operate control equipment and in some cases, notably dry cooling towers, the plant's gross output per unit of fuel input is reduced. Again, it appears that these penalties will not differ enough among different methods of generation to alter the relative cost position significantly.

Having noted the relationship between price per million Btu and price per kwh, it may be noted further that any cost can be put on either basis. However, the critical question is which method produces a specific amount of electricity most cheaply. A "price" per million Btu must measure the costs of a specific number of kwh. Thus, the price per kwh for each system must be converted to a price per million Btu by use of the kwh/million Btu of a *specific* generating method. For example, we can multiply the costs per kwh by 111. This gives the costs of the amount of electricty generated by a million Btu in a modern fossil-fired plant. By definition, the fuel cost of 111 kwh by 111. This gives the costs of the amount of electricity generated by a we have made all other costs comparable with the fuel prices presented in chapter 5. We have simply multiplied everything by a positive constant so that the relative cost position is unchanged. [Let TC_i and TC_j be the costs per kwh of two generating methods. Then if $TC_i < TC_j$, $111\ TC_i < 111\ TC_j$.]

A critical point in this process is noting that the price per 111 kwh of a fuel used in a generating technique with a heat rate different from 9,000 Btu/kwh is *not* its price per million Btu. This can be seen by viewing how the price per 111 kwh is calculated. If the process has a heat rate H_k, a million Btu produces $R_k = 1,000,000/H_k$ kwh. The cost per kwh then is P_k/R_k—the price of a million Btu divided by the number of kwh produced by a million Btu. The cost per 111 kwh then is $111\ P_k/R_k$. Noting that $111 = 1,000,000/9,000$ and recalling the definition of R_k, this reduces to $H_kP_k/9,000$—the price per 111 kwh is the price per million Btu times the ratio of the heat rates.

This proposition is most relevant when we consider new fossil generating technologies with heat rates below 9,000 Btu. Care must be taken to distinguish between the fuel price per 111 kwh generated by the new system and the system's fuel cost per million Btu consumed. Moreover, as chapter 5 showed, the price of a synthetic fuel differs from the price of input fuel because of other conversion costs and losses in conversion. Thus, it is necessary to distinguish input fuel cost from total synthetic fuel costs. Since synthetics may be used in new generating techniques, we may encounter cost distinctions simultaneously in both the cost of synthetic vs. cost of input fuel and cost per 111 kwh generated vs. cost per million Btu.

Having noted the two possible conventions about the dimension in which total costs are measured, we can return to the question of how to levelize in practice. An 18 percent capital charge means that $0.18 must be earned each year for every dollar of investment. To prorate this cost to each unit of output, an assumption, as noted, must be made about annual outputs. The usual method of presentation is in terms of the percent rate of capacity utilization. It may be recalled that a kilowatt is a measure of power intensity and a kilowatt hour represents the maintenance of one kilowatt of power for one hour. Therefore, over the course of a year, each kilowatt of capacity can produce at most 365 times 24 or 8760 kwh of output. An operating rate is simply the percent of 8760 that is actually used. For example, the Atomic Energy Commission indicates that 80 percent utilization of nuclear plants is likely so that each kilowatt of capacity produces 7008 kwh a year. By division of 0.18 by 7008, we get a cost per kwh of 0.026 mills. By multiplication by 111, we get a cost of 0.28 cents per 111 kwh. Similar calculations for other rates are shown in table 7.6. It also tabulates the levelized costs associated with different capital cost levels.

Considerable controversy has arisen over what constitutes an appropriate operating rate assumption for nuclear and fossil plants. As noted, higher rates improve the position of the more capital-using technique. Thus, if all generating methods are credited with excessive utilization rates, this makes the most capital-using approach seem more attractive than it really is. However, when the degree of overestimation differs among techniques, this produces a bias towards the method most excessively favored. There is no neat way to resolve these issues, so the expedient adopted here is to examine the implications of different operating rate assumptions.

Nevertheless, some observations may be made. First, the much publicized reliability problems of nuclear plants probably represent the normal breakin difficulties of a new technology. Nuclear plants should ultimately have a high availability and retain a favorable position on the load curve. The 80 percent rate, however, is unlikely to be maintained throughout the 1980s simply because there may be too many nuclear plants for all to operate at high rates. However, fossil-fuel plants may all have much lower operating rates because of a less favored position on the load curve. This may be aggravated for coal-fired plants using sulfur scrubbers by persistent difficulties in maintaining availability. At best, considerable amounts of preventive maintenance may be required. Thus, it seems appropriate to assume nuclear power will maintain operating rates less than 80 percent but greater than rates for coal-fired plants. A 75 percent rate, therefore, is chosen here for nuclear plants.

Another critical standard assumption is that the construction proceeds expeditiously. Delays, of course, mean that capital is tied up longer, raising the cost of the plant and the benefits (retirement of old plants, avoidance of construction of more expensive alternatives, and lesser purchase of power) are postponed. Although such difficulties have become chronic, particularly for nuclear plants, it seems best here to ignore them. The case of what is most economical without unusual construction delays provides a useful benchmark. Besides, it is not clear whether future problems will be more severe for coal or for nuclear power. Those nuclear delays reflecting technical problems promise to become much less frequent as more experience develops. Coal plants with scrubbers will undoubtedly

TABLE 7.6

Levelized Capital Costs at 18 Percent Annual Change, Selected Operating Rates, and Costs per Kilowatt

(cents per 111 kwh unless otherwise stated)

	40 percent	50 percent	64 percent	75 percent	80 percent
1. Utilization rate	40 percent	50 percent	64 percent	75 percent	80 percent
2. Hour per year (1 × 8760)	3504	4380	5606.4	6570	7008
3. Levelized cost in mills per kilowatt hour of $1 investment[a]	.051	.041	.032	.027	.026
4. Levelized cost in cents/111 kwh for investment of $1[b]	.571	.457	.357	.304	.285
$10	5.7	4.6	3.6	3.0	2.9
$20	11.4	9.1	7.1	6.1	5.7
$30	17.1	13.7	10.7	9.1	8.6
$40	22.8	18.3	14.3	12.2	11.4
$50	28.5	22.8	17.8	15.2	14.3
$60	34.2	27.4	21.4	18.3	17.1
$70	40.0	32.0	25.0	21.3	20.0
$80	45.7	36.5	28.5	24.4	22.8
$90	51.4	41.1	32.1	27.4	25.7
$100	57.1	45.7	35.7	30.4	28.5
$110	62.8	50.2	39.2	33.5	31.4
$120	68.4	54.8	42.8	36.5	34.2
$130	74.2	59.4	46.4	39.6	37.1
$140	79.9	63.9	49.9	42.6	40.0
$150	85.6	68.5	53.5	45.7	42.8
$160	91.3	73.1	57.1	48.7	45.7
$170	97.0	77.6	60.6	51.8	48.5
$180	103	82.2	64.2	54.8	51.4
$190	108	86.8	67.8	57.8	54.2
$200	114	91.3	71.3	60.9	57.1
$250	143	114	89.2	76.1	71.3
$300	171	137	107	91.3	85.6
$350	200	160	125	107	99.9
$400	228	183	143	122	114
$450	257	205	161	137	128
$500	285	228	178	152	143

[a] The actual calculations were made on an electronic hand calculator with a 10 significant digit capacity and then rounded to three significant digits after manipulation. The cost per kwh is found by dividing .18 by line 2.

[b] Line 3 multiplied by 111.1111111; subsequent lines are multiples of the unrounded values of the line 4 figures.

experience comparable problems. Regulation, similarly, may become less of a barrier to use of nuclear power plants and more of one to coal-fired plants.

Viability of using a particular fuel is defined here as a levelized cost less than that of *using* alternative fuels. The standard economic criterion that past costs are irrelevant applies here. In viewing the economics of existing plants, the only capital outlays germane to fuel choice are new ones required to adapt the plant to use a different fuel or permit compliance with environmental regulations. New plants, by definition, require new investment that must be considered.

In the present analysis, it is convenient at times to fix the value of certain costs and see what these assumptions imply for allowable values of other costs. Two approaches are possible. In the first, we assume a specific value for each component of the cost of using fuel j but divide the total costs (TC_i) of using fuel i into a portion assumed known (KC_i) and an "unknown" portion (UC_i). If fuel i is to be competitive, $UC_i + KC_i \equiv TC_i \leqq TC_j$ or $UC_i \leqq TC_j - KC_i$. The highest allowable or "breakeven" level for the component of the cost of using fuel i assumed to be unknown is the postulated total costs of using fuel j less the components of the cost of using fuel i that are presumed known.

The distinction between known and unknown costs, of course, is merely an expositional device since all cost component forecasts may be erroneous. In any case, a standard application of this technique is to fix all nuclear costs and all fossil-fuel-use costs except those for actual fuel and determine the maximum price at which fossil fuel would still be competitive with nuclear power. One might, however, use the technique for other purposes such as determining the maximum allowable levelized capital cost for nuclear power or setting the sum of coal prices and sulfur emission controls as an unknown.

The method may be adapted for the case in which components of the cost of using both fuels are considered unknown. Then we require $KC_i + UC_i \leqq KC_j + UC_j$ or $UC_i - UC_j \leqq KC_j - KC_i$. If we choose i and j so that the right-hand term of the inequality is positive, it measures the premium that the unknown components of the cost of using fuel i can enjoy over the unknown components of the cost of using fuel j because of the lower known costs of using fuel i. For example, here $UC_i - UC_j$ is often defined to represent the difference between the price of two fuels. $KC_j - KC_i$ would then refer to various penalties for using the lower priced fuel— the higher cost of a nuclear compared to a fossil plant, the retrofitting cost for converting an existing fossil plant to a new fuel, or the scrubbers needed to permit coal use in such existing plants.

In what follows, nonfuel operating costs for all plants will be considered components of KC. Indeed since these costs are generally assumed to be equal among steam turbine fossil plants using different fuels and between fossil and nuclear plants, they cancel out of the analysis. The only exception is that the combined cycle (see Appendix E) has somewhat higher operating costs. Similarly nuclear fuel costs are considered part of KC. Comparisons between nuclear power and other alternatives is on a breakeven basis. The method generally emphasized is to compute the breakeven value of either fossil-fuel prices or the sum of such prices and emission control expenses. Comparisons among fossil-fuel systems emphasize premiums that may be paid for a fuel and control of its regulated environmental impacts, if any.

Because of the complexities of the algebra, when the advanced combined cycle is considered, the breakeven price of fuel per 111 kwh is first computed, and then the price per million Btu of fossil fuel is inferred.

Appendix B

THE COST OF CONVENTIONAL FOSSIL AND NUCLEAR PLANTS

The previous section indicated how estimates of capital costs could be levelized and combined with estimates of other cost elements to produce measures of the comparative economics of different alternatives. It now becomes possible to employ the available data to develop such comparisons. A chronic problem in practice is inconsistency among data. Aside from the normal inconsistencies in accounting practices, there are many sources of differences. For example, the comparison may relate to the generating plant alone or include ancillaries such as switchyards and transmission lines. Another problem arises from treatment of construction cost trends. Some studies do not properly normalize for this, and, for example, show the costs of two plants started, rather than completed, at the same date.

Perhaps the most useful set of consistently compiled cost estimates is that produced by the U.S. government's appraisal of nuclear power. Through late 1969, the major source was a series of papers by Philip Sporn, former president of American Electric Power. He prepared for the Congressional Joint Committee on Atomic Energy periodic evaluations of the comparative economics of coal and nuclear generation. These in turn often inspired alternative calculations from the Atomic Energy Commission (AEC) and others.[5]

Since Sporn's last paper, the AEC has itself issued several cost comparisons, based on data supplied by the utilities, in both Congressional testimony and separate publications. These later studies involve a critical change in methodology. The figures up to 1969 ignored the cost of sulfur emission control, but it is now included in AEC data. These data include an adjustment for inflation, and so are in current rather than constant dollars.

[5] All but Sporn's 1969 paper were collected in one volume by the Joint Committee (1968). A 1971 Joint Committee Publication contains the 1969 Sporn paper and extensive comments on it. (See bibliography under U.S. Congress. Joint Committee on Atomic Energy.)

Both to preserve historical comparability and to allow for explicit treatment of different estimates of sulfur emission control, the older basis of calculation is employed in this review of estimates.

Table 7.7 lists these forecasts and the breakeven prices that they imply. It may be seen that Sporn's initial paper contended that the AEC had been overly optimistic about nuclear power's ability to compete with coal. However, later developments caused all Sporn's subsequent estimates of the breakeven price to lie at or below the initial AEC estimate of about $0.29 per million Btu. AEC testimony in 1971 produced similar conclusions (see table 7.8 for details).

Unfortunately, it is quite difficult to place later AEC figures on a basis comparable to earlier ones because sulfur emission control costs are included but the numerical assumptions often are not provided. Thus, the (late) 1971 annual survey of the nuclear industry (p. 93) reports a $360 a kilowatt cost for a nuclear plant and $295 a kilowatt for a coal plant with emission control—a $65 a kilowatt differential. Assuming that the $40 a kilowatt estimate for emission control used in the 1971 testimony also applied, the differential between nuclear and coal plants without emission controls would be $105.

TABLE 7.7
Selected Estimates of Comparative Costs of Fossil and Nuclear Plants

	Capital costs (dollars per kilowatt)			Coal breakeven price (cents per million Btu)
	Nuclear	Coal	Difference	
1962 AEC estimates				
for 1966	182	132	50	34*
for early seventies	165	132	33	29*
Sporn 1962				
for 1966	190	120	70	39*
for early seventies	160	100	60	36*
1962 AEC revised				
for early seventies	135	100	35	30*
Sporn 1964	139	107	32	27.0
Sporn 1966	123	112	11	24.0
Sporn 1967	140–150	117	23–33	22–23
Sporn 1969	203.5	170.6	33	28–29.5
AEC 1971a	319–377	268–335†	37–46	31–34*
AEC 1971b	360	255	105	52*
AEC 1972	383	314	69	40*
AEC 1973	435	355	80	44*

Sources: Estimates through Sporn 1967 in Joint Committee on Atomic Energy, 1968; Sporn 1969 in Joint Committee, 1970a. See text for source of subsequent forecasts.

* Calculated by author assuming 75 percent utilization; 20.1 cent nuclear fuel cost and a 16 percent capital charge in 1960s and 18 percent in 1970s.

† Excludes the AEC's $40 cost estimate (see text) for sulfur emission control.

TABLE 7.8

Breakeven Cost of Coal and Oil with Nuclear Power—Atomic Energy Commission
Estimates

Plant location	Nuclear plant with radiation waste controls and cooling tower	Coal plant with sulfur emission control and cooling tower *(dollars per kilowatt)*	Oil plant with cooling tower	Breakeven price of fuel *(cents per million Btu)* High sulfur coal	Low sulfur fuel oil
Northeast Seaboard	377	375	271	19.2	43.6
Southeast	314	308	219	20.6	41.2
Midwest/Great Lakes	342	342	245	19.2	41.6
South Central	319	322	230	18.2	39.7
Rocky Mountain	323	318	227	20.2	41.4
Pacific Southwest	328	323	231	20.2	41.7
Pacific Northwest	333	330	236	19.7	41.5

Note: Calculations by AEC (Shaw, 1971, p. 636) based on a 1,000 megawatt plant ordered in mid-1971 for 1977 delivery. No adjustments for inflation are provided, and the assumption is that sulfur control costs $40 a kilowatt. Operating costs of these control facilities are apparently thought negligible.

While the commission's 1972 testimony provided only summary figures, their basis can be determined from a report from an Oak Ridge National Laboratory group that aided the work. The AEC testimony (U.S. Congress Joint Committee on Atomic Energy, 1972, p. 1092) set costs of a nuclear plant at $390 a kilowatt and a coal plant with scrubbers at $360. The Oak Ridge group presented respective figures of $383 and $361. The group also set scrubber costs at $47 a kilowatt implying a $314 a kilowatt cost for plants without scrubbers (Bennett, Bowers, and Myers, 1971).

Power Engineering (Olds, 1973) provided a summary of later Oak Ridge estimates in its January 1973 issue. These set nuclear costs at $435 a kilowatt in 1980 dollars and coal at $409 with $54 for scrubbers. Thus, a coal plant without scrubbers would cost $355.

While Sporn did not treat oil, the later AEC reports did. The first set a cost range of $219–$271 (the variation reflects regional construction cost differences). This meant an oil plant cost from $89 to $106 a kilowatt less than a nuclear plant in the same region, $89–$104 less than a coal plant with scrubbers, and $49–$64 less than a coal plant without scrubbers (see table 7.8). The 1971 survey set oil costs at $240 a kilowatt; the 1972 testimony, at $330. The Oak Ridge reports show that this last figure included $47 for sulfur scrubbing. Thus, an oil plant without scrubbers would cost $287 (using Oak Ridge's total of $334). The Oak Ridge figures reported by *Power Engineering* in 1973 set oil costs at $377 a kilowatt including $54 for scrubbers implying a cost without scrubbers of $323.

These figures suggest that the differential between nuclear and fossil plant capital costs (excluding sulfur stack gas scrubbers) has been more stable than the absolute levels. Therefore, the differences are stressed in the analysis although the absolute levels are considered when an effort is made to consider differences between nuclear and fossil plants in operating rates. The basic assumptions are that a nuclear plant costs $40 to $100 a kilowatt more than a coal-fired plant without scrubbers and $70 to $160 more than an oil-fired plant. Similarly, a new coal plant without scrubbers is assumed to cost $30 to $60 more than a new oil-fired plant.

It is assumed here that these are costs in 1973 dollars. This may slightly bias the figures against nuclear power since the data were derived from estimates that do attempt to add in the accounts of inflation and thus show a wider cost disadvantage for nuclear power than might arise from comparison based on 1980 prices. The approach can be justified in several ways; the most obvious rationale is that the uncertainties about costs are such that it is quite possible that real forces will have the same effect on relative costs as would the inflation assumed by the sources.

The literature is relatively thin on the costs of retrofitting oil use capacity, but a survey of electric company annual reports provides figures suggesting that such costs would run from $10–$20 a kilowatt.

Turning to calculation of breakeven prices per 111 kwh, we must add to these capital cost figures an estimate of nuclear fuel and insurance costs. A standard estimate is that fuel runs 1.7 mills/kwh and insurance 0.11 mills, and the 1.81 mill total becomes 20.1 cents when multiplied by 111. The breakeven price then is the sum of nuclear fuel prices and the difference in levelized capital costs. When a 75 percent operating rate is assumed for all fuels, the coal "breakeven price" with nuclear ranges from 32.3 to 50.5 cents. This, it may be recalled, is the amount available to pay for coal and sulfur emission control. Lowering the assumed operating rate for both fuels to 50 percent would raise the range to 38.4 to 65.8 cents (see table 7.6).

However, if a coal plant has a lower operating rate than a nuclear plant, significantly different results follow. Commonwealth Edison (1973) indicates that even in the early years of a coal plant's life only a 64 percent operating rate is possible. A plant with an initial cost of $350 a kilowatt— roughly the Oak Ridge National Laboratories figure for a coal plant without scrubbers—has a $1.25 levelized capital cost per 111 kwh at a 64 percent operating rate. If a nuclear plant were only $40 more expensive (i.e., $390) and operated at 75 percent, its levelized costs would only be $1.19— $0.06 less than the levelized coal capital cost—leaving a breakeven price of $0.14. At a $450 per kilowatt nuclear cost, the levelized cost per 111 kwh is $1.37 or $0.12 more than for fossil fuel, leaving a $0.32 breakeven price.

Similarly, the oil breakeven price with nuclear power ranges from 41.4 to 68.8 cents when both operate at 75 percent rates. This rises to 52.1 to 93.2 cents when both operate at 50 percent. If a $300 per kilowatt oil plant is utilized at a 64 percent rate, its breakeven price range with a $390 to $450 nuclear plant operating at 75 percent is $0.32 to $0.50 per 111 kwh. In short, nuclear breakeven prices are extremely sensitive to the assumptions about costs and operating rates. How significant this sensitivity is may be seen after sulfur scrubbing costs are analyzed.

In the case of oil vs. coal in new plants, the capital cost saving imposes a penalty on coal of 13.7 to 27.4 cents at a 50 percent operating rate; 10.7 to 21.4 cents at 64 percent and 9.1 to 18.3 cents at 75 percent. This is summarized here as a $0.10 to $0.25 advantage for oil. Conversely at the same respective operating rates, the retrofitting penalties for oil are 4.6 to 9.1, 3.6 to 7.1, and 3.0 to 6.1 cents. For expositional purposes a $0.05 to $0.10 range is used here.

After these figures were prepared, another study of comparative costs, made for Northeast Utilities by Arthur D. Little, Inc., became available. Direct comparisons are not possible because the Little report was presented in a different manner from those already cited. The Little report indicates the costs in future dollars (of an unspecified year that is apparently 1981). Little sets prices at $389 per kilowatt for an oil-fired unit, $588 for a coal-fired unit with scrubbers, and $702 per kilowatt for a nuclear unit. The report also suggests that scrubber costs will run around $100 a kilowatt. Thus, in terms of future dollars, the data indicate a coal plant without scrubbers has a cost advantage of more than $200 a kilowatt over a nuclear plant but a $100 cost disadvantage compared to an oil plant. Without trying to reverse the escalation formulas used in the Little report, it can be seen that its figures suggest that coal is worse off relative to oil and better off relative to nuclear power than my figures indicate. Given the wide range of my figures and the material provided for the reader to make further calculations, adjustment for the Little numbers seemed unnecessary at this stage.

Appendix C

THE COST OF SULFUR OXIDE STACK GAS SCRUBBING

An enormous literature exists appraising both quantitatively and qualitatively the economics of stack gas scrubbing systems for power plants. However, three 1973 studies suffice to provide a full review of cost estimates since the reports encompass the range of the prevailing opinion. At one extreme are estimates by a U.S. government study group providing quite low estimates. The direct antithesis appears in a memorandum issued by the Commonwealth Edison Company. An intermediate approach is taken in a paper by two members of the Federal Power Commission staff.

The government group—the Sulfur Oxide Control Technology Assessment Panel (SOCTAP)—presents the costs of six sulfur oxide control methods (see table 7.9). Since one of these processes is much less efficient than the others, it is ignored here. The capital costs of the processes are expected to run from $25 to $41 a kilowatt. At the 18 percent capital charge and 80 percent operating rate the report assumes, the levelized cost ranges from 7.1 to 11.7 cents per million Btu. The total cost is set at 1.1 to 1.5 mills per kwh (12.2 to 16.7 cents/million Btu). This could fall to 1.1 to 1.3 mills per kwh (12.2 to 14.4 cents/million Btu) if credits can be earned by selling recoverable products such as sulfur or sulfuric acid (not shown in table). Retrofitted plants would have capital costs ranging from $45 to $65 (12.8 to 18.6 cents per million Btu levelized costs). Total costs would range from 2.1 to 3.0 mills/kwh (23.3 to 33.3 cents/million Btu) without by-product credit and otherwise 2.1 to 2.7 mills/kwh (23.3 to 30.0 cents/million Btu).

The FPC writers (Gakner and Jimeson, 1973) indicate that with a 64 percent operating rate and 18 percent capital charge, capital costs would range from 1.83 to 2.47 mills, and operating costs would run about 75 percent of capital costs (see table 7.10). This implies operating costs of 1.37 to 1.85 mills per kwh or 15.3 to 20.6 cents per million Btu. Total costs then range from 3.2 to 4.3 mills or 35.6 to 48.0 cents. Assuming operating costs are independent of operating *rates,* the use of an 80 percent operating rate lowers costs to 2.8 to 3.8 mills or $0.31 to $0.43.

The Commonwealth Edison Company has responded to the publicity about scrubber costs by issuing a memorandum outlining its cost estimates for a scrubber it plans to install in a new unit. The memorandum indicated that the scrubber could be purchased for $51–$63 a kilowatt but this is only a part of the capital cost (see table 7.11). Such considerations as indirect expenses, loss of capacity, and interest during construction raise the installed cost of the scrubber to $73–$87 a kilowatt. In addition, a waste treatment system is needed to dispose of what Commonwealth describes as a toothpaste-like residue. Two waste disposal alternatives are conceivable—a treatment plant or a sludge pond. The former involves lower installed capital costs than a pond—$16 vs. $37 to $53 but has much higher operating costs—7 to 10.5 cents per million Btu treated vs. 0.5 cents. In any case, the total installed capital costs would range from $89 to $103 if a treatment plant were built and $110 to $140 if a pond were used. Scrubber operating costs would run $0.11 to $0.15 per million Btu treated.

Thus, if scrubber costs are levelized assuming an 18 percent annual charge and 80 percent plant utilization, the capital costs when treatment

TABLE 7.9
SOCTAP Estimates of Sulfur Oxide Emission Control Costs, by Process Used

	Dry limestone injection	Wet limestone Ca(OH)$_2$ slurry scrubbing	Magnesium oxide scrubbing	Catalytic oxidation	Soluble sodium scrubbing	Double alkali
Percent control efficiency	22–45	80–90	90	85–90	90	90
New plant capital cost dollars/kilowatt[a] cents/million Btu[b]	17	27	33	41	38	25
at 64 percent utilization	6.1	9.6	11.8	14.6	13.6	8.9
at 75 percent utilization	5.2	8.2	10.0	12.5	11.6	7.6
at 80 percent utilization	4.9	7.7	9.4	11.7	10.8	7.1
Operating costs cents/million Btu	1.8	4.5	7.2	5.0	4.7	5.1
Total cost cents/million Btu						
at 64 percent utilization	7.9	14.1	19.0	19.6	18.3	14.0
at 75 percent utilization	7.0	12.7	17.2	17.5	16.3	12.7
at 80 percent utilization	6.7	12.2	16.7	16.7	15.6	12.2
Total cost mills/kwh at 80 percent utilization[a]	0.6	1.1	1.5	1.5	1.4	1.1

	19	46	58	64	65	45
Retrofitted plant capital cost dollars/kilowatt[a] cents/million Btu						
at 50 percent utilization	8.7	21.0	26.5	29.2	29.7	20.5
at 64 percent utilization	6.8	16.4	20.7	22.8	23.2	16.1
at 75 percent utilization	5.8	14.0	17.7	19.5	19.8	13.7
at 80 percent utilization	5.4	13.1	16.6	18.3	18.6	12.8
Operating costs cents/million Btu	3.5	11.3	16.8	10.6	14.8	10.5
Total cost cents/million Btu						
at 50 percent utilization	12.2	32.3	43.3	39.8	44.5	31.0
at 64 percent utilization	10.3	27.7	37.5	33.4	38.0	26.6
at 75 percent utilization	9.3	25.3	34.5	30.1	34.6	24.2
at 80 percent utilization	8.9	24.4	33.3	28.9	33.3	23.3
Total cost mills/kwh at 80 percent utilization[a]	0.8	2.2	3.0	2.6	3.0	2.1

Source: SOCTAP 1973.
[a] These are items explicitly shown in report; all other figures are calculated.
[b] 18 percent capital change.

175

TABLE 7.10

Gakner and Jimeson Estimates of Sulfur Oxide Emission Control Costs

	Low cost	High cost
Capital costs dollars/kilowatt[a]		
Scrubber	45	65
Sludge treatment	12	12
Total	57	77
Capital costs levelized at 64 percent		
Utilization mills/kwh[a]	1.83	2.47
cents/million Btu	20.3	27.4
Levelized at 75 percent cents/million Btu	17.4	23.4
Levilized at 80 percent cents/million Btu	16.3	22.0
Operating cost/(.75 capital cost at 64 percent utilization)[b]	15.3	20.6
Total costs cents/million Btu		
at 64 percent utilization	35.6	48.0
at 75 percent utilization	32.6	44.0
at 80 percent utilization	31.5	42.6

Source: Gakner and Jimeson 1973.
[a] Data in source; other numbers calculated.
[b] 75 percent factor used by Gakner and Jimeson.

plants are used runs from $0.25 to $0.29 per million Btu treated. Adding in the scrubber and treatment plant operating costs raises the total to $0.43–$0.55. The analogous ranges for a scrubber with settling pond are $0.31 to $0.40 for capital and $0.43 to $0.56 for total costs. Commonwealth argues that 80 percent is an unrealistically high operating rate. It suggests that for the first four or five years of a plant's life a 64 percent rate can be maintained but that the rate falls sharply in later years.

Commonwealth's levelized cost data using the 64 percent assumption (and a slightly different approach to levelizing) imply total costs of $0.51 to $0.59 with a treatment plant and $0.52 to $0.63 with a settling pond. Commonwealth suggests that a $0.54 to $0.57 range is most likely. However, in later years costs will rise to match those of a retrofitted plant. A detailed calculation in table 7.11 shows that the range implied by Commonwealth's data extends from $0.70 to $0.91. Again, the memorandum suggests a narrower $0.75 to $0.85 range is more appropriate.

The first point to note about these figures is that the criticism of SOCTAP's methodology implicit in the Commonwealth Edison memorandum seems quite valid. Whether the numbers Commonwealth proposes are correct is more difficult to determine. Therefore, for present purposes, I employ a range of scrubber costs of $0.15 to $0.57 for new plants and $0.30 to $0.85 for retrofitting. The lows are roughly equal to the average of the figures (without sulfur by-product credits) presented by SOCTAP; the highs are the highest numbers used by Commonwealth Edison. Since the cost range encompasses the influence of differences in operating rates, no further adjustments for such differences in operating rates are needed.

In using these figures, it is also imperative to recall the arguments discussed in chapter 6 about when satisfactory scrubber technology would be perfected. All the data in this appendix relate to a process that everyone agrees remains unperfected. Debate is considerable whether the remaining problems are minor or require many years to resolve.

Addendum. Since this was written, the EPA has continued to insist and most utilities have persisted in denying that scrubbers are nearly perfected. The most recent process attracting attention is one developed by General Motors. Phone discussions in May 1974 with people involved in the project indicated that it was not fully perfected. Cost data provided by General Motors (Phillips, 1974) indicated a cost of $10 per ton or for the 12,500 Btu/pound coal used, $0.40 per million Btu treated. However, the capital cost estimate of $0.17/billion Btu included only depreciation and, given the estimated $80 per kilowatt, capital cost levelizes to $0.24/million Btu if a 75 percent plant utilization rate prevails and to $0.29/million Btu if a 64 percent plant utilization rate prevails. Therefore, total costs would range between $0.47 and $0.52/million Btu. This suggests that EPA endorsement of the General Motors process implicitly represents acceptance of utility criticism that prior EPA cost estimates were far too low.

TABLE 7.11
Commonwealth Edison Estimates of Sulfur Oxide Emission Control
(dollars/kilowatt)

	Treatment plant		Settling pond	
	Low	High	Low	High
a. Capital costs				
Direct scrubber cost	51	63	51	63
Direct waste disposal facility cost	10	10	26	36
Total direct cost[a]	61	73	77	99
Scrubber cost including indirect	73	87	73	87
Waste disposal cost including indirect	16	16	37	53
Total direct and indirect costs	89	103	110	140

(*Continued*)

TABLE 7.11 *Continued*

	Treatment plant		settling pond	
	Low	High	Low	High

b. Levelized costs as computed by Commonwealth Edison—new plant 64 percent utilization

	(cents/million Btu)			
Scrubber levelized capital costs	27.0	28.0	27.0	28.0
Waste treatment levelized capital costs	5.5	5.5	13.0	19.0
Total levelized capital cost[a]	32.5	33.5	40.0	47.0
Operating costs				
Scrubber	11.0	15.0	11.0	15.0
Waste treatment	7.0	10.5	.5	.5
Total operating costs	18.0	25.5	11.5	15.5
Total costs	50.5	59.0	51.5	62.5

c. Levelized costs as computed by Commonwealth Edison—older plant utilization

	(cents/million Btu)			
Scrubber levelized capital costs	43.0	45.0	43.0	45.0
Waste treatment levelized capital costs	9.0	9.0	20.0	30.0
Total levelized capital costs[a]	52.0	54.0	63.0	75.0
Total operating costs[a]	18.0	25.5	11.5	15.5
Total costs	70.0	79.5	74.5	90.5

d. Levelized costs for new plants adjusted to higher operating rate assumptions

Total levelized capital costs at:				
75 percent utilization	27.1	31.4	33.5	42.6
80 percent utilization	25.4	29.4	31.4	40.0
Total costs at:[b]				
75 percent utilization	45.1	56.9	45.0	58.1
80 percent utilization	43.4	54.9	42.9	55.5

Source: Commonwealth Edison 1973.

[a] Actual sum of components, Commonwealth reports slightly different sums.

[b] Sum of total levelized capital costs and total operating costs given in section C above.

Appendix D

THE ECONOMICS OF A SULFUR TAX

Two approaches are possible in analyzing a sulfur or other effluent tax. One can first postulate specific goals such as forcing immediate adoption of scrubbers or their use only in new plants. Then the tax can be made high enough to exceed the cost of using a scrubber. Alternatively, a tax rate could be set and its implications considered. The basis for the first approach has already been provided by the review of scrubber costs. This appendix, therefore, can discuss only the implications of specific tax rates. Those chosen for review are those proposed by the U.S. government.

The Nixon Administration originally proposed a tax that would start at a penny a pound of sulfur contained in the fuel in 1972 and rise to $0.10 a pound by 1976. Refunds would be provided in proportion to the sulfur level equivalent of the emission control employed. A more complex alternative was proposed in 1972. A three-level system was to take effect in 1976. Regions would be classified on the basis of their compliance in 1975 with air quality standards (see chapter 6). No tax would prevail if all standards were met; a $0.10 a pound tax would be charged if the primary—but not secondary standards—were met; if neither standard was attained, a $0.15 tax would prevail.

Clearly the impact of this system would be widely variable—particularly when applied to coal. Both sulfur and heat contents of particular coals differ considerably so that, with any given tax rate, different coals would have quite different taxes per million Btu. Similarly, it is not yet clear exactly what reduction of sulfur emissions and, therefore, of taxes would be secured from a stack scrubber.

For present purposes, it seems desirable to deal with a few illustrative cases to demonstrate the possibilities. Sulfur levels in coal range from around 0.5 percent for the best western resources and, for limited amounts of eastern coal, to levels in excess of 4 percent. Thus, a $0.10 per pound sulfur tax would lead to taxes between $1 to $8 a ton; a $0.15 tax, $1.50 to $12.

The cost per million Btu is further affected by differences in heat contents of the coals. Thus, the western coals may have contents of only 8,500 Btu per pound. A 0.5 percent sulfur western coal would bear a $0.06 per million Btu tax if a $0.10 per pound rate applied; $0.09, if a $0.15 rate prevailed. Representative figures for the Middle West might be 4 percent sulfur and 10,500 Btu per pound. Thus, the $0.10 per pound tax is $8 a ton or $0.38 per million Btu; this rises to $0.57 with a $0.15 per pound tax rate. Alternatively we might have a 3 percent sulfur 12,000 Btu per pound Appalachian coal. At the $0.10 a pound rate, the tax is $6 per ton of coal or $0.25 per million Btu; the tax per million Btu rises to $0.38 if the tax becomes $0.15 per pound of sulfur.

Similarly, typical figures are that residual fuel oil contains around 2.5 percent sulfur, weighs 331 pounds, and contains about 6.3 million Btu. Thus, a barrel contains about 8 pounds of sulfur and bears an $0.83 tax at the $0.10 rate and $1.24, at $0.15. The corresponding costs per million Btu are $0.13 and $0.20. Low-sulfur oil has a content of around 0.3 percent sulfur but is lighter and has a lower heat content (about 6 million Btu per barrel). It contains less than a pound of sulfur. The tax can roughly be set at $0.02 per million Btu when the $0.10 per pound tax rate prevails and $0.03, when $0.15 per pound is charged.

Finally, since no emission control method is perfectly effective, installation of such approaches reduces rather than eliminates the tax. This is obvious when the strategy is to switch to a lower sulfur fuel. The tax falls from the level on the old fuel to the level on the new one. Such savings are listed in table 7.2 for the critical cases. The table also shows the savings due to use of stack gas scrubbers using the SOCTAP assumption of 90 percent efficiency.

Appendix E

NEW TECHNOLOGIES FOR FOSSIL-FUEL GENERATION
OF ELECTRICITY

Numerous concepts for new technologies to generate electricity from fossil fuels are discussed in the literature, and each has its own devoted adherents. However, attention here is confined to a single alternative—the advanced combined cycle. This approach involves coupling a gas turbine to a waste heat utilization system to secure increased overall thermal efficiency.

The choice of emphasis is dictated by three main, interrelated considerations. The technique seems to have secured at least as much favor as any alternative discussed in the literature. The basic concept is already in use, and the proposed improvements seem reasonably well assured. Extensive, if somewhat obsolete, data are available on prospective costs. The last condition arises precisely because the developments are relatively straightforward extrapolations of proven technology. This certainty and the quantification it permits are clearly a major cause for the selection of this example. In any case, the combined cycle illustrates a general property of new fossil-fuel-based systems of power generation that is critical here—the need to transform coal before use in generation.

The interest in the combined cycle is largely due to an extensive report by the United Aircraft Research Laboratories for the National Air Pollution Control Administration. This report provided an exhaustive review of the possibilities of the combined cycle and of securing the fuel it required.[6]

---

[6] The acceptance of the report seems to have secured, as represented by the treatment of combined cycles in the various appraisals of new technology cited here, is all the more remarkable considering that United Aircraft's Pratt and Whitney Division is a leading manufacturer of gas turbines. In another report, United Aircraft proposed the use of the gas turbine alone as a way to avoid thermal pollution of water (United Aircraft Research Laboratories, 1971).

Briefly, the critical element of the analysis is that already realized, and prospective improvements in aircraft engine performance could, when incorporated into industrial steam turbines, greatly improve their technical and economic characteristics. Such changes as improved materials that would permit turbine inlet temperatures to rise to 3,100 degrees by the 1990s would lead to greatly increased thermal efficiencies. The first generation of gas turbines available in the 1970s would have 35.2 percent efficiencies—a heat rate of about 9,700 Btu. Efficiency would rise to 41.5 percent (about 8,200) in the 1980s and reach 43.6 percent (about 7,800) by the 1990s (p. 259).

The inlet temperatures in all generations are significantly higher than fossil plant steam temperatures, but so are the turbine gas exit temperatures—another major influence on thermal efficiency. Indeed, these exit temperatures are high enough to justify use of the waste heat in a recovery system involving a heat recovery boiler and steam turbine. To improve system performance, the gas turbines operate at slightly lower thermal efficiencies in the combined cycle than when used alone. The rates are 27.3 percent in the 1970s, 34.2 in the 1980s, and 40.4 in the 1990s. This is more than offset by the benefits of waste heat recovery that raises overall power plant thermal efficiencies to 47.0 percent (7,250 Btu), 54.5 percent (6,250), and 57.7 (5,900) respectively (p. 278). The NPC (1972, p. 233) sees 1972 efficiencies as 40 percent and expects a rise to 48 percent by 1985.

A final potential advantage of the combined cycle is that it has lower capital costs than a conventional steam turbine plant. Moreover, this cost advantage could widen over time. Combined cycle plants could be largely manufactured in factories so that a much smaller portion of the work would involve on-site construction. The greater possibilities for productivity advance in manufacturing than in construction would cause more favorable cost trends for the combined cycle than for conventional plants.

The basic difficulty with widespread use of combined cycles is the need for clean fuels. Traditionally gas turbines were powered only with middle distillate fuel oil or natural gas. More recently methods are being developed to treat residual fuel oils to permit their use in gas turbines. Numerous future fuel choice options might emerge. It is possible to imagine conditions in which natural gas and distillate fuel oil prove the cheapest combined cycle fuel. However, the standard presumption in public discussions is that either treated residual fuel oil or synthetic gas from coal or oil will be the preferable fuels. This view is employed here.

It may also be noted that because of losses in the fuel conversion process a combined cycle plant using low Btu gas would have lower overall efficiencies than those of the power plant. The figures for overall efficiency when coal gasification is involved for the three generations postulated by United Aircraft are 36.1, 47.6, and 49.9 percent (Robson, p. 403–8). The

NPC (1972, p. 233) similarly sees a 1982 efficiency of 40 percent and a 1992 level of 48 percent.

Since the United Aircraft data are now obsolete because of the subsequent sharp rises in prices, some adjustments are necessary. Unfortunately, little more than a few price quotations for current combined cycle plants are available. One manufacturer indicated in a phone conversation that his 1973 price quotation ran $130 a kilowatt installed for a combined cycle plant. This contrasts to the $89 a kilowatt figure used in the United Aircraft report (p. 418–19). However, it is not clear that all this difference is due to inflation; another industry source suggested that the original estimates may have been somewhat unrealistic even as an indicator of 1969 costs.

Nevertheless, for present purposes, a cost range of $150–$250 a kilowatt is assumed for the combined cycle. The lower figure accepts the view that technical progress will keep the costs of a combined cycle plant from rising more rapidly than 2 percent a year from its 1973 level, even when changes to improve thermal efficiency are incorporated. The $250 a kilowatt estimate is based on the pessimistic assumption of continuation of the nearly 10 percent a year increase from 1969 to 1973 implied if the $89 a kilowatt estimate for 1969 were an accurate measure of true prevailing prices. The choice is arbitrary but may be justified by arguing that unexpected difficulties in improvement of the thermal efficiency of the combined cycle may have the same effects as recent inflation.

The most convenient way to develop figures on the capital cost differential between the combined cycle and other plant types is to use the respective absolute per kilowatt price estimates of Appendix B—$390–$450 for nuclear, $350 for coal and $300 for oil. The respective differences between the combined cycle and each of the other plant types are $140–$300 a kilowatt compared to nuclear, $100–$200 a kilowatt, to a conventional coal plant without scrubber, and $50–$150, to a conventional oil plant.

Before presenting the levelized data, it may be noted that United Aircraft estimates that nonfuel operating costs are 0.3 mills/kwh or $0.03 per 111 kilowatt hours higher than other plants. A further refinement of charging the plant for the capacity used to gasify when synthetic fuels are used is ignored here since its effect is implicitly handled by the broad range used. Thus, the net levelized cost advantages consist of the capital cost advantage less the operating cost advantages. Table 7.5 lists the relevant breakeven prices implied. It also uses the fuel price assumptions of table 7.1 to determine, on the basis for the formulas in chapter 5, implied synthetic gas prices per million Btu of gas. Using the calculation method outlined in Appendix B, these are then converted to prices per 111 kilowatts generated by the combined cycle.

8

Forecasts of Coal Consumption: 1980, 1985, and 1990

INTRODUCTION

The prior chapter suggests that forecasts of electric utility coal consumption levels cannot be meaningfully constructed. For that matter, it would be incredibly difficult even to trace the consequences of the different cost assumptions of chapter 7. This chapter, therefore, takes the alternative approach of developing the argument that the standard coal forecast for 1980 does not account for problems created by prevailing environmental policies. This will be done by examining a typical example of the standard forecast, comparing some of its elements and conclusions to other studies, and suggesting the probable errors.

SELECTED FORECASTS
OF ELECTRIC UTILITY CONSUMPTION
OF COAL

The forecast chosen as representative was undertaken as part of this coal research project in a thesis by Charles J. Johnson.[1] He was particularly careful in developing and specifying a logically complete forecasting model. Before reviewing his work, it is useful to outline the structure of his model. The basic questions are the levels of electric power to be generated, the capacities of each type of plant available to meet demands, their operating rates, and the amounts of fuel each plant uses per unit of output. The answers to these questions combine to determine total fuel use so we may now examine how he handled these issues.

To appraise Johnson's electric power demand forecasts, it is necessary to review the basic controversies about such projections and the other studies that have been made. A growing current tendency exists to attack these usual forecasts for failing to consider reduction of demands on environmental or cost increase grounds, but Johnson chose to ignore this problem and tried a more traditional approach. However, he was confronted with a

---

[1] The author, therefore, must assume considerable responsibility for the design and results; the criticism that follows simply reflects the fact the data that become available after Johnson completed his work necessitated a revised outlook.

long-standing problem in electric power forecasting—the extent to which electric power can continue growing at historic rates. No sector can grow forever at a rate in excess of that for the total economy. Indefinite continuation of a higher growth rate means the part eventually would be bigger than the whole—a logical absurdity. Thus, forecasters often assume a slowdown in growth of electric power production and often have been premature. Johnson, therefore, chose to deal with the case in which at least recent trends continued. In particular, he simply fitted trend lines to recent data and used their extrapolations for forecasts.[2]

This may be compared to other forecasts available to Johnson. The only detailed projections available were those from the *1970 National Power Survey* (which were separately released well before the issue of the survey). The *Power Survey* forecast for 1980 was for about 3.1 trillion kilowatt hours, which was significantly higher than most of the forecasts for 1980 made during the sixties (see EEI, 1969); the *1964 Power Survey,* for example, set 1980 output at 2.7 trillion kilowatt hours. Johnson's estimate—3.26 trillion kilowatt hours—exceeded the *1970 Power Survey* estimate by 6 percent but is roughly equal to that of Gerard Gambs of Ford, Bacon, and Davis who estimated an output of 3.3 trillion kilowatt hours (1970b). However, other readily available forecasts for 1990 are lower than Johnson's because the others expect a growth slowdown. Thus, the respective estimates are 7.1 trillion by Johnson, 6.4 by Gambs, and 5.8 by the *1970 National Power Survey.* Thus, Johnson's estimate is about 21 percent above that of the *Power Survey* and 11 percent above Gambs' number. Many observers would, therefore, consider Johnson's numbers as far too high; indeed some consider the *Power Survey* figures as overly optimistic (see the discussion on forecasting in volume 4 of the survey). The Johnson figures can be defended, however, as providing the basis of forecasts of coal use that cover all conceivable favorable developments including higher than expected demands.

In moving to coal forecasts, it may first be noted that clearly coal use will be confined to plants equipped for its use. Future capacity can be divided into three basic groups—the portion of presently existing capacity that is not retired, the capacity already ordered, and capacity yet to be ordered. In each case, only part of the capacity will have coal-burning capacity. The forecast of survival of existing coal plants was made by assuming retirements would follow their historical trend; this approach was selected after testing several alternatives.

The commitments for new coal plants were then determined from the

[2] He explored various time series and finally chose a synthetic series consisting of actual data for 1960–1969 and FPC forecasts for 1970–1972. Since he was using a deliberately naive method, he used the naive criterion of better fit to select this time series.

literature. Similar calculations indicated the probable surviving capacity of old noncoal plants and of capacity on order of such plants. From all this, Johnson could determine how much additional capacity remained to be ordered. He than made various assumptions about coal's share of these orders. For the eastern portion of the country (i.e., FPC Regions I–IV), this was done by estimates of the viability of coal in different markets. Four cases were employed. In each case, each electric power company was assumed to buy coal plants if its expected future coal cost was below the estimated breakeven price. The individual cases combined different pairs of assumptions about the actual and breakeven prices. For example, in the case most favorable to coal, each company was assumed to be able to supply new plants with coal at a cost $0.03 above that company's average coal cost in 1969; the breakeven price was set at $0.42 (based on a $120 a kilowatt difference between capital costs of a nuclear plant without scrubber and $0.11 per million Btu levelized scrubbing costs). In his next most favorable case, he lowered the breakeven price to 32.6 cents and assumed a $0.05 coal price rise. The other two cases involved further breakeven price drops and actual coal price rises sufficient to make coal plants uneconomic. For the rest of the country, he simply assumed plausible but arbitrary shares for coal plants of future orders. For example, in FPC Region V (roughly the South Central States and part of Missouri) he used ratios of 25, 10, and 5 percent. This reflects rough evaluations of the prospects of local coals and purchases from the West. Different ratios reflecting local conditions were used for other regions.

Heat rate and coal Btu content assumptions were then made for each region, and a variety of plant utilization assumptions were employed. Only these last need explicit discussion here. He established a dichotomy between plants already operating and those, ordered or unordered, yet to operate. The first were expected to have gradual declines in operating rates. The others were expected to be less flexible (see chapter 7) and thus have a steady operating rate.

Operating rate declines are difficult to measure from existing data. Age figures reported by the FPC relate to plants, and these may include subsequently added units. Indeed, the bulk of the capacity often consists of such units. Thus, the historical behavior of plant operating rates is the net effect of declines for each unit and the periodic addition of new units. Johnson, nevertheless, attempted to use this historical record as a basis for projecting declines. He correlated FPC data on age with operating rates of plants and determined that each one year rise in age lowered operating rates 0.72 percent. Projections of utilization using this rate assume that new units will continue to be added to these plants, but in practice it is inordinately difficult to determine how much new capacity actually is added to old plants. To compensate roughly for this problem, Johnson examined the consequences of a decline in operating rates double that indicated by the regression analysis.

While he assumed that new plants would operate at some constant rate, Johnson recognized that several different assumptions could be made about the particular level of that rate. He explored three cases—a nationwide rate of 65 percent, a combination of a 70 percent rate in FPC Regions I–IV, and 75 percent elsewhere, and a uniform 75 percent national rate. Table 8.1 shows the implications of this approach. Line one shows coal use of existing plants using his assumption of utilization declines double the computed rate. To this, line two adds coal use in plants on order, assuming 65 percent utilization. The sum, shown in line three, amounts to 441 million tons in 1980 and 391 million in 1990. Line four then shows the coal use if old plant utilization only falls 0.72 percent a year. Line five gives coal use for plants on order if they maintain 70 percent utilization in the East and 75 percent in the West. The total (line six) is 488 million in 1980 and 464 million in 1990. Further calculations, not shown here, added the impacts of both the assumption of 75 percent utilization nationwide and additional orders of coal plants. Johnson calculated that maximum success in meeting nuclear competition would raise the 1980 total to 566 million tons but hypothesized that a 515 million ton figure was most probable. In short, his model indicates that the great bulk of 1980 coal use will be in plants existing or already ordered, and at best subsequent orders would have a modest effect on the total. Of course, newly ordered plants will make a much greater contribution to 1990 electric power output. Should coal manage to conquer its competition, its consumption would hit 1.4 billion tons. Johnson, however, estimated that 650 million was a more probable level.

Johnson's forecasts are quite similar to many others issued around the same time period. The *National Power Survey* projected that electric utility coal use would be 500 million tons in 1980 and 700 million in 1990 (p. I–1–20).

The National Petroleum Council released in 1971 a massive study of prospective energy market trends assuming "unchanged" policies. This essentially seems to have meant continued gas price control and preservation of the implicit policy of allowing oil imports to rise to cover excess demands in the U.S. The study was broken up into task forces, and each followed a somewhat independent course, which precludes an accurate synthesis.

The coal task force sets 1980 coal consumption by electric utilities at 525 million tons and 1985 consumption at 654 million (vol. 2, p. 128). The forecast was prepared by accepting the demand task force estimate that electric power output would grow at an average annual rate of 7.2 percent.

TABLE 8.1

Forecasts of Coal Consumption by FPC Regions in Existing and Ordered Power Plants, 1980 and 1990

(*million tons*)

Forecast	Region								Total
	I	II	III	IV	V	VI	VII	VIII	
1969 Actual	49.7	106.8	78.0	51.9	4.6	9.8	1.9	3.8	306.5
Forecasts for 1980									
1. Lower forecast of coal use in existing plants	41.3	88.1	64.3	42.8	3.8	8.1	1.5	3.1	253.0
2. Lower forecast of coal use in plants on order	12.7	70.6	39.4	25.2	10.9	4.2	12.3	12.3	187.6
3. Total (1 + 2)[a]	54.0	158.7	103.7	68.0	14.7	12.3	13.8	15.4	440.6
4. Higher forecasts of coal use in existing plants	45.3	97.5	71.2	47.3	4.2	9.0	1.7	3.5	279.7
5. Higher forecasts of coal use in plants on order	13.7	76.1	45.5	27.2	12.6	4.9	14.2	14.2	208.4
6. Total (4 + 5)	59.0	173.6	116.7	74.5	16.8	13.9	15.9	17.7	488.1
Forecasts for 1990									
1. Lower forecast of coal use in existing plants	33.0	71.0	51.9	34.5	3.1	6.5	1.2	2.5	203.7
2. Lower forecast of coal use in plants on order	12.7	70.6	39.4	25.2	10.9	4.2	12.3	12.3	187.6
3. Total (1 + 2)	45.7	141.6	91.3	59.7	14.0	10.7	13.5	14.8	391.3
4. Higher forecast of coal use in existing plants	41.4	88.9	64.9	43.2	3.8	8.2	1.6	3.2	255.2
5. Higher forecast of coal use in plants on order	13.7	76.1	45.5	27.2	12.6	4.9	14.2	14.2	208.4
6. Total (4 + 5)	55.1	165.0	110.4	70.4	16.4	13.1	15.8	17.4	463.6

Source: Worksheets of Charles J. Johnson.

[a] Figures in parentheses refer to line numbers within this table.

Nuclear output was deduced by assuming respective capacities of 127 and 251 million kilowatts in 1980 and 1985 and 74 percent utilization. The remaining output was allocated on the basis of capabilities of plants existing, or on order, to use different fuels and appraisals of the probable choice of fuel in new plants.

In the 1972 NPC final report, four different models of electric utility coal use were considered. One case was the possibility of maintaining consumption at the 1970 level because of environmental pressures. In another case, considered "*most feasible* from the point of view of electric utilities," consumption rises to 14.3 quadrillion Btu by 1980 and falls to 13.9 quadrillion in 1985. Using a 24 million Btu per ton conversion factor, this implies 596 million tons in 1980 and 579 in 1985. A pattern associated with heavier reliance on nuclear power in 1985 involves a 15.6 quadrillion Btu–650 million ton level of electric utility coal consumption in 1980. In anticipation of post-1980 availability of nuclear plants, lesser shifts to oil and gas occur. By 1985 coal consumption would fall to 12.5 quadrillion Btu or 521 million tons. In the case of a moratorium on nuclear plant building after 1980, 1980 consumption would be at 15.6 quadrillion Btu (650 million tons) but would rise to 21.5 quadrillion Btu or 894 million tons in 1985.

Similarly, the U.S. Department of Interior (1972, p. 16–17) projects 1980 electric utility consumption of coal of 10.7 quadrillion Btu or 460 million tons. This would rise to 14.2 quadrillion Btu or 613 million tons by 1985.[3] Less optimistic figures were prepared by National Economic Research Associates (NERA). It predicts 1980 electric utility coal consumption of 442 million tons and 471 million in 1985 (p. 29).

Gerard Gambs (1970b), in contrast, has argued that the pressures of nuclear competition and environmental regulations would cause electric power industry coal use to fall. He predicted coal use would reach its peak of 330 million tons in 1975 and begin a decline. His forecast for 1980 was 280 million tons; declines would continue to 1984 when a level of 240 million tons would be reached. Electric power coal use would then be stable until 1995, when consumption would fall—to 160 million tons in 2000.

His initial forecast assumed that oil would be the main beneficiary of this fall in coal use, but that after 1977 nuclear capacity additions would be proceeding at a pace that would also cause oil use to decline. The subsequent delays in nuclear plants have caused him to revise this appraisal. His position seems to be that the thrust of public policy is inspiring a level of oil use that may cause balance of payments problems (Gambs, 1972).

EVALUATION OF THE FORECASTS

The factors on the new plant purchase side that tended to be ignored include both the economic considerations discussed in chapter 7 and political

---

[3] The report presented both the tonnage and Btu figures.

barriers. For example, the EPA standards discussed in chapter 6 cannot yet be met with a coal-fired plant, and many pressures are arising to halt construction of further mine mouth plants in the Southwest. The net impact may be to encourage both nuclear plant building and, where time permits only a fossil plant, adoption of the oil alternative. This is most likely to occur in the eastern half of the United States and on the West Coast, for reasons discussed in chapter 7. Whether 1973 proposals to alleviate these pressures will be adopted, remains unclear. In what follows, I presume such efforts will be abortive. Clearly, the concerns expressed in the slogan "Project Independence" could alleviate the pressure on coal.

By and large, however, nuclear decisions since Johnson's work was completed have largely been ones that were predicted by his analysis. The main exceptions are that both Union Electric and Illinois Power, companies with fairly good proximity to coal, have announced their first nuclear plants for 1980 operation (see Appendix).

However, announcements of oil plant construction have occurred in many former totally coal-using regions. Pennsylvania Power and Light plans to construct two 800 megawatt (mw) oil units for 1975 and 1977 use; a pipeline will be constructed to serve the plant. Metropolitan Edison in Pennsylvania also plans oil use. In 1974 Niagara Mohawk in upstate New York added an 825 mw oil unit to its Oswego plant.

Consumers Power in Michigan plans two 600 mw plus oil units for 1975 and 1976, and Detroit Edison will add 800 mw in 1978. Commonwealth Edison in Chicago will oil fire three 500 mw units for use in 1977, 1978, and 1979. South Carolina Gas and Electric will add two 600 mw oil units in 1973 and 1979, and at least one of Carolina Power's additions will include oil firing capabilities.

Just how much oil conversion is likely is unclear at least outside the Northeast. Here, it is quite apparent by now that only the mine mouth plants in Pennsylvania have a high probability of continued coal use. Conversions have already become widespread, and the plans for oil use elsewhere in inland eastern Pennsylvania may well extend eventually to old plants.

Elsewhere, it would be fatuous to guess the exact combination of scrubbing technology and economics, fuel prices, and public policy that will prevail. However, the prior discussions suggest that it would certainly be quite likely that considerable conversions could occur. The main possible exceptions are areas near the western coal fields and the markets identified in chapter 7 where western coal might compete.

Such possibilities provide the basis only for general expectations about the basic direction of coal use to 1980 but leave the actual magnitudes quite uncertain. Clearly, public policy will greatly influence the outcome, and it seems desirable to design policy to handle developments most effectively.

Under some circumstances, an immediate shift away from coal could prove intolerably expensive or even physically impossible.

Thus, what we need clearly is, not a better forecast, but public policies that are flexible enough to adapt to these developments. As chapter 1 indicated, many observers feel that the principle of a sulfur tax may be an attractive one for providing the desired flexibility. All that must be added here to the debate over the most appropriate level of the tax, is recognition of the implications of the analysis in chapter 7. It was suggested that the tax probably would only encourage an accelerated shift to nuclear power or oil. Clearly, the wisdom of limiting pressures to this level can only be evaluated when the urgency of abatement has been more explicitly determined. Should the pace prove intolerably slow, a higher tax rate could be adopted.

A coal comeback could be effected by 1990, but this requires substantial success with new technology and other elements of good luck. Indeed, the best advice for 1990 is that we should carefully follow actual developments and be able to move rapidly into what really proves the socially preferable pattern.

Appendix[4]

NOTES ON NUCLEAR COMMITMENTS
BY MAJOR UTILITIES

Practically all the logically possible patterns of commitment to nuclear power ranging from plans for total reliance on it for new base load plants to noninvolvement were prevailing in 1973. However, the basic models of participation were:

1. A few companies, TVA, Duke, and Virginia Electric and Power, hope to stop building base load fossil plants by the middle seventies and rely on nuclear power for new capacity.
2. A somewhat larger group of companies is heavily committed to nuclear power but, probably because of nuclear delays, has decided also to build fossil plants in the late seventies.
3. Companies that made relatively early commitments to nuclear power but have no nuclear plants scheduled for the late seventies.
4. Companies that announced since 1971 that they would build their first nuclear plants for operation in the early eighties.
5. The special case of the Wisconsin companies and Northern State Power in Minnesota. These companies were until 1973 examples of model 3, but then they announced nuclear plants for the 1980s.

Where nuclear commitments are heavy, most companies, nevertheless,

[4] This section is based on the September 1973 list of nuclear plants, existing, ordered, or announced, issued by the AEC (Wash 1208, 9–73) and 1972 annual reports of the companies.

are likely to have found it necessary to include base load fossil plants in their construction plans for the late seventies. This pattern characterizes the overall situation in New England, New York, the Pennsylvania-New Jersey-Maryland (PJM) power pool, and the Pacific States. (The PJM pool encompasses the eastern half of Pennsylvania, all of Delaware, the District of Columbia, and most of Maryland except for the portion served by the Allegheny System.)

The rest of Pennsylvania and Maryland and West Virginia are best treated together with the East North Central States. Here the degree of nuclear involvement ranges quite broadly. Three groups meet the criterion of heavy but incomplete commitment—the Capco group of companies in western Pennsylvania and northern Ohio, Detroit Edison, and Consumers Power in Michigan, which plan joint construction programs, and Commonwealth Edison. Otherwise, the companies had by 1973 either made only a limited relatively early commitment or just announced their first nuclear plants. The Wisconsin situation was outlined above. A number of companies, most notably American Electric Power, have only ordered one or two nuclear plants for the early or middle seventies. A major total holdout from nuclear power is the Allegheny System. As noted above, Illinois Power is one of those announcing its first nuclear plants in 1972.

In the West North Central States, again the situation is quite mixed. The Minnesota situation was explained above. Union Electric in Missouri and the Kansas City Electric Company in conjunction with a company in Kansas have announced their first nuclear plants for the 1980s. Two Nebraska plants were ordered for the early seventies.

In the South Atlantic States not already discussed, nuclear is predominant. It was noted that two companies in this region expect to stop building base load fossil plants by the middle seventies; the remaining major companies have heavy but not total commitment to nuclear power for the late seventies.

The main consideration in the East South Central region is TVA's plans to move rapidly into nuclear power. In addition, the Southern Company follows the pattern of a heavy but incomplete nuclear commitment.

Until 1972, Middle South Utilities was the only West South Central region company with a heavy commitment to nuclear power. Subsequently, practically all the major companies have announced plants for 1979 or later. These companies include Texas Utilities, Gulf States Utilities, Houston Lighting and Power, and Central and Southwest.

Finally, through the 1970s nuclear power in the Mountain States will be limited to the gas-cooled Fort Saint Vrain reactor in Colorado. However, Arizona Public Service, Tucson Gas and Electric, Public Service of New Mexico, and the Salt River Project announced in 1973 that they would jointly build three 1270 megawatt plants for completion in 1981, 1983, and 1985.

9

Summary and Conclusions

This study has developed the argument that the widespread belief in the likelihood of substantial growth in coal output rests on a weak basis. In fact, the dual threats of rising costs of coal mining and severe environmental restraints on coal production and use may cause a decline in coal consumption. In summary, optimism about coal implicitly involves a variety of presumptions that, while they may be valid, are quite difficult to substantiate.

First, even the optimists recognize that a massive research program would be required to develop better methods to mine and use coal. However, little evidence is available that, even if the support is forthcoming, it will lead to the expected success. Second, the case for coal also rests heavily on the presumption that society will not impose environmental restrictions that seriously impede its competitive position. Again this is a difficult argument to settle. Given the stress on massive strip mining ventures for synthetic fuels, the industry, for example, may prove extremely vulnerable to objections to land disturbance. Finally, and probably most critically, the case for coal centers on expectations of sharply rising costs for rival fuels. Again, counterarguments exist. Should they be correct, this also will aggravate the problems in the realm of research and environmental policies. Funding of research will be less generous, and the accomplishments must be greater to overcome the competition. Similarly, the availability of cheaper fuels will encourage more stringent environmental regulation of coal.

In interpreting the present study, it is critical to recognize the limitations of the scenarios presented. A particularly important point is to note the implications of significant departures from the assumptions used. Three points are critical here—the development of oil supplies, the state of nuclear power, and the nature of environmental problems in coal use.

As has been pointed out in chapters 5 and 7, even if oil prices are significantly higher than those used for illustrative purposes, coal will face substantial difficulties competing in either electric power generation or as a source of close substitutes for crude oil and natural gas. The situation is clearer in the latter case since oil shale competition is so formidable a barrier. The prospects are better but far from assured in the electric power realm.

Neglect of problems in using nuclear power is the logical approach for a study stressing the difficulties facing coal. Clearly, pressures on coal would be greatly alleviated if society discovers that nuclear power is an unsatisfactory energy source. The concerns about nuclear power are far from frivolous, so that one cannot dismiss the possibility of a radical change in policy. However, conversely, the evidence is not so clear that we can be confident of such a reversal. At present, nuclear power remains likely to continue to provide formidable competition for coal, and the prudent assumption is that nuclear power is a relevant option.

Finally, the study has dealt only with the two most tractable cases related to the environmental problems of coal use. The case stressed is that in which stringent environmental regulations and the technology to meet them are both available. However, the implications of removal of sulfur controls were also considered.

In the environmental case and for that matter in the whole study, none of the calculations is a forecast of future developments. On the one hand, the basic argument is that forecasting is inappropriate since the uncertainties are so great. Only suggestions of possible outcomes are relevant. Moreover, the actual outcome depends upon public policies. No analyst can do more than show the possible consequences of different policy postures and leave to the decision makers the choice of an optimal approach. Thus, in the case of environmental problems of coal use, there is the possibility that high scrubber costs or even failure to develop scrubber technology may cause a radical change in sulfur standards or at least a delay in their implementation.

In short, economic and political trends prevailing up to 1973 were seriously worsening the competitive position of coal, not improving it. One cannot be confident either that the trends that depend purely on technical and market developments will reverse, or that public policy should and will alter to change conditions drastically. While considerable debate prevails about the precise form present policies have taken, by and large it is agreed that those affecting coal use have largely been directed at significant problems. Therefore, despite all the limitations of the present study, largely reflecting our limited ability to forecast, it can be reasonably concluded that the future of coal can be bright only if radical policy changes occur and prove highly successful.

As chapter 1 noted, this book is not a complete study of these global and nearly impossible-to-resolve issues. It has the more modest aims of showing the role of coal in U.S. electrical power markets and the policies that influence the position of coal. Stress is on forces within the coal markets.

Both the history of coal use since 1946 and the problems that plague its prospects were examined. However, chapters 1 and 5 did provide a brief overview of some of the broader forces at work, and these should be recalled here. It was pointed out that physical supplies of energy are so ample that physical exhaustion is not a meaningful problem. What is critical is the market price of using these resources. Even here, at least until well into the 1980s, the main threat to prices comes from successful efforts of foreign oil producing countries to keep prices well above costs rather than from rising costs. A further major problem is the existence of a complex assortment of energy policies that may increasingly threaten the ability of energy markets to function effectively.

In summarizing this study, it may be useful to deal with each market issue as it applies to all sectors, rather than sector by sector. Thus, first, the structure of coal markets may be reviewed. Then the policies affecting coal may be summarized. This allows review of historical performance since 1946 and future prospects. In conclusion, some suggestions for further research and public policy may be provided. The discussion here is deliberately qualitative. There are no key numbers in which to restate the argument. The specific data are best left in context so that they are read in conjunction with the caveats surrounding them.

In chapter 3, it was shown that a fairly large number of firms supplied coal in the United States. It was noted that several of the largest firms in the coal industry had been purchased by oil companies and other firms. It was suggested, however, that these purchases had no perceptible effect on competition. In no case did the resulting energy company obtain a large share of the combined market for oil and coal. None of the biggest oil companies bought one of the biggest coal companies. Chapter 2 showed that in the electric utility market the coal was purchased by a fairly small group of companies. The evidence on buying practices (chapter 3) suggests, moreover, that utilities have aggressively and successfully sought to develop advantageous methods of purchasing.

Given the market structure and the sophistication of the buyers, the prospects for monopoly in the coal industry appear very low. Coal seems available to a consumer at a price reasonably close to that which would result from textbook pure competition. Thus, it seems reasonable to doubt the validity of attacks on energy companies as emergent monopolies. Further support to the criticism of the assertions that monopoly prevailed is provided by the market analysis in this study. The outcry about the energy companies arose because coal prices began to rise sharply in 1970. It has been argued here that these developments are better explained as the response of a competitive but relatively inflexible market to short-run developments of supply and demand. The monopoly argument is implausible and redundant.

Turning to public policies, a wide variety have been directed against the production and use of coal. This tendency which arose in the late 1960s sharply contrasts with prior emphasis on policies explicitly concerned with oil, gas, or nuclear power. These only indirectly affected coal. The evidence (chapter 5) suggests that the major policy influence on coal mining costs has been the increased emphasis on safer, healthier methods of coal mining.

These pressures are compounded by other policies, principally those directed at control of damage from surface mining of coal. It has been argued here that the main threat comes from policies that prohibit or severely limit the levels of strip mining. At least in the West, where the greatest strip mine expansion potential exists, reclamation requirements are likely to prove a minor element in costs.

As of 1973, the most critical restraint on coal *use* came from regulations limiting emissions of sulfur oxides (see chapter 6). Most coal users, except perhaps coke oven operators, could control particulate emissions using available technology. Nitrogen oxide emission standards for coal burning facilities remain relatively mild. However, stringent sulfur oxide regulations have been imposed, but satisfactory methods to meet them while still using coal have not yet been devised. Those in regions where local coals are generally higher in sulfur content than regulators desire may find that a lower sulfur coal may be quite expensive to obtain. Some states in which ample amounts of low-sulfur coal are available are insisting that even such coal produces excessive emissions. Of course, these difficulties may cause revisions of sulfur regulations along lines sketched in chapter 1.

The trends of the post-1946 period transformed coal into a far more specialized fuel than it was originally. In 1946 coal both was a general purpose fuel for many industrial, commercial, and household consumers and had special markets in the railroads, electric power generation, and the steel industry. By 1971, the great bulk of sales were concentrated in the electric power and steel sectors. Industrial sales remained but at a reduced level, and the retail and railroad markets had virtually disappeared.

The central consideration about the market position of coal is that it is a much more difficult fuel to use than oil or gas. Handling of solids involves difficulties at every stage from extraction to the disposal of residues after combustion. Pig iron manufacture is the only process in which coal's properties, as improved by coking, are a distinct advantage. Outside the steel industry, coal use will be undertaken only when the overall economics are quite favorable. Under the market conditions prevailing in the United States, only large-scale users of fuel have had the incentives to use coal extensively. In a significant part of the country the delivered price of coal was significantly lower than that of other fossil fuels. These large-scale users found this price advantage more than compensated for the higher other costs of using coal. This was particularly true of the electric utility industry, which over the postwar period as a whole steadily increased its consumption of coal. Throughout the period, coal was the leading electric power fuel source. The electric power industry became coal's leading consumer.

By the early 1970s, signs of pressures on coal's position were becoming quite evident. After the 1966 liberalization of oil import quotas for residual oil delivered to the U.S. East Coast, oil rapidly began to displace coal, particularly in the Northeast, because it was the cheaper fuel. This movement to oil accelerated as ever more stringent sulfur emission standards were imposed on the East Coast. By 1972, most of the electric utilities with plants with easy access to oil by water had heavily and often completely converted from coal to oil. (Chapter 2 provides a full description of the process.) Reconversion is possible but apparently will be difficult in some cases because coal handling facilities were dismantled.

Nuclear power has also emerged as a challenge to coal. To be sure, the threat was more a prospect than a reality by 1972. The contribution of nuclear power was still quite small. The long lead times on nuclear plants, while disadvantageous for the electric utility industry's flexibility, provide ample advance warning of planned shifts and the indications are that electric utilities are moving heavily into nuclear plants. Moreover, although unresolved issues—primarily of safety and the disposal of nuclear wastes—remain, to date it is not apparent that these are as difficult to resolve as those relating to coal. Another critical question is whether nuclear costs can be kept within the ranges assumed here.

Supplementing developments in the domestic market have been the movements of coal exports. Over the period covered, such exports have fluctuated greatly with the vagaries of market conditions and public policies in the consuming industries. The result to date has been a solid but irregular market abroad.

Prospects in all these areas remain highly uncertain with those in the critical electric power market being the most difficult to appraise. It has been shown here that up to 1980, nuclear orders while substantial leave considerable room for fossil-fuel plants. Many of these plants normally would burn coal, but the environmental and economic pressures affecting fuel choice *may* cause oil to capture much of the market. This could result from pure physical necessity. Lack of workable sulfur scrubbing devices combined with rigid application of stringent emission standards could force many electric utilities to switch to oil. It is conceivable, moreover, that even if scrubbers to control sulfur oxides were perfected, the economics would be such that oil use would be preferable. This would depend upon coal and oil prices as well as scrubber costs. This study has argued that sharply rising coal prices are likely in the East. Mine health and safety compliance problems, rising labor costs, and an apparent lack of significant technical advance all are putting pressures on costs.

Defenders of coal can argue that trends in the world oil market are such that imported oil prices may rise so much more rapidly than coal prices that coal will remain competitive. However, the more optimistic estimates of oil and supply prospects in the United States suggest that it is quite possible that domestic resources could be developed at costs not greatly in excess of those assumed in chapter 7. It is quite possible, therefore, that early in the 1980s sufficient supplies of domestic oil and gas would be available at low enough prices to constitute devasting competition to coal. Of course, this development would require drastic reforms in the policies that hinder development of domestic oil and gas resources.

Moreover, an alternative possibility is that western coal would take over the market. This would leave the coal industry as a whole no worse off but still cause enormous readjustments within the industry. Severe declines in production would occur east of the Mississippi. Again, this would depend on relative cost developments and public policy.

In the 1980s, nuclear power could begin to take over base load generation from fossil fuels. Unless a satisfactory resolution of the problems plaguing coal or a sharp deterioration in the position of nuclear power occurs, coal is severely threatened. To be sure, new technologies, epitomized here by the combined cycle using gasified coal, could produce cheaper ways to burn coal in an environmentally satisfactory manner. However, this requires either success with the technologies and an ability to stem the forces causing rising coal prices or serious problems with nuclear power. Given the probable need to increase wages sharply to attract workers, costs can only be lowered if economical methods to mine safely and more productively emerge. Of course, as the policies adopted in late 1973 suggest, it may be decided to relax some of the pressures on coal, but the long-run prospects and efficacy of such a development are far from clearly favorable.

The threat is even more severe in the other industrial markets for coal. These consumers are unlikely to be able to take advantage of the economies of scale applicable to such technologies as stack scrubbing, low Btu gasification at the power plant, and nuclear power. Oil and gas even at high prices are likely to appear more attractive than coal or nuclear power. Thus, unless unforeseen technological advances occur, coal use in this sector is likely to decline.

On the basis of research not included here, it can be concluded that the steel industry is likely to continue its use of coal for blast furnace coke. However, at best this will lead to modest absolute growth in consumption. The steel industry's output is not expected to increase rapidly, and the absolute tonnages involved are smaller than in the electric power market. Moreover, if the lower available forecasts of steel industry growth are combined with expectations of continued significant improvements in the utilization of coke, steel industry coal use for coking could fall.

Export prospects depend heavily on the rate at which Western Europe allows its own coal industry to contract. The prospects are good that this will permit a substantial percent rise in exports. Again, however, the tonnages involved are fairly small. These European sales, moreover, may be the main source of increased exports; growth of sales to Japan may be retarded by strong competition from other countries.

The most promising new markets are for synthetic fuels. Such synthetics clearly will be significantly more expensive than oil and gas prices prevailing in the 1960s and early 1970s. Again, all this study can do is point out that the widely held expectation that both oil and gas prices will rise enough to make synthesis viable may be incorrect. Falling world oil prices, massive Arctic oil finds, a substantial response of gas supply to a free market, and lower costs of shale oil conversion all could prevent the development of coal synthesis.

In summary, the future of coal depends upon the mix of public policies adopted and the cost of using coal and alternative fuels, given these policies. The specific projections provided here suggest that should nuclear power evolve as published projections indicate, it poses a great threat to coal in the long run. In the short run, it is possible even if far from assured that a severe competitive threat will be posed by oil. Failure of this threat to materialize may lead to a shift to western coal. Whether coal can be economically used as an input for synthetic fuel manufacture is quite uncertain.

While many other policy proposals could be made on the basis of this study, further advice will be limited to a qualified endorsement of suggestions that coal research be greatly expanded. However, the claims that crash research programs clearly will save the day need much more searching analyses than they have thus far received. The frequent use of low ratios of research to total sales as evidence of inadequate performance should be viewed skeptically. Such ratios may indeed result from shortsightedness or the inability of the inventor to reap enough benefits because many people can use the idea without paying royalties. However, the situation also may only reflect lack of profitable prospects. It is all too easy to explain behavior one does not like as resulting from defects of a free market. Such shortcomings do exist but often it turns out that the market was, in fact, correct.

Clearly, if we can establish that in fact there are good prospects for research to lower the cost of mining and using coal, then a substantial effort should be mounted. This appears to be coal's main hope. However, research policy must recognize the chance of failure as well as of success. To provide sufficient options, we must explore many prospects. Some will fail and we must recognize this in advance by providing methods to terminate the programs.

The support for coal research is given because the ability to have satisfactory energy supplies without using coal is far from guaranteed. On the basis of instincts, it might be argued that it would be better to forget about coal and start now perfecting fusion, solar energy, deep geothermal, and other essentially inexhaustible energy sources for the twenty-first century. Given our energy needs in the interim cautious men may rightfully argue that a hedge on coal is desirable in case oil, gas, and nuclear power cannot economically carry us to the next century. However, because the task for coal is so enormous, the research should be subjected to continuous review so that, should the effort prove unnecessary, it can be abandoned promptly.

Thus, it becomes imperative that research on energy economics in general and coal in particular be intensified. Emphasis, moreover, should be placed on data gathering. A concerted effort should be made to provide data on the economic availability of fuel. For example, the location of coal seams should be studied so that their availability for exploitation is known. Careful measures of the quality of the coal, the seam size, depth, regularity, and other influences on costs should be assembled. With such data, a more realistic analysis could be produced. In short, the basic question raised here of whether coal output will continue its comeback or enter another decline proved unanswerable. The threat of decline, however, seems quite serious. Only time can resolve many of these questions, but better knowledge of the present would be helpful.

The moral of all this may be inferred from some remarks *New York Times* columnist Russell Baker made in a serious moment. He argued that we suffer from "the fearful late twentieth-century epidemic of verbal bloat." He contends that the belief that overstatement is the only way to get attention is quite invalid. "The overstated argument distracts attention from the merits of the case and focuses it, instead, on the absurdity of the overstatement" (December 16, 1971). The objective of this study has been to remove some of the verbal bloat associated with coal and to encourage a more analytic look at the subject. It is hoped that the warning raised here will assist in this process.

Bibliography

The following references are largely restricted to material explicitly cited here. No effort was made to include all of the vast amount of material consulted, especially the numerous reports from the electric power industry. Annual reports, uniform statistical reports, securities prospectuses, and other material were obtained from all the leading U.S. electric utilities. Similarly, such useful periodical sources as *Coal Age,* the *Wall Street Journal,* and *Electrical World* are not explicitly listed although they were used as guides for much research. Finally, the various press releases in which USBM data appear prior to publication in the *Minerals Yearbook* are not cited since the *Yearbook* is more likely to be consulted. When an organization issues reports without identifying the authors, it is listed here as the author. The absence of a named publisher implies that the organization published the report itself. A number of the reports cited were prepared for the U.S. government. Many such reports are then made available through the National Technical Information Service (NTIS). Whenever such availability was known, it was noted. In addition, the NTIS code number was indicated to ease search. Throughout, the publications of a particular author are in chronological order.

Adelman, M. A., ed. 1971. *Alaskan Oil: Costs and Supply.* New York: Praeger Publishers.
———. 1972a. *The World Petroleum Market.* Baltimore: The Johns Hopkins University Press for Resources for the Future, Inc.
———. 1972b. "Is the Oil Shortage Real? Oil Companies as OPEC Tax Collectors," *Foreign Policy,* no. 9 (Winter): 69–107.
American Petroleum Institute. 1972. *Annual Statistical Review,* U.S. Petroleum Industry Statistics, 1956–1971. Washington: API.
Arizona Public Service and others. 1973. *Kaiparowits Project Environmental Report.* 2 vols. n.p.
Arthur D. Little, Inc. 1973. *A Study of Base Load Alternatives for the Northeast Utilities System.* Cambridge: ADL.
Averitt, Paul. 1969. *Coal Resources of the United States, January 1, 1967.* Washington, D.C.: U.S. Geological Survey Bulletin 1275.

Bailey, Arthur G. 1967. *The Economics of Unit Trains.* Chicago: A. T. Kearney Company, Inc.

Baumol, William J., and Klevorick, Alvin K. 1970. "Input Choices and Rate-of-Return Regulation: An Overview of the Discussion," *The Bell Journal of Economics and Management Science,* 1, no. 2 (Autumn): 162–90.

Bennett, L. L., Bowers, H. I., and Myers, M. L. 1971. *Estimated Future Costs of Central Station Steam-Electric Power Plants.* Mimeographed. Oak Ridge: Oak Ridge National Laboratory.

Brown, Keith C. 1972. *Regulation of the Natural Gas Producing Industry.* Baltimore: The Johns Hopkins University Press for Resources for the Future, Inc.

Canada, Mineral Resources Branch, Department of Energy Mines and Resources. 1971. *Canadian Minerals Yearbook.* Ottawa.

Chemical Week. 1968. "Bulk Transportation." March 16, pp. 65–80.

Cochran, Thomas B. 1974. *The Liquid Metal Fast Breeder Reactor.* Baltimore: The Johns Hopkins University Press for Resources for the Future, Inc.

Commonwealth Edison Company. 1973. *Memorandum Regarding SO₂ Removal Experience and Cost Estimates.* Chicago.

Duchesneau, Thomas D. 1972. *Interfuel Substitutability in the Electric Utility Sector of the U.S. Economy.* Staff Report to the Federal Trade Commission. Washington.

Edison Electric Institute. 1960–73. *Statistical Yearbook.* New York: EEI, annual.

——. 1970–74. *Semiannual Electric Power Survey.* New York: EEI, semiannual.

——. 1962. *Historical Statistics of the Electric Utility Industry.* New York: EEI.

——. 1969. Statistical Committee. *Bibliography and Digest of U.S. Electric and Total Energy Forecasts 1970–2050.* New York: EEI.

——. 1970. Committee on Environment. *Major Electric Power Facilities and the Environment.* New York: EEI.

Elder, H. W. and others. 1972. *Sulfur Oxide Control Technology—Visits in Japan, August 1972.* Muscle Shoals, Alabama.

Electrical World. "Longest Slurry Pipeline Passes Tests," February 15, 1971, pp. 44–47.

Electric Utility Industry Task Force on Environment. 1968. *The Electric Utility Industry and the Environment,* n.p.

Erickson, Edward W., and Spann, Robert M. 1972. "Balancing the Supply and Demand for Natural Gas," in J. J. Schanz, Jr., ed. *Balancing Supply and Demand for Energy in the United States.* Rocky Mountain Petroleum Economics Institute 1972. Denver: University of Denver.

First National City Bank, New York. 1972. *Energy Memo,* 6, no. 1 (January).

Frankel, Richard J. 1969. "Problems of Meeting Multiple Air Quality Objectives for Coal-fired Utility Boilers," *Journal of the Air Pollution Control Association,* 19, no. 1 (January): 18–23.

Gakner, Alexander, and Jimeson, Robert M. 1973. *Environmental and Economic Cost Considerations in Electric Power Supply.* National Meeting of American Institute of Chemical Engineers. New Orleans.

Gambs, Gerard C. 1970a. "The Electric Utility Industry: Future Fuel Requirements 1970–1990," *Mechanical Engineering* (April): 42–48.

———. 1970b. *The Twentieth Century Fossil Fuel Crisis: Current and Projected Requirements.* New York: Ford, Bacon and Davis.

———. 1972. "The Energy Crisis in the United States." Paper for the Advanced Management Research International Energy Crisis Seminars.

Garvey, James R. 1972. "Coal as a Resource: Now and in the Future," in *Symposium on Coal and Public Policies.* Knoxville: University of Tennessee Center for Business and Economic Research.

Glover, T. O., Hinkle, M. E., and Riley, H. L. 1970. *Unit Train Transportation of Coal.* U.S. Bureau of Mines Information Circular 8444. Washington, D.C.

Gordon, Richard L. 1969. "A Reinterpretation of the Pure Theory of Exhaustion," *Journal of Political Economy,* 75, no. 3 (June): 274–86.

———. 1970. *The Evolution of Energy Policy in Western Europe, the Reluctant Retreat from Coal.* New York: Praeger Publishers.

———. 1973. "Coal's Role in a National Materials Policy," in Samuel P. Ellison, Jr., ed., *Towards A National Policy on Energy Resources and Mineral Plant Foods.* Austin: University of Texas, Bureau of Economic Geology: 84–98.

———. 1974a. "Mythology and Reality in Energy Policy," *Energy Policy,* 2:1 (September): 88–109.

———. 1974b. "Optimization of Input Supply Patterns in the Case of Fuels for Electric Power Generation," *Journal of Industrial Economics,* 23:1 (September) pp. 19–37.

Hauser, L. G., and Potter, R. F. 1970. "More Escalation Seen for Coal Costs," *Electrical World,* August 15, pp. 45–48.

Henke, William C. 1970. "The New 'Hot' Electrostatic Precipitator," *Combustion* (October): 50–55.

Hottel, K. C., and Howard, J. B. 1971. *New Energy Technology, Some Facts and Assessments.* Cambridge: The MIT Press.

James, D. W. 1971. "Coping with NO_x: A Growing Problem," *Electrical World,* February 1, pp. 44–47.

Jimeson, Robert M., and Maddocks, Robert R. 1973. *Refined Coal: An Energy Source of the Future.* American Chemical Society Symposium—Fuels of the Future. Dallas.

Johnson, Charles J. 1972. "Coal Demand in the Electric Utility Industry, 1946–1990." Ph.D. dissertation, Pennsylvania State University.

Kasper, William. 1972. *Peak Usage as a Factor in Electric Rate Design.* Albany: State of New York Public Service Commission.

Kellogg, M. W., Co. 1971. *Evaluation of SO_2 Control Processes, Task #5 Final Report.*

Keystone Coal Industry Manual. 1950–74. *U.S. Coal Production by Company.* New York: McGraw-Hill, annual.

MacAvoy, P. W. 1969. *Economic Strategy for Developing Nuclear Breeder Reactors.* Cambridge: The MIT Press.

Massachusetts Institute of Technology. 1970. *Man's Impact on the Global Environment,* Assessment and Recommendations for Action. Report of the Study of Critical Environmental Problems. Cambridge: The MIT Press.

McDonald, Forrest. 1962. *Insull.* Chicago: University of Chicago Press.

Moody's Public Utilities. 1970–74. New York: Moody's Investor Service, annual.

National Academy of Engineering. Committee on Power Plant Siting. 1972. *Engineering for Resolution of the Energy-Environment Dilemma.* Washington: NAE.

National Academy of Engineering. National Research Council. 1972. *Abatement of Nitrogen Oxide Emissions from Stationary Sources.* Washington: NAE.

National Coal Association. 1970. *Bituminous Coal Facts.* Washington: NCA, biennial.

———. 1960–74. *Bituminous Coal Data.* Washington: NCA, annual.

———. 1958–73. *Steam Electric Plant Factors.* Washington: NCA, annual.

———. 1960. *Trends in Electric Utility Industry Experience, 1946–1958.* Washington: NCA.

National Economic Research Associates, Inc. 1972. *Fuels for the Electric Utility Industry.* New York: Edison Electric Institute.

National Petroleum Council. 1971. *U.S. Energy Outlook, an Initial Appraisal 1971–1985.* 2 vols. Washington: NPC.

———. 1972. *U.S. Energy Outlook.* Washington: NPC.

———. 1973. *U.S. Energy Outlook—Coal Availability.* Washington: NPC.

Olds, F. C. 1973. "Capital Cost Calculations for Future Power Plants," *Power Engineering* (January): 61–65.

Phillips, Robert J. 1974. "Operating Experience with a Commercial Dual-Alkali SO_2 Removal System," Annual Meeting, Air Pollution Control Association, Denver, Colo.

Reichl, Eric H. 1962. *Coal by Pipeline.* Address presented to the American Mining Congress, Pittsburgh, Pa.

Robson, F. L. and others. 1970. *Technological and Economic Feasibility of Advanced Power Cycles and Methods of Producing Nonpolluting Fuels for Utility Power Stations.* Springfield, Virginia: National Technical Information Service (PB 198 392).

Schurr, Sam H., Netschert, Bruce C., and others. 1960. *Energy in the American Economy, 1850–1975.* Baltimore: The Johns Hopkins Press for Resources for the Future, Inc.

Schurr, Sam H., and others. 1971. *Energy Research Needs.* Springfield, Virginia: National Technical Information Service (PB 207 516).

Shaw, Milton. 1971. Testimony in U.S. Congress. Joint Committee on Atomic Energy.

Sporn, Philip, and Frankenberg, T. T. 1967. "Pioneering Experience with High Stacks on the OVEC and AEP Systems," in Sporn, Philip, ed. *The Tall Stack for Air Pollution Control on Large Fossil-Fired Power Plants.* Washington: National Coal Policy Conference, Inc.: 34–52.

Straton, John W. 1972a. "Effects of Federal Mine Safety Legislation on Production, Productivity and Cost," *Mining Congress Journal,* (July): 19–24.

———. 1972b. "Survey Measure Impact of the Health and Safety Act on Underground Coal Mining," *Mining Engineering* (October): 64–67.

United Aircraft Research Laboratories. 1971. *Advanced Nonthermally Polluting Gas Turbines in Utility Application.* Washington: U.S. Government Printing Office.

U.S. Atomic Energy Commission. 1971. *The Nuclear Industry 1971.* Washington.
——. 1972. *Environment Statement Liquid Metal Fast Breeder Reactor Demonstration Plant.* Washington.
——. 1973a. *The Safety of Nuclear Power Reactors (Light Water-Cooled) and Related Facilities* (Wash 1250). Washington.
——. 1973b. *Status of Central Station Nuclear Power Reactors Significant Milestones* (Wash 1008-3-73). Washington.
——. 1974. *Reactor Safety Study,* an assessment of accident risks in U.S. Commercial Nuclear Power Plants. (Wash 1400). Washington.
U.S. Bureau of the Census. *Census of Manufactures.* Washington.
U.S. Bureau of Mines. 1950–74. *Minerals Yearbook.* Washington: annual.
——. 1970–74. *Bituminous Coal Distribution.* Washington. quarterly.
——. 1971a. *Analysis of the Availability of Bituminous Coal in the Appalachian Region.* Washington.
——. 1971b. *Strippable Reserves of Bituminous Coal and Lignite in the United States.* Information Circular 8351. Washington.
——. 1972. *Cost Analyses of Model Mines for Strip Mining of Coal in the United States.* Information Circular 8535. Washington.
U.S. Bureau of Reclamation. 1971. *North Central Power Study.* Billings, Montana.
U.S. Congress. Joint Committee on Atomic Energy. 1968. *Nuclear Power Economics—1962 through 1967.* 90 Cong. 2 sess. Washington.
——. 1969. *Selected Materials on Environmental Effects of Producing Electric Power.* 91 Cong. 1 sess. Washington.
——. 1970a. *AEC Authorizing Legislation Fiscal Year 1971.* 4 vols. 91 Cong. 2 sess. Washington.
——. 1970b. *Environmental Effects of Producing Electric Power.* 3 vols. 91 Cong. 2 sess. Washington.
——. 1970c. *Uranium Enrichment Pricing Criteria.* 2 vols. 91 Cong. 2 sess. Washington.
——. 1971a. *AEC Authorizing Legislation Fiscal Year 1972.* 4 vols. 92 Cong. 1 sess. Washington.
——. 1971b. *AEC Licensing Procedure and Related Legislation.* 4 vols. 92 Cong. 1 sess. Washington.
——. 1971c. *Calvert Cliffs Court Decision.* 2 vols. 92 Cong. 1 sess. Washington.
——. 1971d. *Nuclear Power and Related Energy Problems—1968 through 1970.* 92 Cong. 1 sess. Washington.
——. 1972. *AEC Authorizing Legislation Fiscal Year 1973.* 6 vols. 92 Cong. 2 sess. Washington.
U.S. Council on Environmental Quality. 1970–73. *Environmental Quality,* Annual Report of the Council on Environmental Quality. Washington: annual.
——. 1973. *Coal Surface Mining and Reclamation.* Washington.
U.S. Department of the Interior. 1972. *Southwest Energy Study,* (draft). Washington.
——. (Walter G. Dupree, Jr. and James A. West). 1973. *United States Energy through the Year 2000.* Washington.
U.S. Environmental Protection Agency. 1971. *Air Quality Criteria for Nitrogen Oxides.* Washington.

———. 1973a. *Compilation of Air Pollution Emission Factors.* 2nd ed. Research Triangle Park.

———. 1973b. James H. Cavender, David S. Kircher, and Alan J. Hoffman. *Nationwide Air Pollutant Emission Trends 1940–1970.* Research Triangle Park.

———. 1974. *Report of the Hearing Panel National Public Hearings on Power Plant Compliance with Sulfur Oxide Air Pollution Regulations.* Washington.

U.S. Federal Power Commission. 1970–74. *Statistics of Privately Owned Electric Utilities in the United States.* Washington: annual.

———. 1970–74. *Statistics of Publicly Owned Electric Utilities in the United States.* Washington: annual.

———. 1964. *1964 National Power Survey.* 2 vols. Washington.

———. 1968. *Air Pollution and the Regulated Electric Power and Natural Gas Industries.* Washington.

———. 1971. *1970 National Power Survey.* 4 vols. Washington.

———. 1972. *Steam-Electric Plant Construction Cost and Annual Production Expenses Twenty-Third Annual Supplement-1970.* Washington.

———. 1973. *A Staff Report on Monthly Report of Cost and Quantity of Fuels for Steam-Electric Plant* (February and May). Washington.

U.S. Federal Trade Commission. Office of Policy Planning and Evaluation. 1971 *Commission Study: Alternatives in the Energy Sector.* Washington.

U.S. Geological Survey. *1974 Final Environmental Statement.* Proposed *Plan of Mining and Reclamation, Big Sky Mine, Peabody Coal Company, Coal Lease M-15965, Colstrip, Montana.* 2 vols. Billings, Montana.

U.S. Congress, House of Representatives. Subcommittee on Special Small Business Problems of the Select Committee on Small Business. 1970. *The Impact of the Energy and Fuel Crisis on Small Business.* 91 Cong. 2 sess. Washington.

———. 1971. *Concentration by Competing Raw Fuel Industries in the Energy Market and its Impact on Small Business.* 2 vols. 92 Cong. 1 sess. Washington.

U.S. National Air Pollution Control Administration. 1969a. *Air Quality Criteria for Particulate Matter.* Washington.

———. 1969b. *Air Quality Criteria for Sulfur Oxides.* Washington.

———. 1969c. *Control Techniques for Particle Air Pollutants.* Washington.

———. 1969d. *Control Techniques for Sulfur Oxide Air Pollutants.* Washington.

———. 1970a. *Control Techniques for Nitrogen Oxide Emissions from Stationary Sources.* Washington.

U.S. Office of Science and Technology, Energy Policy Staff. 1968. *Considerations Affecting Power Plant Site Selection.* Washington.

———. 1970. *Electric Power and the Environment.* Washington.

U.S. Public Health Service. 1949. *Air Pollution in Donora, Pa.* Washington.

U.S. Congress, Senate. Committee on Interior and Insular Affairs. 1971a. *Problems of Electric Power Production in the Southwest.* 7 vols. 92 Cong. 1 sess. Washington.

———. 1971b. *Surface Mining.* 2 vols. 92 Cong. 1 sess. Washington.

U.S. Sulfur Oxide Control Technology Assessment Panel (SOCTAP). 1973. *Final Report on Projected Utilization of Stack Gas Cleaning Systems by Steam Electric Plants,* n.p.

Working Group on Utilities. 1968. *Report to the Vice President and to the President's Council on Recreation and Natural Beauty.* Washington.

Index

THE JOHNS HOPKINS UNIVERSITY PRESS
This book was composed in Times Roman text and Times
Roman Bold display type by Maryland Composition Co.,
Inc., from a design by Susan Bishop. It was printed on 60-lb.
Warren 1854 regular paper and bound in Columbia Bayside
cloth by Universal Lithographers, Inc.

Library of Congress Cataloging in Publication Data

Gordon, Richard L   1934–
  U. S. coal and the electric power industry.

  Bibliography: p.
  Includes index.
  1. Power resources—United States. 2. Coal trade—United States.
3. Electric utilities—United States. I. Resources for the Future. II.
Title.
HD9502.U52G67   333.8′2   74-24403
  ISBN 0-8018-1697-1